English AHEAD

Grade 3

Janet Bartier • William Young

Printed in China

CONTENTS

Nouns

common nouns, proper nouns, compound proper nouns

1

In this unit, students will:

- learn what compound proper nouns are: names and titles with more than one word.
- identify compound proper nouns in a story and use them to answer questions.
- match some common nouns with their meanings.
- predict the meanings of new words using details in the story.
- look for compound proper nouns with missing capital letters in sentences and correct them.
- make up some compound proper nouns and use them in sentences with the help of pictures.

A. Read this story and look at the words in bold. Underline the words that are compound proper nouns.

Bob was a pirate with very big dreams. He wanted to be **captain** of the ship. **Captain Dan** would soon retire and the job would go to the best pirate. Bob was a good pirate, but **First Mate Steve** also wanted the job.

"If you want to be captain," First Mate Steve said to Bob, "you must first sail to the **top of the world**." Then he winked at the other pirates, "Bob will never sail to the top of the world. He will never be captain! Har!"

But Bob hopped aboard an **icebreaker** on its way to the **North Pole**. There, on the **Northern Queen**, he sailed to the top of the **world**.

"So, you've sailed to the top of the world," First Mate Steve said when Bob returned. "If you want to be captain, you must also read ten **pirate books**." Again, he winked at the **others**, "Bob will never read ten pirate books. He doesn't even know how to read! Har!"

But Bob learned how to read. He started digging into pirate books, from ***Pirates ABC*** to ***War and Seas***.

"So, you've sailed to the top of the world and you've read ten pirate books," said First Mate Steve, pulling out a **sword**. "If you want to be captain, you must first take the **job** from me!" He waved his sword at Bob, but Bob had learned many things from his **travels** and his books. He **somersaulted** and kicked the sword away from his rival's hand.

Bob winked at the other pirates, "Steve will never be captain of the ship because I am the best pirate for the job. Har!"

B. Find the compound proper noun from (A) for each of these. Then finish what Bob says.

1. Steve's title: ____________________

2. The title of a book that Bob read:

   ____

3. The name of the icebreaker that Bob sailed on:

   ____

4. My title is now ____________________ !

C. Write the common noun from (A) for each of these word meanings.

1. ______________ : the Earth
2. ______________ : the leader on a ship
3. ______________ : a robber of ships at sea
4. ______________ : what you do to make money
5. ______________ : a weapon with a long metal blade

Think!

To "predict" the meaning of a word that we have never seen before, we can read what comes before and after it in the story. What do you think these words mean? Explain in your own words.

1. retire: ______________________________
2. icebreaker: ______________________________
3. rival: ______________________________

D. Underline the words that should be compound proper nouns. Then write them with the correct capitalization.

1. My youngest aunt knits crazy sweaters. We all call her
Aunt Crazy
aunt crazy.

2. *black beauty* is my favourite storybook.

3. Tonight, the vancouver canucks will play the toronto maple leafs.

4. You can buy fresh berries at fresh fruit mart.

Look at the girl, the dog, and the boy. Use the picture and the given name to make up a compound proper noun for each of them. Then use it in a sentence to describe what each one is doing.

1. Fiona loves flowers.
   Let's name her "Flower Lover Fiona".
   Flower Lover Fiona is smelling a flower.

2. Ben has a big mouth.
   Let's name him "____________________________".
   ____

3. Willy loves the wind.
   Let's name him "____________________________".
   ____

THINGS TO TRY

- **Go on a "Compound Proper Noun Scavenger Hunt"! Look for one that is:**
  - **the title of a book**
  - **the title of a newspaper or magazine article**
  - **the name of a sports team**
  - **the name of a street**
  - **someone's nickname**
  - **someone's job title**

The first compound proper noun on my list is your nickname, "Sweetie Pie".

My List of Compound Proper Nouns

Book: ______________________

Article: ______________________

Team: ______________________

Street: ______________________

Nickname: ______________________

Job Title: ______________________

Checklist

Skills

- [ ] I know that names and titles with more than one word are compound proper nouns.
- [ ] I can identify compound proper nouns in a story and use them to answer questions.
- [ ] I can match some common nouns with their meanings.
- [ ] I can predict the meanings of new words using details in the story.
- [ ] I can correct mistakes in capitalization in compound proper nouns.
- [ ] I can make up some compound proper nouns and use them in sentences with the help of pictures.

Revising

- [ ] I have capitalized the first letter of each word in my compound proper nouns.
- [ ] I have checked my spelling.

Plural Nouns

regular and irregular plural forms

2

In this unit, students will:

- learn some irregular plural nouns (e.g. fishermen, geese, fish).
- tell irregular plural nouns from regular plural nouns.
- complete sentences using irregular plural nouns and their singular form.
- learn some examples of compound words.
- identify the pattern in some irregular plural nouns and write the plural form given the singular form.
- describe a picture using irregular plural nouns.

A. Read this story and look at the nouns in bold. Circle the ones that are plural.

One morning, when the sun rose over the **mountains**, a fishing boat went out to sea. The old **fisherman** in the boat waved to his **dog** at the water's edge. He waved to the **child** walking on the **beach**. Then he sailed into the **ocean** to catch some **fish**.

On the **shore**, the fisherman's dog chased **seabirds** and sniffed under **rocks**. He went swimming with the **geese**, and even tried to catch a **fish**. In the afternoon, he played with **children** in the sand. In the evening, the fisherman should return, but he didn't. His dog was worried. Through the **night** he sat by the shore, watching and waiting. There was not a **person** in sight. Even the last **goose** had left.

The next **morning** before sunrise, the people from **town** came to the water. Many of them were **fishermen**, and they moved quickly to get their **boats** in the water. The rest of the **people** stayed behind. They watched and waited with the fisherman's dog.

The **sun** was high in the **sky** when the fishing boats returned. At first, the people on the shore saw only the boats, so they shaded their **eyes** and stepped closer to the **water**. Soon they saw the **fishermen**. They saw them waving their hands in the air. They saw the lost fisherman, too. His crippled **boat** was attached to another by a **rope**. People cheered, **geese** fluttered their wings, and the fisherman's dog barked and wagged his tail. The **fisherman** was safe, and his boat was full to the brim with **fish**.

B. Sort the plural nouns from (A) into "Regular" and "Irregular".

Regular	Irregular
______________	______________
______________	______________
______________	______________
______________	______________
______________	______________

C. Complete these sentences with the correct nouns from (A).

1. a. One ______________ went fishing one morning.
   b. Many ______________ went looking for him.

2. a. The fisherman waved to a ______________ .
   b. A bunch of ______________ played with his dog.

3. a. The dog swam with a flock of ______________ .
   b. The last ______________ said goodbye at night.

Think!

Did you notice that some of the words in the story are made up of smaller words? They are called "compound words".

Fill in the blanks.

1. seabird = ________ + ________
2. seabirds = ________ + ________
3. fisherman = ________ + ________
4. fishermen = ________ + ________

D. Write the plural form of the nouns in each group. Then tell the pattern of the change.

Pattern

- a → e
- oo → ee
- no change

1. Pattern: ________

goose → ________

foot → ________

tooth → ________

2. Pattern: ________

fisherman → ________

woman → ________

policeman → ________

fireman → ________

3. Pattern: ________

fish → ________

deer → ________

moose → ________

sheep → ________

Your Turn

There are four irregular plural nouns in this picture. Use them to describe what you see.

Plural nouns: ______________ ______________

______________ ______________

There are two geese eating grass, ______________________________

____

____

THINGS TO TRY

- Cut out 20 pieces of paper.
- Write an irregular plural noun on one piece and its singular form on another piece to make a "singular-plural" pair.
- Write different "singular-plural" pairs until you have used all 20 pieces of paper. Use some regular plurals if you like.
- Put the pieces face down on a table. Mix them up. Then arrange them into four rows.
- Taking turns with a friend:
    - Turn over one piece.
    - Turn over another piece. If it matches with your first piece, keep the pair and take another turn. If not, put the paper back, face down.
- The player with the most pairs wins.

Checklist

Skills

- [ ] I know some irregular plural nouns, and I can tell them apart from regular plural nouns.
- [ ] I can complete sentences using irregular plural nouns and their singular form.
- [ ] I know some compound words.
- [ ] I can identify the pattern in some irregular plural nouns and write the plural form given the singular form.
- [ ] I can describe a picture using irregular plural nouns.

Revising

- [ ] I have written the correct plural form of the irregular plural nouns.
- [ ] I have checked my spelling.

Possessive
Adjectives / Pronouns

to show to whom something belongs

3

Where do you want your bookshelf, Louise?
possessive adjective

Here, "your bookshelf" refers to Louise's bookshelf.

Right next to yours, Ben.
possessive pronoun

Here, "yours" refers to Ben's bookshelf.

In this unit, students will:

- know what possessive adjectives are: my, your, his, her, its, our, their.
- know what possessive pronouns are: mine, yours, his, hers, ours, theirs.
- know how to use possessive adjectives and possessive pronouns in sentences.
- learn the difference between "its" and "it's".
- describe a picture using possessive adjectives.

3 Possessive Adjectives / Pronouns

A. Complete the table. Then use the words to finish the poem.

There is no possessive pronoun for "it".

Possessive

adjectives	my	your	his		its		their
pronouns				hers		ours	

My friend, Louise, lives downtown.

1. ____________ apartment is what she prefers.

She eats and sleeps twelve floors into the sky.

A home in the city is 2. ____________ .

My cousins, the twins, live in the woods.

3. ____________ home is among trees – and bears!

They chop wood for heat, and for cooking their food.

A log house in the forest is 4. ____________ .

5. ____________ home is linked to others.

It is brown in a row of nine

On a street in a quiet suburb.

A townhouse on Oak Street is 6. ____________ .

B. Use the correct possessive adjective in a sentence to answer each of these questions.

1. Where is Louise's apartment?

___

2. What kind of house is the twins' home?

___

3. On which street is Jack's house?

___

4. What is the colour of Jack's house?

___

Think!

Do you use "its" and "it's" correctly? "Its" is a possessive adjective like "his" and "her" while "it's" is the contraction for "it is". Don't confuse the two! Circle the wrong "it's" below and write "its" above it.

1. It's too hot today, so the plant has lost it's flowers.

2. It's so funny when my dog chases after it's tail!

C. Circle the correct possessive adjective or possessive pronoun for each sentence.

1. On picture day, I will wear mine / my red sweater to school.
2. The children made the cake, so it is their / theirs .
3. Mike brushed her / his teeth before he went to the dentist.
4. The horse in the pasture over there is our / ours .
5. Sara takes her / hers dog for a walk every day.
6. The blue and white backpack is my / mine .
7. The robot has lost its / it's batteries.
8. "Have you finished your / yours homework yet?" Mom asks.
9. My brother points to the crumbs on the floor and asks me, "Are they your / yours or my / mine ?"

Who are they and what do they have? Circle the correct words and fill in the blanks to finish the description of this picture.

These children are having their / theirs Summer Wheel Parade. ______________ leads the way on his / her ______________. It's / Its wheels are fast! Becky is behind him on her / hers ______________, and her brother ______________ rides his / hers ______________ beside her. ______________ wheels his way on his / her handy ______________, and ______________ cruises down the path on her / hers ______________.

THINGS TO TRY

- Find two different things at home and make thumbnail sketches of each one.
- Find out to whom the objects belong.
- Write about each object in three different sentences using possessive adjectives and possessive pronouns.

This is my brother's storybook.

This is his storybook.

This storybook is his.

Checklist

Skills

- ☐ I know what possessive adjectives and possessive pronouns are.
- ☐ I know how to use possessive adjectives and possessive pronouns in sentences.
- ☐ I know that "its" is a possessive adjective and that "it's" means "it is".
- ☐ I can describe a picture using possessive adjectives.

Revising

- ☐ I have used the correct possessive adjectives and possessive pronouns to tell to whom something belongs.
- ☐ I have checked my spelling.

Verbs

present tense and past tense

4

In this unit, students will:

- identify verbs in a story.
- know that there are regular and irregular verbs.
- learn the past tense of some regular and irregular verbs.
- make up sentences using the past tense of some irregular verbs with or without the help of pictures.
- know that the same action can be described by different verbs.

A. Read this story and look at the words in bold. Underline the ones that are verbs.

It was Friday. It was after school. It was time to play! But wait, Ben had a list of things to do:

Read a story.
Eat an apple.
Drink a glass of water.
Call Grandma to say hello.

When Ben **finished** his list of things to do, he **ran** to the park. He **climbed** a tree and **slid** down the slide. But while he **played**, he had a feeling he **forgot** something.

"I **read** a story, I **ate** an apple, and I **drank** a glass of **water**," Ben thought. "What else did I have to do?"

Ben **walked** down the **street**. He **kicked** a stone and he **waved** to his **friends**. But while **he** walked, he still had a **feeling** that he forgot something.

"I'll go to Grandma's **house**. Maybe **she** could help me remember."

When Ben got to Grandma's house, she was so happy. "What a good boy you are, Ben!" She exclaimed. "I only expected you to call, but you **came** to visit me instead!"

"So that's what I forgot to do!" Ben thought. "I forgot to call Grandma after school!"

B. **Look at (A) again to help you write the present tense or past tense of these verbs. Then finish the sentences with the correct verbs.**

1. **Regular Verb**

present	past
	called
finish	
climb	
play	
walk	
kick	
wave	

2. **Irregular Verb**

present	past
	read
	ate
	drank
run	
slide	
forget	
come	

3. a. Two days ago, Ben ______________ Aunt May to say hello.

b. Grandma ______________ a good story to Ben last week.

c. Ben's sister ______________ to return his yo-yo to him.

d. Oh no! Ben was late, so he quickly got out of the house and ______________ to school.

e. Before going inside the house, Ben ______________ goodbye to his buddy Sam.

f. When Ben and his sister ______________ their homework, they went out to play.

C. Write these sentences in the past tense.

1. Walter takes his dog to the park today.

   ____

2. Felix draws a picture of colourful clowns.

   ____

3. The children sing "O Canada" in the school assembly this morning.

   ____

   ____

Think!

The same action can be described in different words. Which three verbs mean the same as each one of these?

gallop	**gobble**	**chew**	**hop**	**graze**
sniff	**speak**	**scurry**	**speed**	**jump**

1. run: __________ __________ __________
2. eat: __________ __________ __________

Look at each picture and circle the verb that describes the action. Write the past tense of the verb. Then make up a sentence in the past tense.

1.

write / speak / talk

past tense: ________________

____

____

2.

jump / swing / hop

past tense: ________________

____

____

3.

drive / walk / fly

past tense: ________________

____

____

4.

sail / ride / skip

past tense: ________________

____

____

THINGS TO TRY

- **Think of some action words (e.g. run, walk, talk, munch, whistle, cough). Use books, magazines, and newspapers to help you.**
- **Write down each word on a piece of paper.**
- **Act out each verb and have a friend guess what it is: have him or her say it in the present tense. If correct, then have him or her say it in the past tense.**
- **Have your friend find and write down some action words. This time, you be the one to guess what they are.**

Checklist

Skills

- ☐ I can identify verbs in a story.
- ☐ I know the past tense of some regular and irregular verbs.
- ☐ I can make up sentences using the past tense of some irregular verbs.
- ☐ I know we can describe an action using different verbs.

Revising

- ☐ I have written the correct past tense of regular and irregular verbs.
- ☐ I have checked the spelling of my past tense verbs.

Adjectives

positive, comparative, superlative

5

I've just served this table three different sizes of cake. Do you know how to use adjectives to compare them? Read below to find out.

Mrs. Green has a **big** (positive) slice of cake, but her son Bobby has a **bigger** (comparative) slice, and her daughter Cindy has the **biggest** (superlative) slice of cake.

In this unit, students will:

- learn that there are three different forms of adjectives: positive (e.g. small), comparative (e.g. smaller), and superlative (e.g. smallest).
- identify adjectives on a menu and the things that they describe.
- understand what synonyms are and learn a few examples.
- learn the comparative and superlative forms of some adjectives and use them in sentences.
- learn to double the last consonant of some adjectives to spell their comparative and superlative forms (e.g. big, bigger, biggest).
- describe pictures using positive, comparative, and superlative adjectives.

A. **Read this takeout menu and pay close attention to the description underneath each food item. Underline the adjectives there. Then colour the ☆ beside what you would like to order.**

Tasty Place Takeout Menu

☆ **Fish and Chips**

- big and fresh catch of the day, with crispy chips on the side

☆ **Chicken Noodle Soup**

- delicious and healthy, this yummy soup will give you a boost

☆ **Cheese Bread**

- home-baked and cheesy, hot out of the oven

☆ **Chocolate Cake**

- lighter than air, richer than gold, to cheer you up when you are feeling blue

☆ **Ice Cream Sundae**

- creamy chocolate sauce and fresh strawberries on velvety vanilla ice cream

☆ **Lemonade**

- chilled and tart, a refreshing drink for the hottest days

☆ **Hot Chocolate**

- steaming, rich chocolate in a fat mug, to warm you up on the coldest days

B. Read what Bobby and Cindy ask. Find the answers from the menu.

1.

What are the menu items that are described by these adjectives?

a. steaming ____________________

b. chilled and tart ____________________

c. delicious and healthy ____________________

d. home-baked and cheesy ____________________

2.

What are the adjectives that describe these ingredients?

a. chips ____________________

b. strawberries ____________________

c. chocolate sauce ____________________

d. vanilla ice cream ____________________

Think!

Synonyms are words that have similar meanings. Write an adjective from the menu that is a synonym for each of these.

1.

____

2.

____

3.

____

C. Fill in the blanks. Then finish what Cindy and Bobby say with the correct adjectives.

1. light (positive) → ________ (comparative) → ________ (superlative)

2. ________ (positive) → richer (comparative) → ________ (superlative)

3. Air is the ________ thing, so if a chocolate cake is " ________ than air", then the cake is really ________ !

4. Gold is one of the ________ things, so if a chocolate cake is " ________ than gold", then it is really ________ !

D. Read what Mrs. Green says. Write the comparative and superlative forms of the following adjectives.

Letters like "d", "g", "n", and "t" are consonants. When an adjective has a vowel before its last consonant, we double the consonant to make the comparative and superlative forms.

1. sad ____sadder____ ____saddest____
2. big ________ ________
3. thin ________ ________
4. hot ________ ________

Look at each series of pictures. Use positive, comparative, and superlative adjectives in sentences to compare them. Remember to write "the" in front of the superlative form.

1. **Winter months**

November **December** **January**

November was __________ , but December was __________ , and January was the __________ !

2. **The catch of the day**

Friday **Saturday** **Sunday**

The catch of the day was __________ on Friday, but it was ______________________________ ,
______________________________ !

THINGS TO TRY

- **Find comparative or superlative adjectives in newspapers and cut them out.**
- **Glue each adjective under "Comparative" or "Superlative" below.**
- **Spell the other two forms of the adjective based on the one you have.**

Positive	Comparative	Superlative
great	greater	greatest

Checklist

Skills

- ☐ I know that there are three different forms of adjectives: positive, comparative, and superlative.
- ☐ I can identify adjectives on a menu and the things that they describe.
- ☐ I know what synonyms are and I know a few examples.
- ☐ I know the comparative and superlative forms of some adjectives and I know how to use them in sentences.
- ☐ I know when to double the last consonant of an adjective to spell its comparative and superlative forms.
- ☐ I can describe series of pictures using positive, comparative, and superlative adjectives.

Revising

- ☐ I have checked the spelling of my comparative and superlative adjectives, especially the ones where I need to double the last consonant.
- ☐ My writing is neat.

Adverbs

words that describe verbs

6

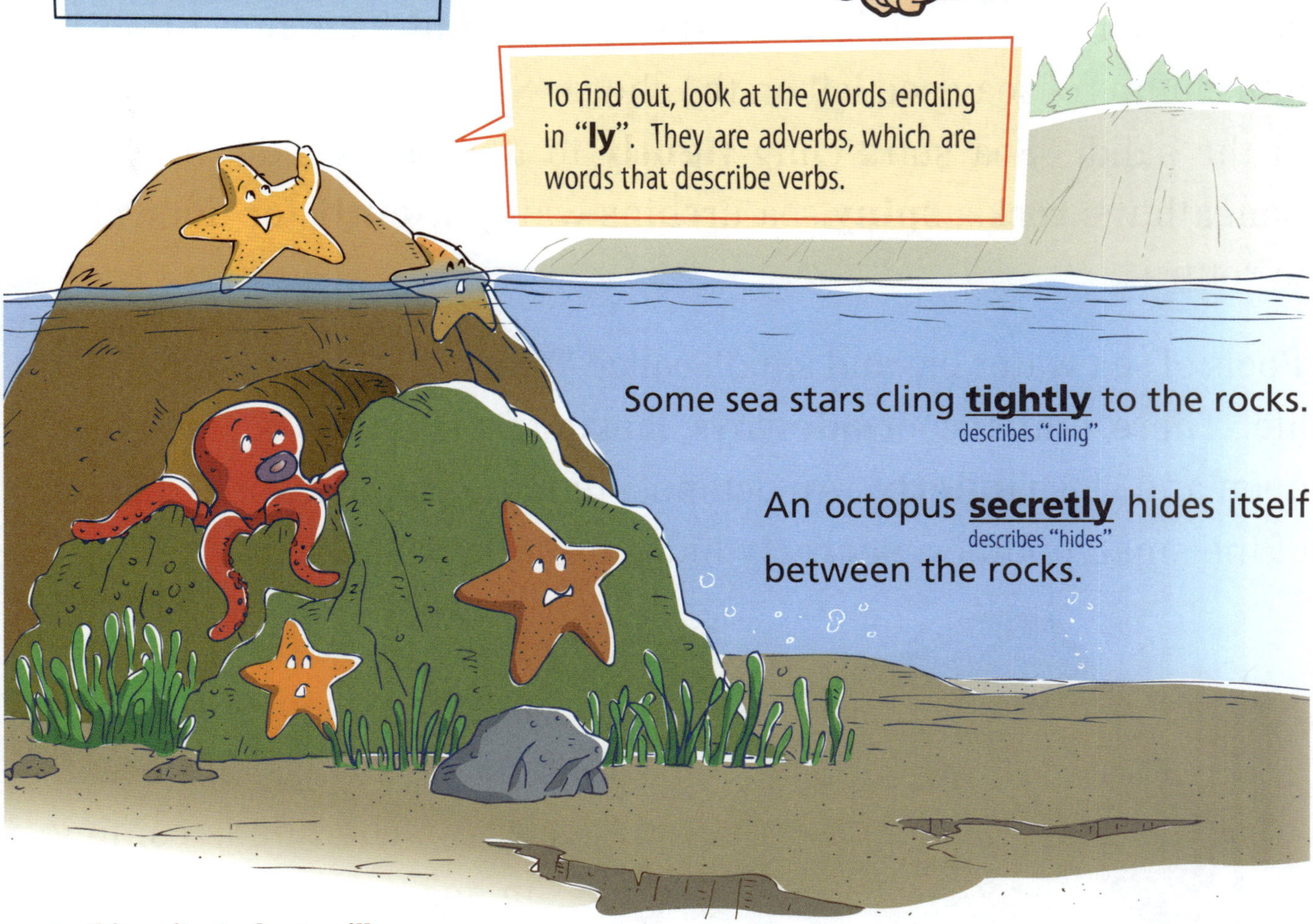

In this unit, students will:

- understand that adverbs describe verbs and identify them.
- complete a crossword puzzle of adverbs.
- learn some examples of adverbs that do not end in "ly".
- know that they can form adverbs out of some adjectives by adding "ly".
- learn how to form adverbs out of adjectives that end in "y".
- describe pictures using verbs and adverbs.

A. Read and look at the words in bold. Underline the ones that are adverbs.

Twice a day, every day, the ocean waves **gracefully** flow out to the sea. The water's edge **becomes** farther and farther away, and the shore widens. Land that was **under** water is now exposed. Sand and rocks **quickly** dry. The beach is **empty**.

Or is it?

Not all sea animals follow the **low** tide. Sand fleas hop **happily** into clumps of seaweed left on the shore. Sand dollars laze **sleepily** in the sand. Sea stars cling **tightly** to the **shady** side of rocks. Beneath the rocks, **spiny** sea urchins wait **patiently** for the water to return.

Pools of sea water big and small, called "tide pools", also hold ocean life. There, crabs scoot **sideways**, looking for shade. Sea anemones open and close **quietly**. An octopus, unhappy to be trapped in one of the small puddles, **secretly** hides itself between rocks.

Then the gaps **between** the tide pools and the ocean **slowly** fill. Each wave brings the ocean closer. The tide is coming in again.

B. Read the clues and complete this crossword puzzle with the correct adverbs from (A).

How do...

A. the sea urchins wait for the water to return?

B. the ocean waves flow out to the sea?

C. the sea anemones open and close?

D. the sand and rocks dry?

E. the sand dollars laze in the sand?

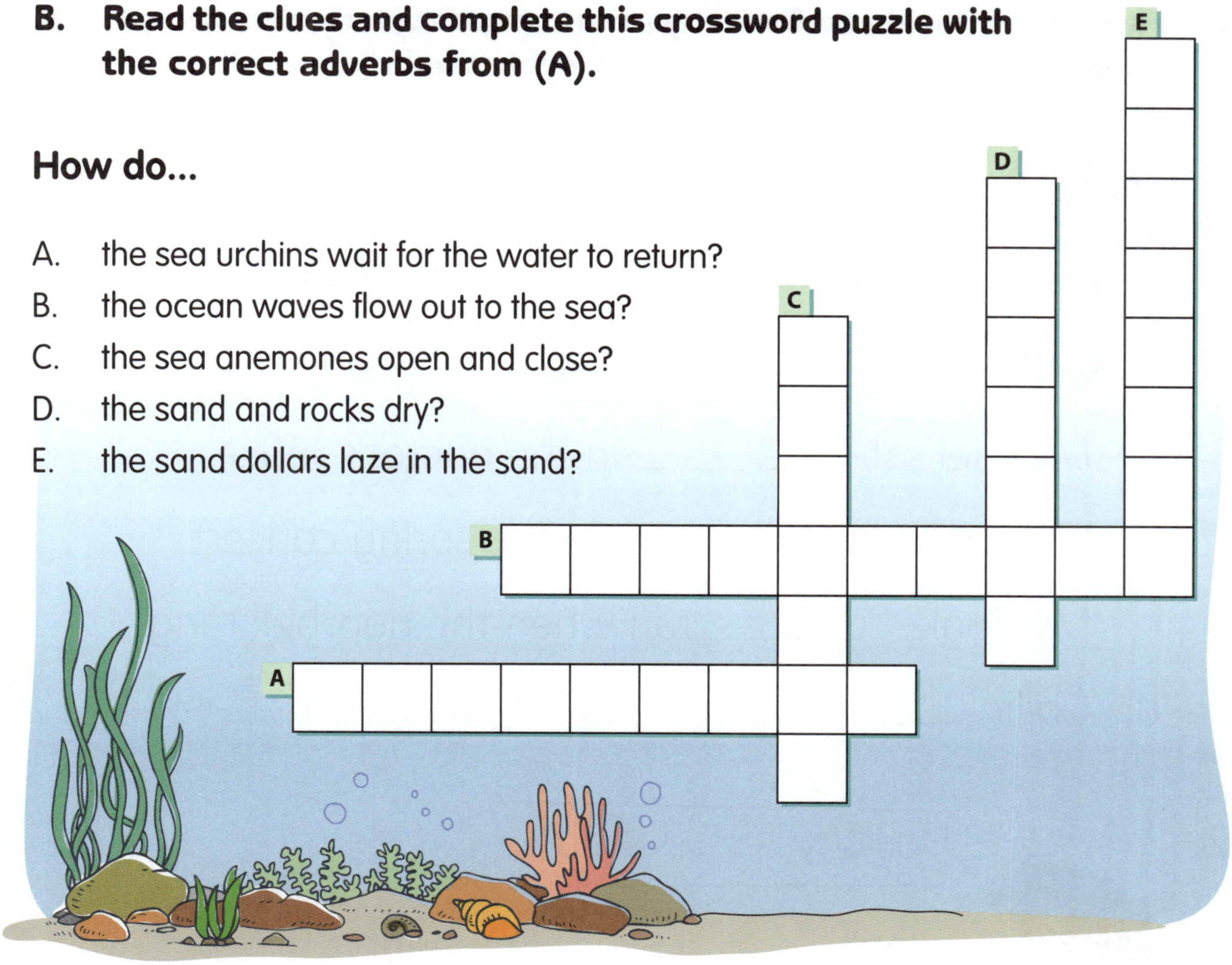

Think!

Some adverbs don't end in "ly". Find the adverb from (A) that doesn't end in "ly". Then unscramble the letters to spell some more adverbs to finish the sentences.

1. Adverb without "ly": ____________

2. Crabs don't move ____________ .
(frowrad)

3. A crab crawls ____________ a seashell.
(isnide)

C. Read what David and Sara say to turn each adjective into an adverb. Then use the adverbs to finish the sentences.

1\.

Add "**ly**".

sudden	__________	nervous	__________
careful	__________	beautiful	__________

a. Michael sat __________ in the doctor's office.

b. Winnie sang __________ in the spring concert.

c. My dog __________ ran when the doorbell rang.

d. Collin __________ washed his paintbrush.

2\.

Change "**y**" to "**i**", and then add "**ly**".

lazy	__________	angry	__________
happy	__________	crazy	__________

a. Michael __________ played music for the whole night!

b. Winnie __________ danced in her new shoes.

c. My dog barked __________ at a stranger.

d. Collin is tired and is lying __________ on the couch.

As you can see, we can form adverbs out of adjectives.

Your Turn

I am singing loudly! See what these people are doing and how they are doing it. Use the correct verb and adverb in a sentence to describe each one.

Verb	singing	dancing	running	lying
Adverb	quickly	beautifully	lazily	wildly

1 

2 

3 

4 

1. ______________________________

2. ______________________________

3. ______________________________

4. ______________________________

THINGS TO TRY

- **Read or sing the words to the popular children's song "Row, Row, Row Your Boat", paying special attention to the adverbs (in bold).**
- **Come up with different adverbs (e.g. quickly, cheerily, rapidly, speedily) to make a new version of the song.**

Original Version

Row, row, row your boat
Gently down the stream.
Merrily, **merrily**, **merrily**, **merrily**,
Life is but a dream.

My Version

Row, row, row your boat
__________ down the stream.
__________ , __________ , __________ , __________ ,
Row it for the team!

Checklist

Skills

- ☐ I know what adverbs are, and I can identify them.
- ☐ I can use adverbs to complete a crossword puzzle.
- ☐ I know some examples of adverbs that do not end in "ly".
- ☐ I know how to form adverbs out of adjectives, including the ones that end in "y".
- ☐ I can use a verb and an adverb to describe a picture.

Revising

- ☐ I have checked the spelling of my adverbs, especially the ones formed out of adjectives that end in "y".
- ☐ I have used a suitable adverb to describe each of my verbs.

Prepositions

words to tell place and direction

7

In this unit, students will:

- learn prepositions that tell about place (e.g. over, under) and prepositions that tell about direction (e.g. from, to).
- use prepositions to finish a piece of writing.
- use prepositions to tell where a train has travelled.
- learn the synonyms of some prepositions.
- complete a crossword puzzle of prepositions and use the prepositions in sentences to describe a picture.
- write sentences using prepositions with the help of a picture.

A. Read and pay special attention to the words in bold. Use the given prepositions to finish this piece of writing.

on
from
through
in front of
above
to

A train starts its journey **from** the west coast **to** the east. It chuffs **through** valleys, first **between** hills, and then **amid** taller and taller mountains. It winds **around** mountain passes. It goes **over** bridges and 1. ____________ tunnels until it reaches the foothills. The train is back 2. ____________ low ground.

Through the prairies, the train steams ahead **beside** fields of wheat and flax. The land is so flat that the scene **ahead of** the train is the same as the scene **behind** it. The sky 3. ____________ the train is so wide that it touches the ground. Suddenly, there is something 4. ____________ the train. The whistle blows, the train slows, so that the cattle can move away.

The train moves onward **under** the endless sky. It follows rivers. It passes lakes. It meets cold nights and sunny days. **In** the distance, children see the train and imagine that they are running **beside** it. The train has travelled **across** the wide country 5. ____________ coast 6. ____________ coast. It will soon stop, drop off and pick up passengers, before going back west.

B. Fill in the blanks with the correct prepositions from (A).

1. ____________ west ____________ east
2. ____________ valleys, tunnels, and the prairies
3. ____________ hills and ____________ mountains
4. ____________ mountain passes
5. ____________ bridges
6. ____________ fields of wheat and flax
7. ____________ a wide country

Think!

Remember what synonyms are? They are words that have similar meanings. Each preposition below has a synonym in (A). Find and write it down.

1. over ____________ 2. amid ____________

3. across ____________ 4. ahead of ____________

C. Write the opposite of each clue word to finish this crossword puzzle. Then choose the correct prepositions from the answers and the clues to finish the sentences.

1.

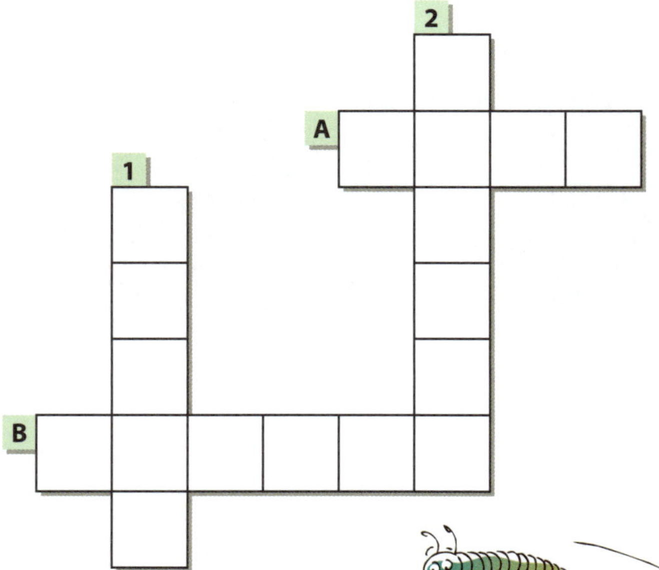

Across

A. to

B. in front of

Down

1. over
2. through

2. The toy bus is ________________ the toy car.

3. The ball is ________________ the table.

4. Leo is ________________ his robot.

5. The bug is flying ________________ the bus.

6. It is flying ________________ the box ________________ Jack.

Use each of the given prepositions to write a different sentence. Look at this picture to help you.

1. Santa is pulling his sleigh across the sky.
2. ______________________________
3. ______________________________
4. ______________________________
5. ______________________________
6. ______________________________

THINGS TO TRY

- Write down five prepositions in the green area.
- Find a picture of a person or thing from kids' magazines or cereal boxes.
- Glue the picture somewhere in the dollhouse below.
- Describe its location in the house using one of your prepositions in a sentence.

Checklist

Skills

- [ ] I know the prepositions that tell about place and the prepositions that tell about direction, and I can use them to finish a piece of writing.
- [ ] I can use prepositions to tell where the train has travelled.
- [ ] I know the synonyms of some prepositions.
- [ ] I can use prepositions to finish a crossword puzzle and use them in sentences to describe a picture.
- [ ] I can use prepositions to write sentences with the help of a picture.

Revising

- [ ] I have checked my spelling.
- [ ] I have written in complete sentences.

Sentences

combining them with conjunctions

8

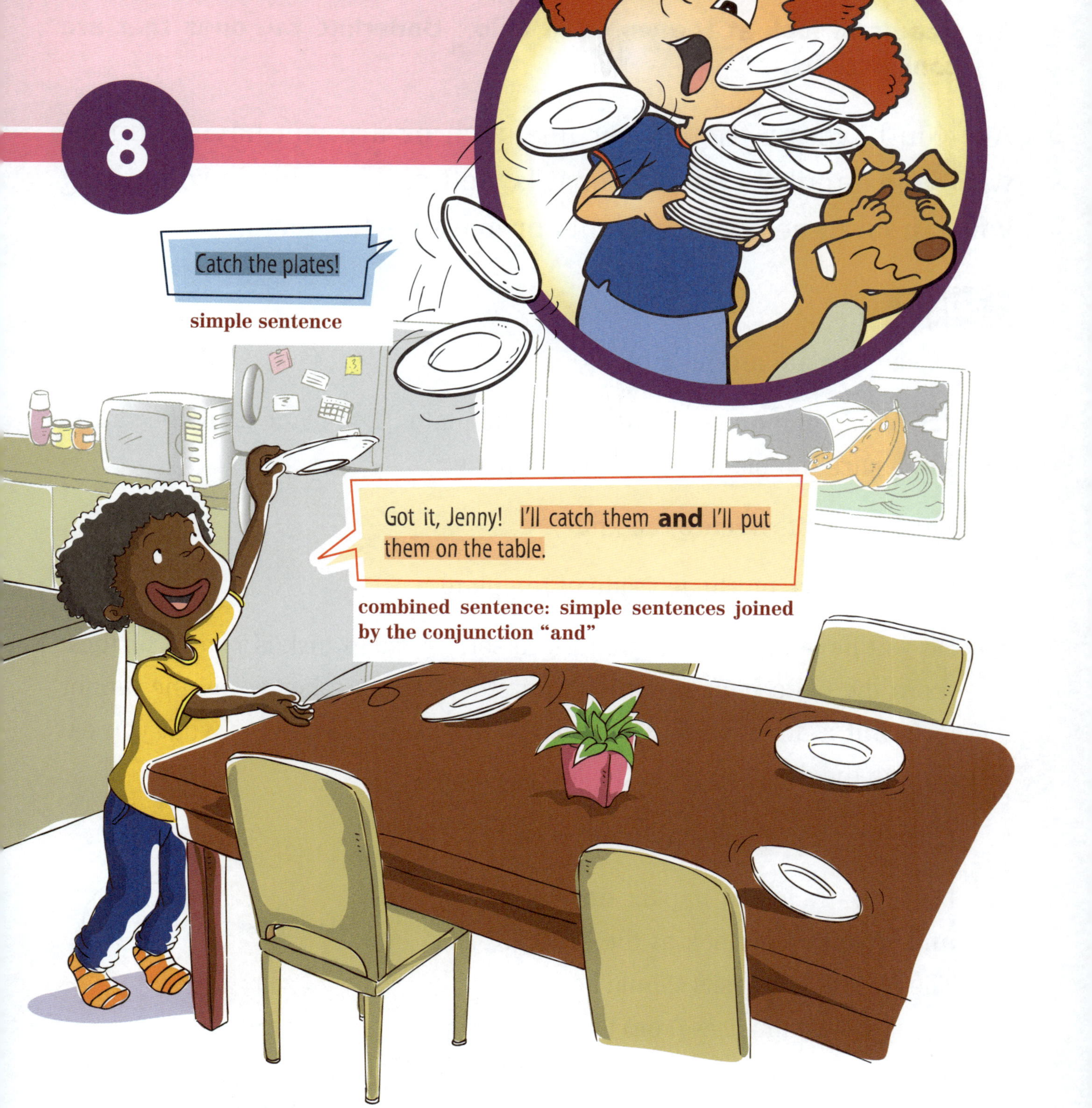

In this unit, students will:

- learn what simple sentences are (without conjunctions) and what "combined" sentences are (with conjunctions), and identify them.
- identify conjunctions in a piece of writing.
- know when to put a comma in a combined sentence: before "so", but not before "because".
- use conjunctions to combine simple sentences.
- describe a picture in a combined sentence.

A. Read and look at the words in bold. Underline the ones that are conjunctions.

Are you having a friend over for lunch **or** are you having dinner with your family? Whichever it is, setting the table is something you can do to help your parents prepare for the meal.

Steps

1. Place the plate **on** the table.
2. Place the knife **on** the right side of the plate. The blade could be sharp, **so** be sure the blade side faces the plate.
3. The spoon sits **beside** the knife.
4. Place the fork on the left side of the plate.
5. Do you have more than one fork to set? A salad fork is placed furthest **from** the plate **because** it is the first fork used, followed by the dinner fork, **but** a dessert fork goes next to the plate. Dessert is what you eat last, **so** the dessert fork is the last one used.
6. Place the water glass **above** the knife.
7. Put a neatly folded napkin **on** the plate **and** step back to look at the setting. The plate and utensils should be about two centimetres **from** the edge of the table.

Set one place setting for each person **at** the meal. You may want to add a centrepiece like a vase of flowers to the table setting.

B. Read each sentence. Write "simple" or "combined".

1. Place the water glass above the knife. ______________
2. Are you having a friend over for lunch or are you having dinner with your family? ______________
3. Dessert is what you eat last, so the dessert fork is the last one used. ______________
4. Place the fork on the left side of the plate. ______________
5. Put a neatly folded napkin on the plate and step back to look at the setting. ______________

Think!

Some combined sentences need a comma, but some don't. As a general rule, we put a comma before "so", but not before "because". Which combined sentences below have missing commas? Put them in.

1. I have a blister on my toe so I won't walk far.
2. I won't walk far because I have a blister on my toe.
3. Amy adopted two kittens because she loves animals.
4. Amy loves animals so she adopted two kittens.

C. Use the given conjunctions to combine these simple sentences.

1. Tammy loves volleyball. She loves basketball.

____

2. I love going to the amusement park. I don't like waiting in line.

____

____

3. The table is set. We can serve dinner now.

____

4. School is cancelled today. There is a snowstorm.

____

5. You can have fish and chips. You can have burger and fries. You can't have both.

____

____

Look at each picture. Describe it in a combined sentence using the given conjunction.

but

because

so

and

1. ______________________________

____

2. ______________________________

____

3. ______________________________

____

4. ______________________________

____

THINGS TO TRY

- **Find a short, simple sentence from a book that you have read.**
- **Copy the sentence on a piece of paper.**
- **Add "and", "but", "so", and "because" to make it into four different combined sentences.**
- **Try the example below as practice first.**

Simple sentence

Neal looked up at the stars.

Combined sentences

1. Neal looked up at the stars **and** ______________________ .
2. Neal looked up at the stars **but** ______________________ .
3. Neal looked up at the stars **because** ______________________
   ____ .
4. Neal looked up at the stars, **so** ______________________
   ____ .

Checklist

Skills

- ☐ I know what simple sentences are: sentences with no conjunctions.
- ☐ I can identify conjunctions in a piece of writing.
- ☐ I know what "combined" sentences are: simple sentences joined by conjunctions.
- ☐ I know when to put a comma: before "so", but not before "because".
- ☐ I know how to use conjunctions to combine simple sentences.
- ☐ I can use a conjunction in a combined sentence to describe a picture.

Revising

- ☐ My sentences begin with a capital letter and end with a period, a question mark, or an exclamation mark.

Punctuation

comma, apostrophe

9

It's (1) August 15, (1) 2007.

Roberta's (2) cat, Muffin, is taking a picture of her rabbits.

They are Snowball, Patches, Peter, and Cotton. (2)

apostrophe:

1 to form the contraction of "it is"

2 to show possession, meaning "Muffin belongs to Roberta"

comma:

1 to separate the month and day from the year in the date

2 to separate names or things in a list

In this unit, students will:

- learn when to use the apostrophe: to show possession and to form contractions (e.g. they're).
- learn how to use the comma in dates and in lists.
- identify words that use the apostrophe to show possession.
- learn where to put the apostrophe when showing possession with plural nouns.
- write some common contractions in full.
- use the apostrophe and the comma in an integrated activity.

A. Read Roberta's photo captions and underline the words that use the apostrophe to show possession. Then write the correct photo numbers on the two photos.

Photo 1 — These are my rabbits. They're so cute! From left to right, they are Snowball, Patches, Peter, and Cotton.

Photo 2 — Snowball's ears are the longest. He has the longest whiskers, too.

Photo 3 — Muffin, my cat, is playing with Cotton's ears.

Photo 4 — Patches and Cotton are wondering why Muffin's tail is different from theirs. It's so much longer!

Photo 5 — Why aren't the rabbits in their cage? That's because they're following Peter. He isn't in the picture because he hopped away when he saw the camera.

Think!

When we show possession with plural nouns, the apostrophe goes after the "s", not before. Which sentence in each group shows possession with plural nouns? Check ✔.

1. ◯ The rabbit's home is very comfortable.
   ◯ The rabbits' home is very comfortable.

2. ◯ The kids' mom is making mango pudding.
   ◯ The kid's mom is making mango pudding.

B. Find and write down the contractions from the passage. Then write them out in full.

	Contraction	Word in Full
1.	They're	They are
2.		
3.		
4.		
5.		
6.		

C. Read what Jessie and Jan say about the comma. Check ✔ the date and the sentence that use the comma correctly.

1. This is where the comma goes in a date.

- ◯ August, 25, 2004
- ◯ January 13, 1996
- ◯ February 20 2009,

2. When we have three or more things in a sentence, we have a "list". Here's how we use the comma in a list:

   I want to visit Mexico, Russia, and China.

- ◯ My favourite colours are red blue green and yellow.
- ◯ My friends are Nancy, David Tim and Tom.
- ◯ My mom bought apples, oranges, peaches, and bananas.

D. The following is the index page of Roberta's photo album. Help her put the comma in the correct places.

Index

Date	Photo
July 15 2007	Snowball
July 22 2007	Snowball and Muffin
August 10 2007	Patches Cotton and Muffin
August 10 2007	Cotton Patches and Snowball
August 15 2007	Peter Patches Cotton and Snowball

Put the apostrophe in the correct place in each photo caption. Then complete the rest of the activity.

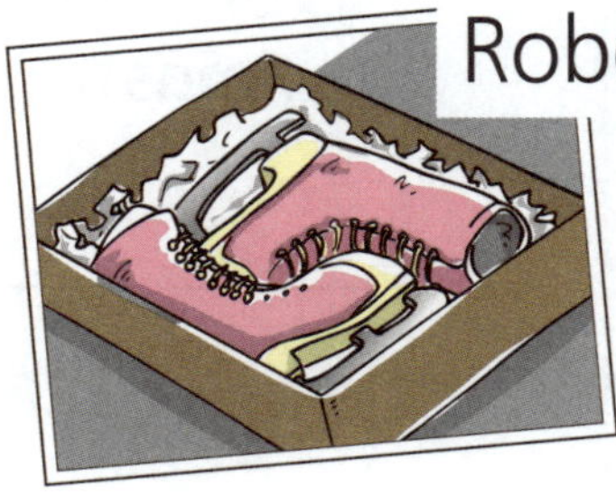

Robertas skates!

Her pets dinner

Glue a picture of you and your friends here.

____

list of names (from left to right)

Think of a sentence that contains "we are" and "I am" to describe your picture. Then write your sentence again using contractions.

- ______________________________
- ______________________________

THINGS TO TRY

- Look through some old newspapers and magazines.
- Find a picture with a caption that has at least one use of the apostrophe.
- Cut out the picture, caption included, and glue it below.
- Write down the word(s) with the apostrophe and underline "possession" or "contraction". If it is a contraction, write it out in full in the ( ).

a picture with a caption that has at least one use of the apostrophe

Words with the Apostrophe

- ____________________
  possession
  contraction (   )
- ____________________
  possession
  contraction (   )
- ____________________
  possession
  contraction (   )

Checklist

Skills

- ☐ I know when to use the apostrophe: to show possession and to form contractions.
- ☐ I know how to use the comma in dates and in lists.
- ☐ I can identify words that use the apostrophe to show possession.
- ☐ I know where to put the apostrophe when showing possession with plural nouns: after the "s".
- ☐ I know how to write some common contractions in full.
- ☐ I know how to use the comma and the apostrophe in an integrated activity.

Revising

- ☐ I have put the apostrophe after the "s" when showing possession with plural nouns.
- ☐ I have used the comma to write dates and to separate things in a list.

A. Read. Then answer the questions with the correct words in bold.

Every year, the students and teachers of **Farmers Public School** put together a show. This year, they are going to perform *Oliver!*, which is a musical about homeless children in 19th century England. It is based on the book titled ***Oliver Twist*** by **Charles Dickens**.

The **children** of the story are all played by students, while the **men** and **women** are played by the **teachers** and the principal. **Ben** plays the role of Oliver, the main character who learns to be a **pickpocket**. His buddy **Paul** plays **The Artful Dodger**, the smartest pickpocket in the story. Their math teacher Mr. Vine plays a **thief** named **Fagin** – he is the man who teaches the homeless children how to steal. The band teacher Ms. Hartley plays a kind-hearted **woman** named **Nancy**. The principal plays a kind **gentleman** named Mr. Brownlow.

The students are very excited because on the day of the **performance**, they get to stain their **teeth** with chocolate sauce to look dirty. Their teachers will also let them run around the **schoolyard** without shoes to get dirty **feet**. The teachers will do the same, of course. When the performers get on stage with their **costumes**, they will all look like poor **people** from 19th century England. It's going to be a great show!

REVIEW

1. What are...

   a. the four compound proper nouns?

   ______________________ ______________________

   ______________________ ______________________

   b. the six irregular plural nouns?

   ______________________ ______________________

   ______________________ ______________________

   ______________________ ______________________

2. 

   I know that ______________ , ______________ , and ______________ are compound words.

B. Read (A) again. Use possessive adjectives to answer these questions.

1. What are the students' roles?

   ____

2. What are the teachers' roles?

   ____

3. What is Mr. Vine's role?

   ____

4. What is Ms. Hartley's role?

   ____

C. Write the past tense of the given verbs to finish these sentences.

1. For months, everyone ______________ (read) their lines over and over so that they would know them by heart.

2. Ben was so excited that he almost ______________ (forget) to take his costume to school.

3. A lot of people ______________ (come) to see the students, teachers, and the principal perform.

4. The students and teachers ______________ (walk) on the stage with dirty feet!

5. Because *Oliver!* is a musical, the performers ______________ (sing) and danced on the stage.

6. When the show was over, the performers bowed and ______________ (wave) to the audience.

7. Ben was so happy that he ______________ (play) the role of Oliver.

REVIEW

D. Complete the chart. Then finish each sentence with the correct adjective or adverb.

1.

Positive	Comparative	Superlative	Adverb
light			lightly
	warmer		
		coldest	
sad			sadly

2. a. At the party, Ms. Lo greeted us ______________ .

   b. The sun gets into my room but not my brother's, so my room is ______________ than his.

3. a. This cake is very fluffy. It's ______________ than air!

   b. Mary doesn't want the floor to creak, so she is walking very ______________ .

4. a. This winter, January was the ______________ month.

   b. Mr. Brown is not very friendly. He talks to everyone very ______________ .

5. a. Mr. Chips will not teach at our school anymore. We ______________ waved goodbye to him.

   b. Tom looks ______________ than usual because he just lost his turtle.

E. Look at this picture and finish the sentences with the given prepositions.

1. Amy is putting a house ______________ the trees.

2. Tom is sitting ______________ a tree.

3. There is a window ______________ Amy.

4. There is a bookshelf ______________ the window.

5. A bee is flying ______________ the room.

6. The toy train is going ______________ the tunnel and ______________ the track.

REVIEW

F. Use the correct conjunctions to combine the following simple sentences.

and or but so because

1. Amy and Tom are playing at home. It is Saturday morning.

2. The kids usually watch TV on weekend mornings. Their parents bought them a train set. They want to play with it.

G. Read Tom's journal and put in the missing commas and apostrophes.

September 20 2007

Mom and Dad bought us a train set! It includes the cars of the train the pieces for the track a tunnel and some houses and trees to make a town. At first, we couldnt get the train to start because we forgot to put in batteries! It was so funny. Now, Amy and I love to play with the train set so much that we dont want to watch TV anymore.

Stories

They're written in paragraphs!

10

In this unit, students will:

- learn the purpose of paragraphs: to make our writing more organized.
- read a story and tell how many paragraphs it has.
- identify the setting, characters, problem, and solution in different paragraphs of a story.
- learn some new words.
- use sequence words (e.g. then, finally) to retell a story.
- write a story that has three paragraphs with the help of pictures.

A. Mother Mouse wrote a story. Read it first. Then finish what her children say.

Mouse of the Gourmet Café

Mouse lived in a cozy hole in a wall in the Gourmet Café. She was happy. Every evening, after Chef Goulet said goodbye to the last customers and locked the doors, Mouse and her children scurried along the floor. All night they gnawed on pieces of bread under the tables. They nibbled on morsels of fine cheese beneath the chairs. But they especially enjoyed crumbs of the café's daily special. When the mice had stuffed themselves, they checked the chef's chalkboard for the next day's special. Full and satisfied, they went back to their cozy little hole to dream of their next feast.

But one night, instead of the next day's special, Mouse saw a message on the chalkboard. She stared at the first two words, gathered her children, and dashed into their hole. The words "REMOVE MOUSE" were scribbled at the top of the board. Mouse knew that their easy days were over.

That night, Mouse and her little ones packed up their things. Just as the sun was rising, they tiptoed out of their hole, and said goodbye to the floor that had given them so much food. Mouse closed her eyes and wondered where they would live: in a scratchy nest in a pile of garbage in some back alley? Then she opened her eyes, and froze: Chef Goulet's big shoes stood in front of her. Slowly looking up, she saw that he was adding another "S" to "MOUSE". "REMOVE MOUSSE", it now said. What she saw before was just a spelling mistake, so Mouse and her children were still safe! Chef Goulet drew a line through "CHOCOLATE MOUSSE" and printed "MANGO PUDDING". With happy thoughts of marvellous meals, Mouse and her children went back to their cozy little hole.

There are ______________ paragraphs in Mom's story.

B. Read what Mother Mouse says to complete this activity.

Remember the following? They're called "story elements". Find the paragraph where I introduce each one and write it in the circle. Then describe each one in your own words.

Setting ◯ : ______________________________

Characters ◯ : ______________________________

Problem ◯ : ______________________________

Solution ◯ : ______________________________

Think!

Use what you know from the story to underline the word that means the same as the given word.

gnawed	dashed	marvellous
cooked nibbled	walked rushed	wonderful beautiful

C. Use the given sequence words and story details to retell the story "Mouse of the Gourmet Café".

Sequence Words

Then

Finally

Later

Story Details

- Mouse realized that the message was not about her and so she did not have to leave.
- Mouse and her children dined on crumbs on the floor of the café.
- Mouse and her children got their things together to move out.
- Mouse thought that Chef Goulet had found out she was living in the café.

When we retell a story, we can finish it in one paragraph because it is supposed to be shorter.

In the beginning, ______________________________

Use the pictures to write a story with paragraphs. Introduce the setting and characters in the first paragraph, the problem in the second paragraph, and the solution in the third paragraph. Remember to give a title.

BOOKS TO READ

Title:
My Father's Dragon

Author:
Ruth Stiles Garret

Publisher:
Random House Books for Young Readers (1987)

Leo's Rating: ★★★★½

"This book makes me want to keep reading to find out what happens next. It's about a boy who leaves home to save a baby dragon. In the beginning, a cat tells the boy about the dragon and gives him advice on how to save it. Then, we follow the boy as he travels to the dragon's faraway island. Finally...well, you'll have to read the book to find out."

Title:
Akimbo and the Elephants

Author:
Alexander McCall Smith

Publisher:
Bloomsbury USA Children's Books (reprint edition, 2005)

Marie's Rating: ★★★★★

"I like this book because I like animals. Akimbo lives in Africa where his dad works at a game reserve: a place where wild animals are protected. But poachers are killing elephants for their ivory tusks. Akimbo needs to do something about it. The middle of the story is full of suspense, so it's very exciting!"

Checklist

Skills

- [ ] I know that organized writing is divided into chunks called "paragraphs".
- [ ] I can tell how many paragraphs there are in a story.
- [ ] I can identify the setting, characters, problem, and solution of a story in different paragraphs.
- [ ] I have learned some new words.
- [ ] I know how to use sequence words like "then" and "finally" to retell a story.
- [ ] I can write a story that has three paragraphs with the help of pictures.

Revising

- [ ] I have checked my spelling.
- [ ] My sentences begin with a capital letter and end with a period, a question mark, or an exclamation mark.

Setting

Use your five senses to describe it!

11

In this unit, students will:

- understand that we can describe the setting of a story using our five senses: see, hear, smell, taste, touch.
- read a story and draw a picture of its setting.
- identify the place and season of a story.
- identify adjectives that tell how something "feels".
- match the five senses with story details about the setting.
- rewrite a paragraph from a story using a different setting.

A. Read this story. Then draw a picture of its setting.

Simon's Fish

Simon moved to his new home and he learned more than he ever did. He learned how to kayak. He knew which flowers smelled nice. He knew which plants on the forest trail would make him itch. He knew which berries were edible and sweet. He knew where to have a refreshing drink of water. He also knew how to catch a fish. But today, he was walking home without one.

Simon's uncle was a fisherman, and bragged to Simon all the time. He had caught fish from all the lakes and rivers. The only place he hadn't fished was from the sky. If only Simon had a fish to take home today, he could show his uncle that he was as good as he was.

It had rained every day since the new school year started. The air smelled fresh. The forest floor was spongy. Beneath Simon's feet, the leaves formed a very wet mat. The sound of the river teased him. "Fish, fish, fish," it seemed to say. The river was full of salmon, yet Simon had no luck in catching any one of them.

Then Simon heard the scream of an eagle. When he looked up, all he saw was a large fish. Hooked on the claws of the bald eagle, the fish seemed to be flying in the sky. The eagle soared higher towards another eagle. The two birds tumbled somersaults. "They have my fish!" Simon thought. Just then, the fish fell on his head and he caught it with his hand. He picked up a stick and hooked the fish on one end. Walking tall with a fish over his shoulder, Simon went home and told his uncle that he had caught a big fish from the sky!

B. Circle the correct place and season of the story. Then tell how you got each answer by writing the sentence that gave you the clue.

Hint: you find out **where** my story takes place in the first paragraph, but you don't know **when** it is until the third paragraph. That's when you know about the weather, which is part of the setting because it is a clue to the season.

Place: city / ocean / forest / farm

Clue sentence: ____________________

____

Season: spring / summer / fall / winter

Clue sentence: ____________________

____

Think!

Read the third paragraph again. What are the adjectives that tell you how something "feels"? Write them down and tell what they describe. Then make up a sentence using both adjectives.

- ____________ : describes the ____________
- ____________ : describes the ____________

____

____

C. Write the word for each of the five senses and the matching given sentence. Then write another matching sentence from the story.

> We learn about the setting in terms of the five senses throughout the story.

- The air smelled fresh.
- The forest floor was spongy.
- "Fish, fish, fish," it seemed to say.
- The two birds tumbled somersaults.
- He knew which berries were edible and sweet.

Five Senses

1. 

2. 

3. 

4. 

5. 

Your Turn

Imagine that the story "Simon's Fish" takes place in winter. Think of adjectives that describe this new setting in terms of the five senses. Then use these adjectives to rewrite the third paragraph of the story.

Third paragraph from "Simon's fish":

It had rained every day since the new school year started. The air smelled fresh. The forest floor was spongy. Beneath Simon's feet, the leaves formed a very wet mat. The sound of the river teased him. "Fish, fish, fish," it seemed to say. The river was full of salmon, yet Simon had no luck in catching any one of them.

Adjectives:

see
white

hear
loud

smell

taste

touch

My rewrite:

____

____

____

____

____

____

____

____

____

____

THINGS TO TRY

- **Look through some newspapers and magazines.**
- **Find a picture of a "setting". There can be people, animals, and/or things in your picture.**
- **Think about what you can see, hear, smell, taste, and touch in this "setting" and write them down.**

Glue your picture here.

see: ______________________

hear: ______________________

smell: ______________________

taste: ______________________

touch: ______________________

Checklist

Skills

- ☐ I know that we can describe the setting of a story using our five senses.
- ☐ I can draw a picture of a story's setting.
- ☐ I can identify the place and season of a story.
- ☐ I can identify adjectives that tell how something "feels".
- ☐ I can match the five senses with the story details about the setting.
- ☐ I can rewrite a paragraph from a story using a different setting.

Revising

- ☐ I have checked my spelling.
- ☐ I have written in complete sentences.

Characters

Some may be very popular!

12

In this unit, students will:

- identify the main and supporting characters in a story.
- make inferences about a character from information in the story.
- understand that setting may affect a character's actions.
- match a character's different actions with different settings.
- describe the main character from the points of view of some supporting characters.

A. Read and fill in the blanks with the main character's first name. Then answer the questions with names of the supporting characters.

Bertie Boyle

In the small town of Littleton, people got around on tractors and horses. Some drove old cars, and some rode their bikes. They had many ways to travel, but because of __________ Boyle, their favourite was by bus.

__________ drove Littleton's only bus. Everybody knew him and he knew everybody. When Mrs. Martin wasn't at her bus stop one morning, he waited a few minutes in case she was running a little late. When Bonnie had to take her budgie to the vet and asked if it could board the bus too, __________ said "Of course!" and turned up the heat so that the budgie would be more comfortable.

Everything was great for __________ in Littleton until one day when his boss at the Big Bus Company gave him a promotion. "You're ready to drive in the big city, __________," he said. "Megacity has grown, and they need experienced drivers like you."

__________ had only dreamed of working in a big city. He never expected it to come true! He would have many more friends. Perhaps he would even be famous. Of course, he would be more sophisticated in the city: people would call him Mr. Boyle, not __________ .

And so Megacity's new bus driver, Mr. Boyle, learned his new route.

His passengers were many – so many, in fact, that he never learned their names! Once, he waited for an old lady who was late, but the others angrily pointed at their watches. When a boy asked if he could bring his new kitten on board, Mr. Boyle glanced at the disapproving passengers in his mirror. He shook his head. "No pets on the bus," he said importantly. "It's in the rules."

__________ Boyle thought things were just fine in Megacity until one day when his boss gave him a package of letters from Littleton. "They miss you, __________," he said. And that is when __________ realized that things were not so fine in Megacity. __________ Boyle went back to his job in Littleton, where he knew everybody and everybody knew him.

1. Who brought a budgie aboard Bertie's bus? __________
2. Whom did Bertie wait for one morning in Littleton? __________
3. Who gave Bertie a promotion? __________

Think!

What do you think the people of Littleton said in their letters about Bertie? Check ✔ what they might have said.

- ◯ **Bring back Bertie! He was the best!**
- ◯ **Bertie was a mean driver. He never waited for me.**
- ◯ **Our new bus driver doesn't wait for late passengers. How we wish that our old driver could come back!**

B. Read what Bertie says. Use your own words to write the opposite of each action. Then write the names of the two settings on the buses and match them with Bertie's actions.

> I moved from a small town called Littleton to a big city called Megacity, and then back again. A change of setting can change a character's actions. That's why I was different in the two different settings.

Bertie's Actions

(A) Bertie knew every passenger's name.

(B) ______________________________

(C) Bertie did not allow any pets on board.

(D) ______________________________

(E) Bertie always waited for his passengers.

(F) ______________________________

Settings

Pretend you are the following characters. Write about Bertie from their different points of view.

Bonnie

- was allowed to bring her budgie on board

____

____

____

____

Mrs. Martin

- was a little late one day but Bertie waited

____

____

____

____

boy with kitten

- was not allowed to bring his kitten on board

____

____

____

____

THINGS TO TRY

- **Look at the characters below and think about their personalities.**
- **Draw each of them a setting that matches the character. Look through picture books, newspapers, and magazines to get ideas. Give each setting a name.**
- **Think of two things to describe each character in his/her setting (e.g. In Littleton, Bertie knew everybody, and he let his passengers' pets board the bus.)**

Setting: ______________________

____

____

____

Setting: ______________________

____

____

____

Checklist

Skills

- ☐ I can identify the main and supporting characters in a story.
- ☐ I can make inferences about a character from information in the story.
- ☐ I know that setting may affect a character's actions.
- ☐ I can match a character's different actions with different settings.
- ☐ I can describe the main character from the points of view of some supporting characters.

Revising

- ☐ I have checked my spelling.
- ☐ I have written in complete sentences.

Problem and Solution

Oh no!

13

In this unit, students will:

- identify where in a story the problem and the solution are.
- answer questions about the story to learn more about the problem.
- write their opinion on what happens in the story.
- match descriptions from different parts of the story with the story elements (setting, characters, problem, solution).
- come up with a different solution to give the story a new ending.

A. Read this story. Then fill in the blanks to finish what Boris says.

The Careless Giant

Boris was everything that a giant should be. He was strong. He was smart. He was hard-working. In the world of giants, he was really, really big. Unfortunately, Boris was careless. He stomped carelessly through puddles, and he sneezed without covering his mouth.

Whenever Boris stepped in a puddle, the little people's ocean had enormous waves. The other giants cared about the little people, and told Boris to watch his step. They said to Boris, "We step in the water gently, two times a day, so that the little people just call it the tide."

Whenever Boris sneezed, the little people had violent storms. The other giants tried to teach him manners, and said to him, "Cover your mouth when you sneeze. And breathe in and out slowly so that the little people just call it wind."

But Boris went on being careless. He could not see or hear the little people. He wasn't even sure if there really were little people!

Then one evening, the little people had a party. There were food and drinks, music and fireworks. But the little people were careless. They were too loud. And they dumped their garbage into the clean oceans, which made the puddles too dirty even for giants.

Now, Boris heard the loud noise and felt the garbage in the puddles. "Little people do exist," Boris thought. And it was not nice when they were careless. From then on, Boris stepped carefully in the puddles, like the other giants, and he covered his mouth when he sneezed.

The problem is introduced in the __________ paragraph. The solution is described in the __________ paragraph.

B. Answer these questions.

1. Look again at the paragraph that introduces the problem. What are the two sentences that talk about the problem?

____

____

2. What happened whenever Boris stepped in a puddle?

____

3. What happened whenever Boris sneezed?

____

Think!

If the little people hadn't had a party, do you think Boris would have learned to be careful? Why or why not?

____

____

C. Write "Problem" and "Solution" to complete the list of story elements. Then write one more description for each story element.

- Besides the giants, there were little people.
- Boris learned it was not nice to be careless.
- The other giants worried about Boris's carelessness.
- There were waves in the ocean sometimes.

Story Element	Description
1.  Setting	There were storms because of Boris's sneezes. __________ __________
2.  Characters	Boris was a giant. __________ __________
3.  ______	Boris did not cover his sneezes. __________ __________
4.  ______	The people's party taught Boris to be careful. __________ __________

Read the following change in the story "The Careless Giant". Write a new ending for the story that gives a different solution.

My Ending to "The Careless Giant"

But Boris went on being careless. He could not see or hear the little people. He wasn't even sure if there really were little people!

Then one evening, Boris heard a tiny sound. Someone, someone very small, was calling his name.

THINGS TO TRY

- Think of a story that you have read.
- Describe the problem and the solution in your own words.
- Ask a friend and a teacher what they would do if they were the characters, and write down their solutions.

Title of the story: ______________________________

Problem: ______________________________

____

Solution: ______________________________

____

Solution from a friend:

Solution from a teacher:

Checklist

Skills

- [ ] I can identify where in a story the problem and the solution are.
- [ ] I can answer questions about the story to learn more about the problem.
- [ ] I know how to write my opinion on what happens in the story.
- [ ] I can match descriptions from different parts of the story with the story elements.
- [ ] I can think of a different solution to give the story a new ending.

Revising

- [ ] I have checked my spelling.
- [ ] I have written in complete sentences.

Fables

stories with a lesson

14

In this unit, students will:

- learn that fables are stories that teach a lesson: the "moral" of the story.
- read a fable and identify its moral.
- put the events of a fable in the correct order.
- use conjunctions to retell a fable in fewer sentences.
- learn the characteristics of a fable.
- write their own fable.

A. Read this fable. Fill in the blanks with "mouse". Then underline the moral of the story.

The Lion and the Mouse

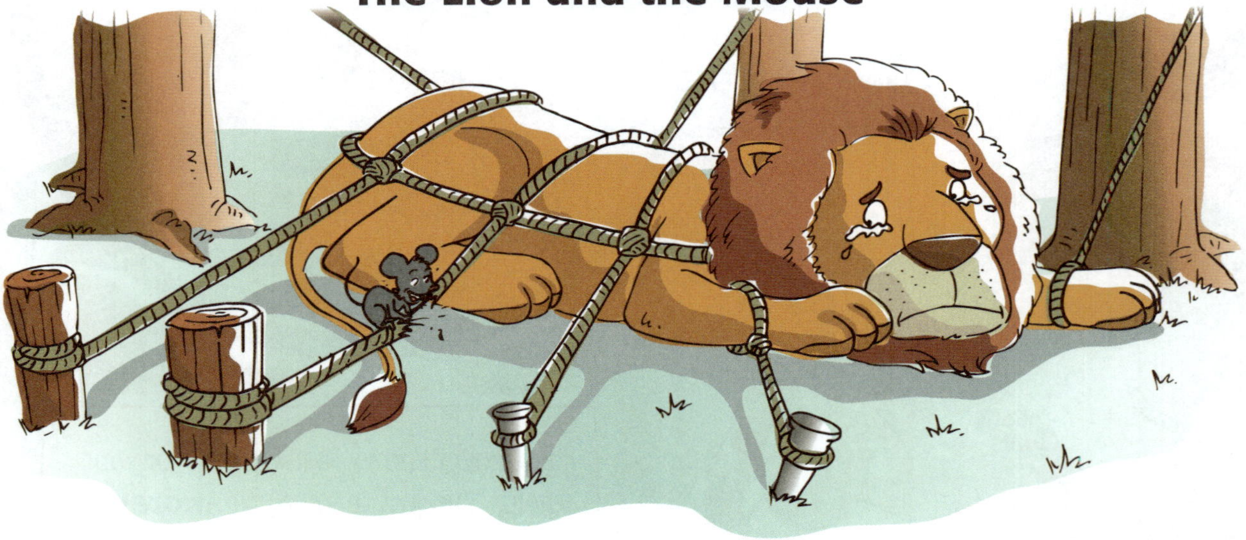

One day, deep in a forest, a ____________ came upon a sleeping lion. Thinking it was safe to walk over him, the ____________ was startled when the lion woke up. The lion was not pleased to be used as a mat. He raised his big paw, and with one swipe, caught the ____________ and brought him to his hungry, wide open mouth.

"Don't eat me!" the ____________ pleaded. "Let me go this time, and next time, I will do a favour for you." The lion could not imagine ever needing help from a tiny ____________ . He laughed at the very idea. But the lion admired the ____________ 's courage, and let him go.

Not long after, the lion was caught in a hunter's trap. He roared a pitiful roar, as his paws were held tight by ropes. The ____________ heard the lion's frightened call, and immediately came to gnaw through the ropes until the lion was free.

The lion learned a valuable lesson: small friends can be a big help.

B. Number these sentences 1 to 7 to retell the fable.

☐ The lion caught the mouse.

☐ The lion laughed and let the mouse go.

☐ A mouse walked over a sleeping lion.

☐ The mouse came to the lion's rescue.

☐ The lion was caught in a trap.

☐ The mouse made a promise to the lion.

☐ The lion realized this: small friends can be a big help.

Think!

We can retell the fable in fewer sentences using conjunctions. Finish this paragraph with the given conjunctions to retell the fable.

The mouse walked over the lion 1.____________ he got caught. He promised he would help the lion 2.____________ the lion set him free. He kept his promise 3.____________ the lion was trapped. The lion learned 4.____________ small friends could be a big help.

C. Read the fable again. Then check ✔ the correct sentences to tell about the characteristics of a fable.

Characteristics of a Fable

1. (A) It teaches a lesson, or "moral", at the end.
   (B) It gives you a puzzle to solve at the end.

2. (A) It is a true story.
   (B) It is make-believe.

3. (A) The setting is simple.
   (B) The setting is described in great detail.

4. (A) The characters are usually animals.
   (B) The characters are usually people.

5. (A) We get to know about the characters in great detail.
   (B) We don't know a lot of details about the characters.

6. The most important thing about a fable is the moral, so the story itself doesn't have to be descriptive.

   (A) The beginning, the middle, and the end are long and descriptive.
   (B) The beginning, the middle, and the end tell what happens, but are short and simple.

Your Turn

Write a fable! Read the beginning. Then write the middle and the end. Don't forget the title and the moral of the story. Draw a picture for your fable.

title

One day, a lazy cat was snoozing in the sun. Before long, a little bird flew down to catch some worms. Since the cat was asleep, he hopped over the cat's tail to reach for his food, but he woke the cat when he brushed the tail's fur. With one strike of his paw, the cat caught the bird.

moral

BOOKS TO READ

Title:
Fables

Author:
Arnold Lobel

Publisher:
HarperCollins (1980)

Leo's Rating: ★★★★½

"There are 20 fables in this book, and each one is only one page long. Each one has humour, wonderful illustrations, and a moral at the end. An animal is at the centre of each fable. This is one of my favourite books to read over and over again."

My Rating: ☆☆☆☆☆

Comments: ______________________________

____

____

____

____

Checklist

Skills

- ☐ I know that fables are stories with a moral.
- ☐ I can identify the moral of a fable.
- ☐ I can put the events of a fable in order.
- ☐ I can retell a fable in fewer sentences using conjunctions.
- ☐ I know the characteristics of a fable.
- ☐ I know how to write a fable.

Revising

- ☐ My fable has a title and a moral.
- ☐ I have written in complete sentences.

Mysteries

stories with a puzzle

15

In this unit, students will:

- learn that a mystery is a story with a puzzle to solve.
- read a mystery and identify the puzzle.
- identify the clue that solves the puzzle.
- learn some types of characters in a mystery: detective, suspects, villain.
- complete the outline of a mystery: setting, characters, puzzle, clue, answer.
- make an outline of a mystery with the help of a picture and write their own mystery.

A. Read this mystery. Underline the sentence that tells what the puzzle is. Then fill in the blanks with the words in bold to help Fly the Private Eye solve the puzzle.

The Missing Cake

It is the night of the Animal Costume Party. The place is colourful with balloons, ribbons, and candles. Fly the Private Eye is in charge of the food. He buzzes around the table. "Where is the cake?" he asks. The cake should be in the centre of the table, but it's gone! Then he says, "I, Fly the Private Eye, will solve this mystery even if it takes me all night."

And it does take him all night. First, he sees a suspicious animal in disguise. "Your tummy looks tubby," says Fly. "You could have eaten a whole cake. Show me your face!" The animal shows his face, and it is Pig with a **wig**. "All pigs have tubby tummies," says Pig.

Next, Fly sees a huge animal with an unusual fin. "You are huge," says Fly. "You could have eaten a whole cake. Show me your face!" The animal shows her face, and it is Whale with a **sail**. "All whales are huge," says Whale.

Then Fly spots a big brown animal in camouflage. "You are big," says Fly. "You could have eaten a whole cake. Show me your face!" The animal shows his face, and it is Bear with fake **hair**. "All bears are big," says Bear.

Now it is almost midnight when all the animals should have a slice of cake. Will Fly the Private Eye find the missing **cake** in time?

Suddenly, he spies Snake. "Snake," says Fly, "you are as long and thin as ever. But why do you have a tummy the size of..."

Then Fly the Private Eye quickly thinks to himself:

Pig has a ____________ .

Whale has a ____________ .

Bear has fake ____________ .

Snake has a ____________ !

The mystery is solved, but the party is almost over. Before midnight, Fly the Private Eye flies in with a pie. What for? To share it with everyone, of course!

Think!

At first, I thought only a large animal could eat a whole cake, but later I realized an important clue. Crack the secret code below to see the clue that helped me solve the puzzle.

Secret code: **HMZPV ISBNVH DRGS XZPV**

Decoder:

A	B	C	D	E	F	G	H	I	J	K	L	M	N	O	P	Q	R	S	T	U	V	W	X	Y	Z
Z	**Y**	**X**	**W**	**V**	**U**	**T**	**S**	**R**	**Q**	**P**	**O**	**N**	**M**	**L**	**K**	**J**	**I**	**H**	**G**	**F**	**E**	**D**	**C**	**B**	**A**

Clue: " ________________________________ "

B. Draw lines to match the types of characters with the meanings.

Types of Characters in a Mystery

Detective •	• the "bad guy" in the story
Suspects •	• the character who solves the puzzle
Villain •	• the "possible" bad guys in the story

C. Fill in the information for the outline of "The Missing Cake".

Outline of "The Missing Cake"

Setting

Place/Event: ______________________

Time of day: ______________________

Characters

Detective: ______________________

Suspects: ______________________

Villain: ______________________

 **Puzzle** ______________________

 **Clue** ______________________

 **Answer** ______________________

Your Turn

Look at the picture to write a mystery called "The Missing Cereal". Make an outline first. Then write your story on a piece of lined paper. Remember to have different paragraphs in your story.

Outline of "____________________________"

Setting

____
place/event

____
time of day

Characters

____
detective

____
suspects

____
villain

Puzzle ____________________________

Clue ____________________________

Answer ____________________________

BOOKS TO READ

Title:
The Case of the Wiggling Wig

Author:
E.W. Hildick

Publisher:
Simon & Schuster Children's Publishing (1996)

Leo's Rating: ★★★★★

"I especially like the characters in this book. Jack, who runs the McGurk Detective Agency, is only ten years old. The other detectives in the agency are his friends. Jack notices mysterious happenings in the house down the road from his bedroom window. The children try to solve the mystery even though Jack is recovering from a broken leg."

Title:
Marvelous Marvin and the Pioneer Ghost

Author:
Bonnie Pryor

Publisher:
HarperCollins Publishers (1995)

Marie's Rating: ★★★★½

"The puzzle in this story is to find out who is polluting Marvin's favourite creek. I enjoyed following the clues and trying to figure out who the villain is. One unusual thing about this mystery is that the detectives get help from a ghost."

Checklist

Skills

- ☐ I know that a mystery is a story with a puzzle.
- ☐ I can identify the puzzle of a mystery.
- ☐ I can identify the clue that solves the puzzle.
- ☐ I know some types of characters in a mystery: detective, suspects, villain.
- ☐ I know how to make an outline of a mystery: setting, characters, puzzle, clue, answer.
- ☐ I can write a mystery with the help of a picture.

Revising

- ☐ I have filled in all the information in my mystery outline.
- ☐ I have written in complete sentences.

Descriptions

to give detailed facts

16

In this unit, students will:

- learn that descriptions give detailed facts about something.
- read a description of an animal, and identify the correct picture and true and false statements.
- use descriptive words to write sentences about two different animals.
- draw a picture of an animal of their choice and describe it in one paragraph.

A. Read this description of the bald eagle. Then check ✓ the correct picture.

The Bald Eagle

A bald eagle is easy to spot. It is a big, muscular bird. It has a sleek, white head of feathers and a matching white tail that stand out against its dark brown body. It has yellow eyes and a yellow, hooked bill that is turned downward in a frown.

The bald eagle does not hide in leafy branches. It perches on treetops and looks down on the rest of the world. When it spies a small animal on the ground, it swoops and dives. Without stopping, it grasps its meal with its sharp talons. It can even pluck a large fish from a roaring river.

The eagle looks and behaves as though it were the king of the sky. But not everything about this bird is majestic. Its sound is often like the sound of a much smaller bird. In fact, the mighty bald eagle's call is more like a sweet tweet than a scary screech.

B. Read each sentence about the bald eagle. Circle "T" for true or "F" for false.

1. **How it looks:**
   - The bald eagle has huge brown eyes. T F
   - The head of a bald eagle has no feathers. T F
   - The bald eagle's bill looks like a frown. T F

2. **What it does:**
   - The bald eagle likes to be on treetops. T F
   - It can pluck a fish from a moving river. T F
   - It glides slowly towards the ground to hunt. T F

3. **How it sounds:**
   - The bald eagle's call is a scary screech. T F
   - When the eagle calls, it's very majestic. T F
   - The call of a bald eagle is sweet. T F

Think!

Look again at the correct picture in (A), and read your answers in (B). Think of two reasons why descriptions are important.

Reason One: ______________________________

Reason Two: ______________________________

C. Write the name of each animal. Then use the descriptive words to write a sentence describing how each animal looks, what it does, and how it sounds.

We use **adjectives** to describe how an animal looks.

Descriptive Words

long small slippery furry	scurries coils sniffs around flicks its tongue	hissing sound squeaking sound

We use **verbs** to describe what an animal does.

1. 

The ____________

How it looks:

____

What it does:

____

How it sounds:

____

2. 

The ____________

How it looks:

____

What it does:

____

How it sounds:

____

Your Turn

Think of an animal and draw a picture of it. Then write down descriptive words for how it looks, what it does, and how it sounds. Finally, write one paragraph about your animal using your descriptive words. Give it a title.

The ________________	How it looks:
	What it does:
	How it sounds:

____

____

____

____

____

____

____

____

____

THINGS TO TRY

Play a game of "word charades" with your friends.

- **Think of a noun: a person, thing, or an animal.**
- **Say different words to describe the noun to your friends.**
- **Keep giving your friends descriptive words about your noun until one of them has the answer.**

Example:

Noun: monkey

Descriptive words:

- has long arms
- has a tail
- climbs trees
- eats bananas

Checklist

Skills

- [ ] I know that descriptions give us detailed facts about something.
- [ ] I can identify the correct picture and true and false statements about an animal after reading its description.
- [ ] I know how to use descriptive words to write sentences about two different animals.
- [ ] I know how to draw a picture of an animal and describe it in one paragraph.

Revising

- [ ] I have included enough detailed facts in my animal description.
- [ ] I have written in complete sentences.

Biographies

We can write life stories about animals, too!

17

In this unit, students will:

- know that we can write biographies of animals.
- identify adjectives in a biography that describe an animal.
- retell facts from the biography.
- recall details from the biography that support the title.
- describe the important people in the life of the animal.
- give details about some important people in their own lives.

A. **Read this biography about a bear and underline the adjectives that describe it.**

Everyone Loved Winnie

A forest full of trees and berry bushes is the perfect place for a bear cub. So how did a small bear end up being for sale at a train stop in Ontario? That was where a soldier named Harry Colebourn found it. A hunter had killed its mother, and he knew it would not survive on its own, so the young orphan was sold to Harry.

Harry named his bear cub "Winnipeg", after his hometown in Manitoba. "Winnie" went wherever Harry went. She charmed passengers on the train. She entertained soldiers at their camp, and even travelled with them to England. Winnie was playful, but gentle.

When Harry went to war in France during World War I, Winnie went to live at the London Zoo. There, she was an extraordinary bear, making friends with the children who visited. One of them was a boy named Christopher Robin, who named his own teddy bear after Winnie. She even inspired Christopher Robin's father, the writer A. A. Milne, to create stories about the two. This was how the stories of Winnie the Pooh and Christopher Robin came about.

Harry missed Winnie, but he knew the bear was happy at the London Zoo, where she lived for almost 20 years. At the time, nobody knew that Winnie would become famous as the friendly bear in A. A. Milne's stories!

B. Fill in the blanks to complete the facts from Winnie's biography.

Facts from Winnie's Biography

- A soldier bought a bear cub at a train stop in 1.__________ and named her "2.__________".
- The bear entertained soldiers and travelled to 3.__________ .
- When her owner went to war in 4.__________ , the bear went to the 5.__________ __________ .
- A boy named 6.__________ __________ became really good friends with the bear.

Think!

Think about the title of Winnie's biography. What was it about Winnie that made her so lovable? List four things from her biography.

1. ____________________
2. ____________________
3. ____________________
4. ____________________

C. Make a list of the important people in Winnie's life. Write their details under their names.

Important People in Winnie's Life

Details

- played with Winnie at the zoo
- wrote stories about his son and Winnie
- bought Winnie at a train stop
- named his teddy bear after Winnie
- had to leave his pet behind
- made Winnie a famous bear

Harry Colebourn

- ______________________________
- ______________________________

Christopher Robin

- ______________________________
- ______________________________

A. A. Milne

- ______________________________
- ______________________________

Jot down some facts about you and draw a small picture of yourself. Then name and draw four people in your life and give details that tell how they are important.

Facts about Me

____
when and where I was born

____
where I live now

____
what I like to do

Important People in My Life

Name: ____________________

____

____

____

Name: ____________________

____

____

____

Name: ____________________

____

____

____

Name: ____________________

____

____

____

BOOKS TO READ

Title:
The Days Before Now

Author:
Margaret Wise Brown (adapted by Joan W. Blos)

Publisher:
Simon & Schuster (1994)

Marie's Rating: ★★★★☆

"I have read many books by Margaret Wise Brown, so it's interesting to read about her life. This book is called an 'autobiography' because the person that it is about is the same person who wrote it. I like how Margaret values her childhood as much as she values her adulthood."

Title:
Snowflake Bentley

Author:
Jacqueline Briggs Martin

Publisher:
Houghton Mifflin (1998)

Leo's Rating: ★★★★½

"You don't have to love snow to love this book, which is Bentley's life story told through his fascination with snowflakes. He spent his life taking pictures of snowflakes – one at a time! Even though the people in the hometown didn't care about pictures of snowflakes, Bentley showed everyone what a beautiful mystery they are."

Checklist

Skills

- ☐ I know that we can write biographies of animals.
- ☐ I can identify adjectives in a biography that describe an animal.
- ☐ I can retell facts from the biography.
- ☐ I can recall details from the biography that support the title.
- ☐ I can describe the important people in the life of the animal.
- ☐ I can write about some important people in my own life.

Revising

- ☐ I have checked my spelling.
- ☐ My writing is neat.

Poems

Did you know they don't always rhyme?

18

Alliteration: using the same beginning sound in a series of words

My Puppy

I named my puppy "Playful Paul"
Because he loves to play with me
He runs and jumps
And sometimes goes "woof!"
He chases birds
Like he is a cat!

Simile: using the word "like" to compare different things

In this unit, students will:

- understand that some poems rhyme, but some don't.
- learn two literary devices: alliteration and simile.
- give titles to and complete some poems about the four seasons.
- identify examples of rhyme, alliteration, and simile in a group of poems.
- learn to write a haiku.
- complete some rhymes and recognize their rhyming patterns.
- write their own poems using rhyme, alliteration, and simile.

A. Use the names of the four seasons to finish these poems and give each of them a title.

The Four Seasons

1 ____________

____________ leaves twinkle like stars
But they don't hang in the sky
They fall to the ground
And we jump in them

2 ____________

When ____________
Wears a white wreath
We wear woolly wraps

3 ____________

____________ is lazy
A white daisy
Sandy feet
An ice cream treat

4 ____________

Bright umbrellas
Colourful flowers
Cute birds
Beautiful ____________

B. Use the poems in (A) to complete this activity.

1. **Rhyme:** using words with the same ending sound

   The poem that uses rhyme: ____________

   The rhyming word pairs:

   ____________ ____________ ; ____________ ____________

2. **Alliteration:** using the same beginning sound in a series of words

   The poem that uses alliteration: ____________

   A line with alliteration from the poem:

   ____

3. **Simile:** using the word "like" to compare different things

   The poem that uses simile: ____________

   The line with simile from the poem:

   ____

Think!

A "haiku" is a Japanese poem written in three lines. It is usually about a season, and has a set number of syllables in each line. Look at the syllable count in the circles to write a haiku about autumn.

Autumn

5 Autumn leaves, ____________

7 Twinkle, and ____________

5 Then we ____________

C. Read what Lily says and finish these poems with the given words. Then write the correct rhyming pattern of each poem.

Rhymes 1 and 3 have the same rhyming pattern and rhymes 2 and 4 have another rhyming pattern.

well sky dream me

1. Rain on the green grass,
Rain on the tree
Rain on the rooftop,
But not on ____________

2. Twinkle, twinkle, little star
How I wonder what you are
Up above the world so high
Like a diamond in the ____________

3. Row, row, row your boat
Gently down the stream
Merrily, merrily, merrily, merrily,
Life is but a ____________

4. Peter, Peter, pumpkin eater,
Had a wife and couldn't keep her
He put her in a pumpkin shell
And there he kept her very ____________

Write a poem that uses rhyme, a poem that uses alliteration, and a poem that uses simile. Use the pictures to help you.

Rhyme:

It's raining, it's pouring

Alliteration:

Tiny tails of Tom and Tammy

Simile:

Glow, glow, gentle moon

BOOKS TO READ

Title:
Baaaad Animals

Author:
Tiffany Stone

Publisher:
Tradewind Books (2006)

Leo's Rating: ★★★★★

"This is not what I thought a book of poems would be like. I laughed even when I read them for the tenth time. There are many different poems: ones that rhyme and ones that don't, and ones that are long and ones that are short."

Title:
The Barefoot Book of Classic Poems

Compiled by:
Jackie Morris

Publisher:
Barefoot Books (2006)

Marie's Rating: ★★★★½

"The poems in this book were written by different poets from many different places and times. The beautiful paintings help me understand the poems. Sometimes they are surprising, and it is cool to see how the poems are expressed in paintings."

Checklist

Skills

- [ ] I know that poems do not have to rhyme.
- [ ] I have learned two literary devices: alliteration and simile.
- [ ] I can give titles to and complete some poems about the four seasons.
- [ ] I can identify examples of rhyme, alliteration, and simile in a group of poems.
- [ ] I know how to write a haiku.
- [ ] I can recognize some simple rhyming patterns.
- [ ] I know how to use rhyme, alliteration, and simile to write my own poems.

Revising

- [ ] My haiku has five syllables in the first line, seven syllables in the second line, and five syllables in the third line.
- [ ] I have checked my spelling.

ANSWERS

ANSWERS

1 Nouns

A. Underline these words in bold:
Captain Dan ; First Mate Steve ;
North Pole ; Northern Queen ;
Pirates ABC ; *War and Seas*

B. 1. First Mate Steve
2. *Pirates ABC* / *War and Seas*
3. Northern Queen
4. Captain Bob

C. 1. world 2. captain
3. pirate 4. job
5. sword

Think!
(Individual answers)

D. 2. black beauty → *Black Beauty*
3. vancouver canucks → Vancouver Canucks ;
toronto maple leafs → Toronto Maple Leafs
4. fresh fruit mart → Fresh Fruit Mart

Your Turn
(Suggested writing)
2. Big Mouth Ben ;
Big Mouth Ben is scaring a little mouse.
3. Wind Lover Willy ;
Wind Lover Willy is reading beside the window.

2 Plural Nouns

A. Circle these words in bold:
mountains ; fish ;
seabirds ; rocks ; geese ; children ;
fishermen ; boats ; people ;
eyes ; fishermen ; geese ; fish

B. Regular: mountains ; seabirds ; rocks ; boats ; eyes
Irregular: fish ; geese ; children ; fishermen ; people

C. 1a. fisherman b. fishermen
2a. child b. children
3a. geese b. goose

Think!
1. sea ; bird
2. sea ; birds
3. fisher ; man
4. fisher ; men

D. 1. oo → ee ; geese ; feet ; teeth
2. a → e ; fishermen ; women ; policemen ; firemen
3. no change ; fish ; deer ; moose ; sheep

Your Turn
geese ; moose ; fish ; children
two moose drinking water, two fish jumping out of water to say hello, and two children looking at the fish.

3 Possessive Adjectives / Pronouns

A. my – mine ; your – yours ; his – his ;
her – hers ; our – ours ; their – theirs
1. Her 2. hers
3. Their 4. theirs
5. My 6. mine

B. 1. Her apartment is downtown.
2. Their home is a log house.
3. His house is on Oak Street.
4. Its colour is brown.

Think!

1. It's too hot today, so the plant has lost ~~it's~~ its flowers.
2. It's so funny when my dog chases after ~~it's~~ its tail!

C. 1. my 2. theirs
3. his 4. ours
5. her 6. mine
7. its 8. your
9. yours ; mine

Your Turn

These children are having **their** Summer Wheel Parade. **Mike** leads the way on **his skateboard**. **Its** wheels are fast! Becky is behind him on **her bicycle**, and her brother **Tim** rides **his tricycle** beside her. **Bill** wheels his way on **his** handy **scooter**, and **Jenny** cruises down the path on **her rollerblades**.

C. 1. Walter took his dog to the park today.
2. Felix drew a picture of colourful clowns.
3. The children sang "O Canada" in the school assembly this morning.

Think!

1. gallop ; scurry ; speed
2. gobble ; chew ; graze

Your Turn

(Suggested writing of the sentences)

1. write ; wrote
   The boy wrote in his notebook.
2. swing ; swung
   The girl swung the baseball bat.
3. fly ; flew
   The plane flew in the sky.
4. ride ; rode
   He rode in his bike.

4 Verbs

A. Underline these words in bold:
Read ; Eat ; Drink ; Call ;
finished ; ran ; climbed ; slid ; played ; forgot ;
read ; ate ; drank ;
walked ; kicked ; waved ;
came

B. 1. call ; finished ; climbed ; played ; walked ; kicked ; waved
2. read ; eat ; drink ; ran ; slid ; forgot ; came
3a. called b. read
c. forgot d. ran
e. waved f. finished

5 Adjectives

A. Underline these words:
big ; fresh ; crispy ;
delicious ; healthy ; yummy ;
home-baked ; cheesy ; hot ;
lighter ; richer ; blue ;
creamy ; fresh ; velvety ;
chilled ; tart ; refreshing ; hottest ;
steaming ; rich ; fat ; coldest
(Individual colouring of the stars)

B. 1a. Hot Chocolate
b. Lemonade
c. Chicken Noodle Soup
d. Cheese Bread

ANSWERS

2a. crispy　　b. fresh
c. creamy　　d. velvety

Think!

1. chilled　　2. creamy
3. tart

C. 1. lighter ; lightest
2. rich ; richest
3. lightest ; lighter ; light
4. richest ; richer ; rich

D. 2. bigger ; biggest
3. thinner ; thinnest
4. hotter ; hottest

Your Turn

1. cold ; colder ; coldest
2. big ; bigger on Saturday ; and it was the biggest on Sunday

Think!

1. sideways　　2. forward
3. inside

C. 1. suddenly ; nervously ; carefully ; beautifully
a. nervously　　b. beautifully
c. suddenly　　d. carefully
2. lazily ; angrily ; happily ; crazily
a. crazily　　b. happily
c. angrily　　d. lazily

Your Turn

(Suggested writing)

1. The boy is running quickly.
2. The girl is dancing beautifully.
3. The children are lying lazily on the floor.
4. The rock singer is singing wildly.

6 Adverbs

A. Underline these words in bold:
gracefully ; quickly ;
happily ; sleepily ; tightly ; patiently ;
sideways ; quietly ; secretly ;
slowly

B.

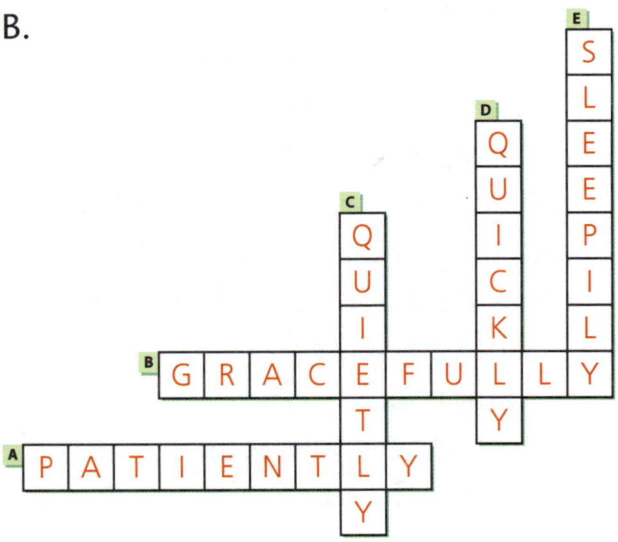

7 Prepositions

A. 1. through　　2. on
3. above　　4. in front of
5. from　　6. to

B. 1. from ; to
2. through
3. between ; amid
4. around
5. over
6. beside
7. across

Think!

1. above　　2. between
3. through　　4. in front of

C. 1.

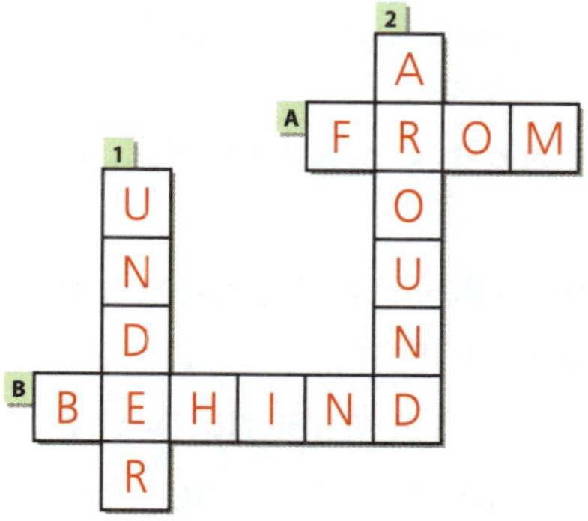

2. behind 3. under
4. in front of 5. over
6. from ; to

Your Turn

(Suggested writing)

2. Rudolph and the gingerbread man are on the sleigh.
3. Rudolph is in front of the box.
4. The gingerbread man is behind Rudolph.
5. There are presents in the box.
6. Everything is under the moon and the star.

4. Amy loves animals, so she adopted two kittens.

C. 1. Tammy loves volleyball and she loves basketball.
2. I love going to the amusement park but I don't like waiting in line.
3. The table is set, so we can serve dinner now.
4. School is cancelled today because there is a snowstorm.
5. You can have fish and chips or you can have burger and fries, but you can't have both.

Your Turn

(Suggested writing)

1. Bill wants to play ball outside, but it is raining.
2. Tammy eats broccoli because it is good for her.
3. Neal is very thirsty, so he drinks a big glass of water.
4. Amy is holding a teddy bear and she is reading a letter.

8 Sentences

A. Underline these words in bold:
or ;
so ;
but ; so ;
and

B. 1. simple 2. combined
3. combined 4. simple
5. combined

Think!

1. I have a blister on my toe, so I won't walk far.

9 Punctuation

A. Photo 2: Snowball's ears
Photo 3: Cotton's ears
Photo 4: Muffin's tail

ANSWERS

Think!

1. The rabbits' home is very comfortable.
2. The kids' mom is making mango pudding.

B. 2. It's ; It is
3. aren't ; are not
4. That's ; That is
5. they're ; they are
6. isn't ; is not

C. 1. January 13, 1996
2. My mom bought apples, oranges, peaches, and bananas.

D. Date:
July 15, 2007
July 22, 2007
August 10, 2007
August 10, 2007
August 15, 2007
Photo:
Patches, Cotton, and Muffin
Cotton, Patches, and Snowball
Peter, Patches, Cotton, and Snowball

Your Turn

Roberta's skates!
Her pets' dinner
(Individual picture and writing)

Review

A. 1a. Farmers Public School ;
Oliver Twist ;
Charles Dickens ;
The Artful Dodger
b. children ; men ; women ; teeth ; feet ; people
2. pickpocket ; gentleman ; schoolyard

B. 1. Their roles are the children of the story.
2. Their roles are the men and women of the story.
3. His role is a thief named Fagin.
4. Her role is a kind-hearted woman named Nancy.

C. 1. read 2. forgot
3. came 4. walked
5. sang 6. waved
7. played

D. 1. lighter ; lightest ;
warm ; warmest ; warmly
cold ; colder ; coldly
sadder ; saddest
2a. warmly b. warmer
3a. lighter b. lightly
4a. coldest b. coldly
5a. sadly b. sadder

E. 1. between 2. beside
3. behind 4. under
5. across
6. through ; around

F. 1. Amy and Tom are playing at home because it is Saturday morning.
2. The kids usually watch TV on weekend mornings, but their parents bought them a train set, so they want to play with it.

G. September 20, 2007
Mom and Dad bought us a train set! It includes the cars of the train, the pieces for the track, a tunnel, and some houses and trees to make a town. At first, we couldn't get the train to start because we forgot to put in batteries! It was so funny. Now, Amy and I love to play with the train set so

much that we don't want to watch TV anymore.

10 Stories

A. three

B. 1 ; the Gourmet Café

1 ; Chef Goulet, Mouse, and her children

2 ; Mouse saw the message "REMOVE MOUSE" on the board.

3 ; What Mouse saw was only a spelling mistake.

Think!

gnawed – nibbled

dashed – rushed

marvellous – wonderful

C. In the beginning, Mouse and her children dined on crumbs on the floor of the café. Later, Mouse thought that Chef Goulet had found out she was living in the café. Then Mouse and her children got their things together to move out. Finally, Mouse realized that the message was not about her and so she did not have to leave.

Your Turn

(Individual writing)

11 Setting

A. (Individual drawing)

B. forest ; He knew which plants on the forest trail would make him itch.

fall ; It had rained every day since the new school year started.

Think!

spongy ; forest floor

wet ; leaves

(Individual writing of the sentence)

C. (Suggested matching sentences)

1. see ;

   The two birds tumbled somersaults.

   When he looked up, all he saw was a large fish.

2. hear ;

   "Fish, fish, fish," it seemed to say.

   Then Simon heard the scream of an eagle.

3. smell ;

   The air smelled fresh.

   He knew which flowers smelled nice.

4. taste ;

   He knew which berries were edible and sweet.

   He knew where to have a refreshing drink of water.

5. touch ;

   The forest floor was spongy.

   Beneath Simon's feet, the leaves formed a very wet mat.

Your Turn

(Individual writing)

12 Characters

A. Fill in all the blanks with this name: Bertie

1. Bonnie
2. Mrs. Martin
3. Bertie's boss

ANSWERS

Think!

- ✔ Bring back Bertie! He was the best!
- ✔ Our new bus driver doesn't wait for late passengers. How we wish that our old driver could come back!

B. (Suggested writing)

B. Bertie did not know his passengers' names.

D. Bertie allowed his passengers' pets on board.

F. Bertie did not wait for his passengers because he had to leave each bus stop on time.

Your Turn

(Individual writing)

13 Problem and Solution

A. first ; sixth / last

B. 1. Unfortunately, Boris was careless. He stomped carelessly through puddles, and he sneezed without covering his mouth.

2. The little people's ocean had enormous waves.

3. The little people had violent storms.

Think!

(Individual answer)

C. 1. There were waves in the ocean sometimes.

2. Besides the giants, there were little people.

3. Problem ;

The other giants worried about Boris's carelessness.

4. Solution ;

Boris learned it was not nice to be careless.

Your Turn

(Individual writing)

14 Fables

A. Fill in all the blanks with this word:

mouse

Underline the last line of the fable:

The lion learned a valuable lesson: small friends can be a big help.

B. 2 ; 4 ; 1 ; 6 ; 5 ; 3 ; 7

Think!

1. but 2. if
3. when 4. that

C. 1. A 2. B
3. A 4. A
5. B 6. B

Your Turn

(Individual writing and drawing)

15 Mysteries

A. Underline this sentence in the first paragraph:

The cake should be in the centre of the table, but it's gone!

wig ; sail ; hair ; cake

Think!

SNAKE RHYMES WITH CAKE

B. Detective – the character who solves the puzzle

Suspects – the "possible" bad guys in the story

Villain – the "bad guy" in the story

C. Place / Event: Animal Costume Party

Time of day: night

Detective: Fly the Private Eye

Suspects: Pig, Whale, and Bear

Villain: Snake

Puzzle: The cake for the party is missing.

Clue: Snake rhymes with cake.

Answer: Snake has the cake.

Your Turn

(Individual writing)

16 Descriptions

A. ✔ C

B. 1. F ; F ; T   2. T ; T ; F

3. F ; F ; T

Think!

They give you a better picture of something.

They give you facts about something.

C. 1. Mouse

It is small and furry.

It scurries and sniffs around.

It makes a squeaking sound.

2. Snake

It is long and slippery.

It coils and flicks its tongue.

It makes a hissing sound.

Your Turn

(Individual drawing and writing)

17 Biographies

A. A forest full of trees and berry bushes is the perfect place for a bear cub. So how did a small bear end up being for sale at a train stop in Ontario? That was where a soldier named Harry Colebourn found it. A hunter had killed its mother, and he knew it would not survive on its own, so the young orphan was sold to Harry.

Harry named his bear cub "Winnipeg", after his hometown in Manitoba. "Winnie" went wherever Harry went. She charmed passengers on the train. She entertained soldiers at their camp, and even travelled with them to England. Winnie was playful, but gentle.

When Harry went to war in France during World War I, Winnie went to live at the London Zoo. There, she was an extraordinary bear, making friends with the children who visited. One of them was a boy named Christopher Robin, who named his own teddy bear after Winnie. She even inspired Christopher Robin's father, the writer A. A. Milne, to create stories about the two. This was how the stories of Winnie the Pooh and Christopher Robin came about.

Harry missed Winnie, but he knew the bear was happy at the London Zoo, where she lived for almost 20 years. At the time, nobody knew that Winnie would become famous as the friendly bear in A. A. Milne's stories!

B. 1. Ontario   2. Winnipeg

3. England   4. France

5. London Zoo

6. Christopher Robin

ANSWERS

Think!

1. Winnie charmed passengers on the train.
2. She entertained soldiers at their camp.
3. She was playful, but gentle.
4. She made friends with the children visiting the London Zoo.

C. Harry Colebourn:
- bought Winnie at a train stop
- had to leave his pet behind

Christopher Robin:
- played with Winnie at the zoo
- named his teddy bear after Winnie

A. A. Milne:
- wrote stories about his son and Winnie
- made Winnie a famous bear

Your Turn

(Individual writing and drawing)

18 Poems

A. 1. Autumn ; Autumn
2. Winter ; winter
3. Summer ; Summer
4. Spring ; spring

B. 1. Summer ;
lazy – daisy ; feet – treat
2. Winter ;
Wears a white wreath / We wear woolly wraps
3. Autumn ;
Autumn leaves twinkle like stars

Think!

(Individual writing)

C. 1. me ; abcb
2. sky ; aabb
3. dream ; abcb
4. well ; aabb

Your Turn

(Individual writing)

ACKNOWLEDGMENT

Resurgence Books would like to acknowledge the talent of Chrissie Wright in the crafting of these children's materials. This series would not have been possible without her expertise in children's education and her discerning mind for sound, engaging, and age-appropriate theology.

Thank you, Chrissie.

Lost and Found Kids: Family Guide
Teaching God's Story from Creation to Kingdom Come

Published by Resurgence Publishing 1411 NW 50th Street

Seattle, WA 98107

First printing, 2012 Printed in the United States of America

ISBN-13: 978-1-938805-08-0

TABLE OF CONTENTS

CHURCH

WORSHIP

STEWARDSHIP

KINGDOM

WHAT'S IN THIS BOOK?

PROCLAMATION

Every week, aim to both proclaim and apply the doctrine you are exploring with your kids. The Proclamation section of the Family Guide provides key lesson content and language you might find useful as you shepherd your kids this week.

BIG IDEA: This is the one-sentence summary of what kids will be learning this week.

FOCUS VOCABULARY: These are words that are featured throughout the lesson this week. You may want to work them into your vocabulary and discussions as a family, and continue to use them in coming weeks as you move on to studying other doctrines. You might find it helpful to create a word wall in your house (e.g., on the refrigerator or in a kid's bedroom), or a word notebook where you add key vocabulary each week. This way both you and your kids can continue to internalize and contextualize what you're learning now with what you've learned so far.

OBJECTIVES: The Objectives describe what we hope kids will be able to say or do by the end of the week. You can assess whether kids have met the lesson's Objectives by reviewing their independent activity with them, or by following up with them during discussion. Objectives help clarify that effective instruction is defined not by whether you as a parent have simply told kids what you want them to know. Rather, instruction is effective when kids can restate, apply, and analyze the ideas you taught them.

KEY POINTS:

- The Key Points break down the Big Idea into three or four bite-sized pieces. Each Key Point is stated explicitly, then supported with additional content. In this section, you will find the exact language your child's teacher used when teaching the lesson on Sunday. By reviewing it, you will be equipping yourself to reinforce what kids heard, and to elaborate and apply the ideas as a family. While reviewing the Key Points together, it can be both entertaining and helpful to use the gestures your child learned on Sunday for the Big Idea. Using gestures helps engage kinesthetic learners, and helps most kids internalize content regardless of learning style.
- **Gospel Link:** This is the part of the lesson where your child's teacher explicitly linked the week's Big Idea to the gospel. This is critical: be sure that you are anchoring each doctrine in the greater narrative of God's Big Story with Jesus as Hero.

APPLICATION

The Application section provides discussion questions, Scripture reading and exploration, and prayer ideas. The goal of this section is to apply the content you're learning and explore how it actually plays out at the heart level.

DISCUSSION:

- These are the questions your child discussed with their Community Group on Sunday. You may want to review them as a family so that you can pursue your child's heart in their responses, and fill in any gaps in understanding.

SCRIPTURE:

Read:

- This section includes several passages you may want to include in your family's Bible reading this week.

Explore:

- It also includes a verse that kids in both age groups explored on Sunday. Feel free to continue breaking it down and studying it as a family. Kids spend two weeks on each verse.

PRAYER:

- This section provides some ideas of things to be praying about as a family this week. Consider keeping a prayer journal as a family, and regularly revisiting the journal to witness evidences of God's grace.

ADDITIONAL RESOURCES:

- This section points you to relevant sections of excellent resources that you may find helpful in shepherding your family this week.

ACTIVITY PAGES

For each doctrine there are activity pages that children of each age group can complete at home with you. The activities are consistent in form with those your child completes on Sundays, but the specific questions are different.

TRINITY: Lesson 1

PROCLAMATION

BIG IDEA:

The Trinity is one God in three persons—God the Father, Jesus the Son, and the Holy Spirit.

FOCUS VOCABULARY:

- **Trinity:** The Trinity is one word we use to describe God, who is one God in three persons.
- **Persons:** The persons of the Trinity are God the Father, Jesus the Son, and the Holy Spirit. Each person is God, and each person is distinct from the others.

OBJECTIVES:

- Kids can articulate that there is only one God.
- Kids can name the three persons of the Trinity.
- Kids can connect God the Trinity to the gospel.

KEY POINTS:

The Trinity is one God.

- There is only one God. The Bible, the book he wrote for us, tells us lots about him. Here are just some of the things that the Bible teaches us about God:
  - God controls the whole world, and he has power over everything.
  - God knows everything—including everything that happened yesterday, everything happening right now, and everything that will happen tomorrow.
    - God knows your name.
    - God even knows the number of hairs you have on your head!
  - God is holy. He is perfectly good and loving.
  - God is helpful.
  - God is happy! He is not lonely, and he does not need anything.
  - God is fun, and God is beautiful.

- God tells the truth, and we can always depend on him.

The Trinity is three distinct persons: Father, Son, and Holy Spirit.

- God the Father is God, Jesus Christ the Son is God, and the Holy Spirit is God.
- Jesus and the Holy Spirit are not the same person. The Father and the Holy Spirit are not the same person. Jesus and the Father are not the same person. Each one is a person, but all three together are one God.

Gospel Link: How does what we know about the Trinity connect to the gospel, the good news of God's Rescue Plan through Jesus?

- All three persons of the Trinity are part of God's Big Plan to rescue the world, and Jesus is the Hero.
- Even though each person is fully and equally God, each person of the Trinity has a special job: God the Father made the plan, Jesus lived the plan, and, when you believe in Jesus as your Savior from sin, the Holy Spirit helps you follow your part in the plan.
  - God the Father made a plan for the whole world to rescue his people and bring them back into his family.
  - God the Son agreed with the plan from before the world began. Then, he lived, died, and rose to make the plan happen.
  - God the Holy Spirit lives in people who love Jesus and believe in Jesus as their Rescuer from sin. The Holy Spirit helps them act out their special little parts in God's Big Plan. The Holy Spirit teaches you how to pray and understand the Bible. He helps you love and serve other people.
- If you want to talk more about God's Big Plan, and how Jesus lived, died, and rose to be your Rescuer and give you the Holy Spirit, feel free to talk to your dad or mom, your teacher or Community Group leader, or to read the Bible and talk to Jesus.

APPLICATION

DISCUSSION:

- What do you know about God the Trinity? What are some words that describe God? For example, I know God is beautiful. Can you think of some more words to describe God?
- Who are the three persons of the Trinity? What do you know about them?
- How does what you know about God the Trinity connect to the gospel, the good news of God's Rescue Plan for the world through Jesus?

SCRIPTURE:

Read:

- Read Genesis 1 and discuss the role of the Trinity in creation.
- Read Matthew 3 and discuss the role of the Trinity at Jesus' baptism.
- Read Matthew 28:19 and discuss the role of the Trinity in our mission.
- Read Titus 3:4–6 and discuss the role of the Trinity in changing our hearts to love Jesus (our salvation).

Explore:

- Genesis 1:26a: "Then God said, 'Let us make man in our image, after our likeness.'"

PRAYER:

- If you have believed in Jesus as your Savior from sin, pray that the Holy Spirit will help you live as part of God's Big Story. If you have not believed in Jesus as your Savior from sin, you can talk to your parents today.
- Pray through Genesis 1:26a, recognizing the Trinity in creation and thanking God for making the world.

ADDITIONAL RESOURCES:

- Joey Allen, *Big Thoughts for Little Thinkers: The Trinity* (Green Forest, AR: New Leaf Press, 2005).
- Sergio Cariello, illus., *The Action Bible: God's Redemptive Story*, ed. Doug Mauss (Colorado Springs, CO: David C. Cook, 2010). See especially "In the Beginning" (17–20), "Born Twice?" (554–555), "Living Water" (556–559), "On Trial!" (627–630), "The Last Command" (645–650), "Waiting for the Spirit" (651–653), and "Tongues of Fire!" (654–658).
- Sally Michael, *God's Names*, Children Desiring God (Phillipsburg, NJ: P&R Publishing, 2011).
- Bruce A. Ware, "God as Three in One," in *Big Truths for Young Hearts: Teaching and Learning the Greatness of God* (Wheaton, IL: Crossway, 2009), 37–57.

TRINITY: Lesson 2

PROCLAMATION

BIG IDEA:

The three persons of the Trinity—God the Father, Jesus the Son, and the Holy Spirit—are each eternally and fully and equally God.

FOCUS VOCABULARY:

- **Eternal:** Always, always, always! Eternal refers to always in the past, always in the world we know, and always in the future. God the Trinity has always existed, exists now, and will exist forever.
- **Fully and equally:** All the way, and in the same amount.

OBJECTIVES:

- Kids can name characteristics that describe all three persons of the Trinity (eternal and fully and equally God).
- Kids can describe the actions of the three persons of the Trinity in connection to the gospel (God the Father made the plan, Jesus lived the plan, and the Holy Spirit helps you follow your part in the plan).

KEY POINTS:

God the Father, Jesus the Son, and the Holy Spirit are each eternally God.

- "Eternal" means God is outside time like we think of it—he never had a beginning, and he will never end.
    - God the Father is eternal—he never had a beginning, and he will never end.
    - Jesus the Son is eternal—he never had a beginning, and he will never end. He existed even before he was born on the earth as both God and man.
    - The Holy Spirit is eternal—he never had a beginning, and he will never end.

God the Father, Jesus the Son, and the Holy Spirit are each fully and equally God.

- Each person being fully God means that each person is all the way God.

- God the Father is God, Jesus the Son is God, and the Holy Spirit is God.

- Each person being equally God means that no person is more God than another. God the Father, Jesus the Son, and the Holy Spirit are equally God.
- Each person being fully and equally God also means that the things we know about God are also true about each person of the Trinity.
  - For example, we know that God is beautiful. This means that God the Father is beautiful, Jesus the Son is beautiful, and the Holy Spirit is beautiful.

Gospel Link: How does what we know about the Trinity connect to the gospel, the good news of God's Rescue Plan through Jesus?

- All three persons of the Trinity are part of God's Big Plan to rescue the world, and Jesus is the Hero.
- Even though each person is fully and equally God, each person of the Trinity has a special job: God the Father made the plan, Jesus lived the plan, and, when you believe in Jesus as your Savior from sin, the Holy Spirit helps you follow your part in the plan.
  - God the Father made a plan for the whole world to rescue his people and bring them back into his family.
  - God the Son agreed with the plan from before the world began. Then, he lived, died, and rose to make the plan happen.
  - God the Holy Spirit lives in people who love Jesus and believe in Jesus as their Rescuer from sin. The Holy Spirit helps them act out their special little parts in God's Big Plan. The Holy Spirit teaches you how to pray and understand the Bible. He helps you love and serve other people.
- If you want to talk more about God's Big Plan, and how Jesus lived, died, and rose to be your Rescuer and give you the Holy Spirit, feel free to talk to your dad or mom, your teacher or Community Group leader, or to read the Bible and talk to Jesus.

APPLICATION

DISCUSSION:

- Each person of the Trinity is eternal. What does that mean?
- Each person of the Trinity is fully and equally God. What does that mean?
- How does what you know about God the Trinity connect to the gospel, the good news of God's Rescue Plan for the world through Jesus?

SCRIPTURE: *Review the Scriptures you began exploring last week.*

Read:

- Read Genesis 1 and discuss the role of the Trinity in creation.
- Read Matthew 3 and discuss the role of the Trinity at Jesus' baptism.
- Read Matthew 28:19 and discuss the role of the Trinity in our mission.
- Read Titus 3:4–6 and discuss the role of the Trinity in changing our hearts to love Jesus (our salvation).

Explore:

- Genesis 1:26a: "Then God said, 'Let us make man in our image, after our likeness.'"
- Matthew 3:16–17: "And when Jesus was baptized, immediately he went up from the water, and behold, the heavens were opened to him, and he saw the Spirit of God descending like a dove and coming to rest on him; and behold, a voice from heaven said, 'This is my beloved Son, with whom I am well pleased.'"

PRAYER:

- Pray that the Holy Spirit will help us live as part of God's Big Story.
- Pray through Genesis 1:26a, recognizing the Trinity in creation and thanking God for making the world.
- Pray through Matthew 3:16–17, thanking God that the gospel is true and that all three persons of the Trinity are involved in our lives.

ADDITIONAL RESOURCES:

- Joey Allen, *Big Thoughts for Little Thinkers: The Trinity* (Green Forest, AR: New Leaf Press, 2005).
- Sergio Cariello, illus., *The Action Bible: God's Redemptive Story*, ed. Doug Mauss (Colorado Springs, CO: David C. Cook, 2010). See especially "In the Beginning" (17–20), "Born Twice?" (554–555), "Living Water" (556–559), "On Trial!" (627–630), "The Last Command" (645–650), "Waiting for the Spirit" (651–653), and "Tongues of Fire!" (654–658).
- Sally Michael, *God's Names*, Children Desiring God (Phillipsburg, NJ: P&R Publishing, 2011).
- Bruce A. Ware, "God as Three in One," in *Big Truths for Young Hearts: Teaching and Learning the Greatness of God* (Wheaton, IL: Crossway, 2009), 37–57.

TRINITY: Lesson 3

PROCLAMATION

BIG IDEA:

God is a Friend, and God has Friends.

FOCUS VOCABULARY:

- **God:** There is one God in three persons: God the Father, Jesus the Son, and the Holy Spirit. We call this the Trinity. Each person of the Trinity is eternally and fully and equally God.
- **Friend:** A friend is someone who is in loving relationship with another person. Each person thinks, acts, feels, speaks, and relates.

OBJECTIVES:

- Kids can list the Friends of each person of the Trinity.
- Kids can describe ways that God is a Friend.
- Kids can describe how thinking of God as a Friend connects to the gospel, the good news of God's Rescue Plan through Jesus.

KEY POINTS:

God is a Friend.

- Saying that each person of the Trinity is a "person" means that each one of them thinks, acts, feels, speaks, and relates. These are each things that a friend can do, so each person of the Trinity is a friend!
  - God the Father is a Friend.
  - Jesus the Son is a Friend.
  - The Holy Spirit is a Friend.
- We also learned that each person of the Trinity is loving, helpful, fun, and good. Those qualities sound like ones a good friend would have! We know that each quality that is true about God is fully and equally true about each person of the Trinity, so we know that each person of the Trinity is a good friend.

- God the Father is loving, helpful, fun, and good.
- Jesus the Son is loving, helpful, fun, and good.
- The Holy Spirit is loving, helpful, fun, and good.

God has Friends.

- The Trinity is something special—it is an eternal friendship! Just like the persons of the Trinity are eternal, their friendship is eternal. It has always existed, and it goes on and on forever.
  - God the Father, Jesus the Son, and the Holy Spirit have always been thinking, acting, feeling, speaking, and relating to each other, and they will keep on doing it forever.
- Each person of the Trinity always has the others as Friends.
  - God the Father has Jesus the Son and the Holy Spirit as Friends.
  - Jesus the Son has God the Father and the Holy Spirit as Friends.
  - The Holy Spirit has God the Father and Jesus the Son as Friends.

Gospel Link: How does what we know about God as Friend connect to the gospel, the good news of God's Rescue Plan through Jesus?

- God's Rescue Plan shows each person of the Trinity acting as a Friend to the others. God the Father wrote the plan, Jesus lived the plan, and the Holy Spirit helps people (including Jesus) act out their part in the plan. The plan couldn't have happened without each person of the Trinity helping his Friends to make it happen.
- God's Rescue Plan also helps us see how Jesus can be our best friend of all. Even though our hearts were dirty because of sin, Jesus came to be our neighbor, love us as his friends, die for our sins to make us family, and share God's love with us. God sent him, and the Holy Spirit helped him. All three persons of the Trinity are in on God's Loving Plan.
  - If we confess with our mouths and believe in our hearts that Jesus is our Rescuer from sin, we can also know that he is our Forever Friend.
  - If you want to talk more about Jesus as your Rescuer, feel free to talk to your dad or mom, your teacher or Community Group leader, or to read the Bible and talk to Jesus.

APPLICATION

DISCUSSION:

- Is God a Friend? How do you know?
- Who are Jesus' Friends? God the Father's? The Holy Spirit's? How long have they been Friends?
- Jesus lived out God's Rescue Plan. How does this show you that he is a Friend?

SCRIPTURE:

Read:

- Read John 3. Identify which members of the Trinity are mentioned and explore their relationship and roles. Discuss:
    - What does this chapter say to you about God as Friend?

Explore:

- John 3:35: "The Father loves the Son and has given all things into his hand."

PRAYER:

- Thank God for his Rescue Plan. Thank Jesus for living, dying, and rising so that we can be saved from the punishment we deserve.
- Thank Jesus for being the best friend of all.
- If you have believed in Jesus as your Savior from sin, pray that the Holy Spirit will help you to be a loving friend to others. If you have not, you can do that today. Talk to your parents or Community Group leader.
- Pray through John 3:35.

ADDITIONAL RESOURCES:

- Joey Allen, *Big Thoughts for Little Thinkers: The Trinity* (Green Forest, AR: New Leaf Press, 2005).
- Mark Driscoll and Gerry Breshears, *Doctrine: What Christians Should Believe* (Wheaton, IL: Crossway, 2010), 12.
- Sally Michael, *God's Names*, Children Desiring God (Phillipsburg, NJ: P&R Publishing, 2011).
- Bruce A. Ware, "God as Three in One," in *Big Truths for Young Hearts: Teaching and Learning the Greatness of God* (Wheaton, IL: Crossway, 2009), 37–57.

TRINITY: Lesson 4

PROCLAMATION

BIG IDEA:

God made us to be friends with him and with other people.

FOCUS VOCABULARY:

- **God:** There is one God in three persons: God the Father, Jesus the Son, and the Holy Spirit. We call this the Trinity. Each person of the Trinity is eternally and fully and equally God.
- **Friend:** A friend is someone who is in loving relationship with another person. Each person thinks, acts, feels, speaks, and relates.

OBJECTIVES:

- Kids can describe ways their friendships with others reflect God's friendships within the Trinity.
- Kids can list reasons Jesus is the best friend of all.

KEY POINTS:

God made us to be friends with him.

- God loves every person he makes, and desires to be in relationship with each person—that definitely includes you!
  - God made man in his image—to be like him in special ways. One special way we are like God is that we were designed to have friendships with God like the persons of the Trinity have friendships with each other.
- Because of sin, we are separated from God and don't automatically get to enjoy friendship with him. But God the Father knew that sin would happen, so he made a Rescue Plan through Jesus.
  - God the Father created the plan to bring us back into relationship with him, Jesus the Son lived out the plan, and the Holy Spirit helps us live our parts in the plan. God's Rescue Plan shows us how the persons of the Trinity are Friends to each other, and to us! We'll talk more about the Rescue Plan later.

- If you have believed in Jesus as your Savior from sin, you can love God as your friend by talking to him in prayer, singing to him in worship, and more.

God made us to be friends with other people.

- God the Father, God the Son, and God the Holy Spirit love each other. God made us like him, so he gave us the desire to love others, too. Because God is Trinity, he created us to have friends, too.
    - You like to talk and play with your friends because God made you in his image to be like him. The Father, Son, and Holy Spirit talk and relate to each other constantly.
    - Not only that, but when we believe in Jesus as our Savior from sin, he gives us new hearts with bigger desires to be good friends and love other people. Jesus is such an amazing friend that he even sends the Holy Spirit to help us be good friends.

Gospel Link: How does what we know about God as Friend connect to the gospel, the good news of God's Rescue Plan through Jesus?

- God's Rescue Plan helps us see how Jesus can be our best friend of all. Even though our hearts were dirty because of sin, Jesus came to be our neighbor, love us as his friends, die for our sins to make us family, and share God's love with us. God sent him, and the Holy Spirit helped him. All three persons of the Trinity are in on God's Loving Plan.
    - If we confess with our mouths and believe in our hearts that Jesus is our Rescuer from sin, we can also know that he is our Forever Friend.
    - If you want to talk more about Jesus as your Rescuer, feel free to talk to your dad or mom, your teacher or Community Group leader, or to read the Bible and talk to Jesus.

APPLICATION

DISCUSSION:

- Is Jesus your friend? How do you know?
- Who helps you to be a good friend?
- Jesus lived out God's Rescue Plan. How does this show you that he is a Friend?

SCRIPTURE: *Review the Scriptures you began exploring last week.*

Read:

- Read John 3. Identify which members of the Trinity are mentioned and explore their relationship and roles. Discuss:
    - What does this chapter say to you about God as Friend?

Explore:

- John 3:35: "The Father loves the Son and has given all things into his hand."

PRAYER:

- Thank God for his Rescue Plan. Thank Jesus for living, dying, and rising so that we can be friends.
- Thank Jesus for being the best friend of all.
- Pray that the Holy Spirit will help us to be loving friends to others.

ADDITIONAL RESOURCES:

- Joey Allen, *Big Thoughts for Little Thinkers: The Trinity* (Green Forest, AR: New Leaf Press, 2005).
- Sally Michael, *God's Names*, Children Desiring God (Phillipsburg, NJ: P&R Publishing, 2011).
- Bruce A. Ware, "God as Three in One," in *Big Truths for Young Hearts: Teaching and Learning the Greatness of God* (Wheaton, IL: Crossway, 2009), 37–57.

TRINITY: 4/5/6 Activity 1

While you create each three-in-one picture, describe each person of the Trinity out loud. For example, while I draw three beautiful flowers, I am thinking about how beautiful God is. To help myself remember that all three persons of the Trinity are beautiful, for each flower I draw I can say a sentence out loud, "God the Father is beautiful, God the Son is beautiful, and God the Holy Spirit is beautiful. All three persons are beautiful." Ask your child questions like, "Is God the Son _____?" "Is God the Father _____?" "Is God the Holy Spirit _____?" and "Is God the Trinity _____?"

Example:

BEAUTIFUL

POWERFUL

TRUSTWORTHY

PERFECT

TRINITY: 4/5/6 Activity 2

God is a Friend, and God has Friends.
God made me a friend, and God gives me friends.

In the boxes below, sketch yourself, your neighbor, and a way the Holy Spirit helps you to love your neighbor (something you do or say to your neighbor to show them you love them).

ME:

MY NEIGHBOR:

SOMETHING THE HOLY SPIRIT HELPS ME DO TO LOVE MY NEIGHBOR:

TRINITY: 7+ Activity 1

Write the verse below.	Which persons of the Trinity are mentioned here?	What does this verse say to me about the character of God?
Matthew 3:16–17		
Acts 1:7–8		
Can you find another verse that mentions at least two persons of the Trinity? Write it here.		

TRINITY: 7+ Activity 2

Write the verse below.	Which persons of the Trinity are mentioned here?	What does this verse say to me about God as Friend?
John 3:16		
Matthew 11:28–30		
Can you find another verse that mentions at least two persons of the Trinity? Write it here.		

REVELATION: Lesson 1

PROCLAMATION

BIG IDEA:

God speaks to everyone through his creation all around us.

FOCUS VOCABULARY:

- **Creation:** God made everything, and we refer to what God has made as "creation." Creation includes people, places, animals, plants, and things.

OBJECTIVES:

- Kids can name at least one way God teaches the world about who he is.
- Kids can list examples of how creation shows who God is.

KEY POINTS:

God speaks to everyone in the whole world.

- God speaks. Whoa! Let's stop right there and think about how amazing that is—the God of the universe who created everything speaks . . . to us!
    - We can't figure out who God is or get to know him by ourselves. But because God knows this about us and loves us, he talks to us in different ways.
    - "Revelation" is the special name for the ways God speaks to us and tells us about himself. Because God speaks, we can tell he wants us to know him.
- God doesn't just speak to some people—he speaks to everyone in the whole world.
    - God loves everyone. He created every single person in the world and he loves each one. That means God loves you. Not everyone chooses to love God back, but God keeps on loving them anyway. God talks to everyone everywhere because he wants us all to know him.

God speaks through creation.

- God shows us who he is through the things he has made in the world.
- When we see a sky full of stars, we think to ourselves, "Wow!" But God made the stars!

So when we think of God, we say, "Wow!!!" God must really be amazing and powerful to make all those stars! He must also be beautiful and great.

- The things God makes show everyone everywhere who he is.

Gospel Link: How does what we know about the ways God speaks connect to the gospel, the good news of God's Rescue Plan through Jesus?

- God speaks to everyone in the world because he wants people to know and understand the good news of his Rescue Plan through Jesus.
  - He knows that because of sin we can't be good on our own, so he sent a Rescuer: his Son, Jesus!
  - Jesus lived a perfect life, then died a brutal death to take the punishment for all the ways we fail to be good. After three days, he rose again so that we can live with him in heaven, telling and singing and shouting the Story of who God is for all of time!
    - In Romans 10:9, it says that "if you confess with your mouth that Jesus is Lord and believe in your heart that God raised him from the dead, you will be saved."
    - If you want to talk more about Jesus as your Rescuer, feel free to talk to your dad or mom, your teacher or Community Group leader, or to read the Bible and talk to Jesus.

APPLICATION

DISCUSSION:

- Who does God speak to?
- What is something that God made that you think is beautiful? How does creation show you about God?
- Who does God want to know about his Rescue Plan through Jesus?

SCRIPTURE:

Read:

- Notice how Jesus uses conscience to apply the grace of the gospel in the following passages:
  - Luke 18:9–14: The Pharisee and the Tax Collector.
  - Can you and your family identify other passages that illustrate Jesus' use of conscience to apply the gospel?

Explore:

- Psalm 19:1: "The heavens declare the glory of God, and the sky above proclaims his handiwork."

PRAYER:

- Thank God for making everything.
- Pray that Jesus would continue to teach our hearts about what sin is, and to help us understand that Jesus is our Always Rescuer.

ADDITIONAL RESOURCES:

- Sally Lloyd-Jones, "The Story and the Song," in *The Jesus Storybook Bible: Every Story Whispers His Name* (Grand Rapids, MI: Zondervan, 2007), 12–17.
- Bruce A. Ware, "God's Word and God's Own Life as God," in *Big Truths for Young Hearts: Teaching and Learning the Greatness of God* (Wheaton, IL: Crossway, 2009), 17–24.

REVELATION: Lesson 2

PROCLAMATION

BIG IDEA:

God speaks to everyone through the conscience right inside us.

FOCUS VOCABULARY:

- **Conscience:** Inside every person, God has built a sense of things that are right and things that are wrong. He has built into us a sense that we are responsible for the things we do. We call this "conscience."

OBJECTIVES:

- Kids can name at least one way God teaches the world about who he is.
- Kids can list examples of times they felt a sense of right and wrong, and connect their conscience to the gospel.

KEY POINTS:

God speaks to everyone in the whole world.

- God speaks. Whoa! Let's stop right there and think about how amazing that is—the God of the universe who created everything speaks . . . to us!
  - We can't figure out who God is or get to know him by ourselves. But because God knows this about us and loves us, he talks to us in different ways.
  - "Revelation" is the special name for the ways God speaks to us and tells us about himself. Because God speaks, we can tell he wants us to know him.
- God doesn't just speak to some people—he speaks to everyone in the whole world.
  - God loves everyone. He created every single person in the world and he loves each one. That means God loves you. Not everyone chooses to love God back, but God keeps on loving them anyway. God talks to everyone everywhere because he wants us all to know him.

God speaks through conscience.

- Last week, we learned that God speaks to everyone through his creation all around us. But that's not the only way he speaks to us. He also speaks through how he made us.
  - Inside every person, God has built a sense of things that are right and things that are wrong. He has built into us a sense that we are responsible for the things we do. We call this "conscience"
  - Not only that, but because we are made in God's image, our conscience also tells us something about God—he not only knows what is right and what is wrong, he always does what is right and good. Every single time!
    - Meanwhile, God knows that because of sin we can't be good on our own, so he sent a Rescuer: his Son, Jesus!

Gospel Link: How does what we know about the ways God speaks connect to the gospel, the good news of God's Rescue Plan through Jesus?

- Again, God knows that because of sin we can't always be good on our own, so he sent a Rescuer: his Son, Jesus!
  - Jesus lived a perfect life, then died a brutal death to take the punishment for all the ways we fail to be good. After three days, he rose again so that we can live with him in heaven, telling and singing and shouting the Story of who God is for all of time!
    - In Romans 10:9, it says that "if you confess with your mouth that Jesus is Lord and believe in your heart that God raised him from the dead, you will be saved."
    - If you want to talk more about Jesus as your Rescuer, feel free to talk to your dad or mom, your teacher or Community Group leader, or to read the Bible and talk to Jesus.

APPLICATION

DISCUSSION:

- Who does God speak to?
- How does God speak through the way he made us? Do you have a sense of things that are right and things that are wrong?
- Who does God want to know about his Rescue Plan through Jesus?

SCRIPTURE: *Review the Scriptures you began exploring last week.*

Read:

- Notice how Jesus uses conscience to apply the grace of the gospel in the following passages:

- Luke 18:9–14: The Pharisee and the Tax Collector.
- Can you and your family identify other passages that illustrate Jesus' use of conscience to apply the gospel?

Explore:

- Psalm 19:1: "The heavens declare the glory of God, and the sky above proclaims his handiwork."

PRAYER:

- Thank God for speaking to us through the conscience right inside us.
- Pray that Jesus would continue to teach your heart about what sin is, and to help you understand that Jesus can be your Rescuer.

ADDITIONAL RESOURCES:

- Sally Lloyd-Jones, "The Story and the Song," in *The Jesus Storybook Bible: Every Story Whispers His Name* (Grand Rapids, MI: Zondervan, 2007), 12–17.
- Bruce A. Ware, "God's Word and God's Own Life as God," in *Big Truths for Young Hearts: Teaching and Learning the Greatness of God* (Wheaton, IL: Crossway, 2009), 17–24.

REVELATION: Lesson 3

PROCLAMATION

BIG IDEA:

God speaks to people who love Jesus through the Bible.

FOCUS VOCABULARY:

- **Bible:** The Bible is God's Word. It is perfect and true, and he uses it to speak to us. Another word for the Bible is "Scripture."

OBJECTIVES:

- Kids can list three or more things they know about the Bible (e.g., author, organization).
- Kids can restate God's purpose for the Bible (to tell his Big Story with Jesus as Hero).

KEY POINTS:

God speaks in special ways to people who love Jesus.

- God speaks to everyone through his creation and through the way he made us with a conscience.
- Those aren't the only ways God speaks, though! He also speaks in special ways to Christians—people who have believed in Jesus as their Savior from sin.

God speaks in words through the Bible.

- The Bible is . . .
    - *A Big Story with Jesus as Hero:* The Bible is one Big Story with Jesus as Hero. *The Jesus Storybook Bible* says it well: "No, the Bible isn't a book of rules, or a book of heroes. The Bible is most of all a Story. It's an adventure story about a young hero who comes from a far country to win back his lost treasure."[1]
        - "It's a love story about a brave Prince who leaves his palace, his throne—everything—to rescue the one he loves. It's like the most wonderful of fairy tales that has come true in real life! You see, the best thing about this Story is—it's true. There are lots of stories in the Bible, but all the stories are telling one Big Story.

[1] Sally Lloyd-Jones, *The Jesus Storybook Bible: Every Story Whispers His Name* (Grand Rapids, MI: Zondervan, 2007), 17.

The Story of how God loves his children and comes to rescue them. And at the center of the Story, there is a baby. Every story in the Bible whispers his name. He is like the missing piece in a puzzle—the piece that makes all the other pieces fit together, and suddenly you can see a beautiful picture."[2]

- Every single bit of the Bible is a piece of God's Big Story. We have to think about how all the pieces fit together (like a puzzle!) to tell us all about Jesus.
- Some people "think the Bible is a book of heroes, showing you people you should copy."[3] But the Bible is really one Big Story with Jesus as Hero! He's not a Hero we need to copy on our own, but one who changes our hearts so we can believe in him as our Savior from sin. Then God sends the Holy Spirit to help us live for him.

- Chapters and verses were added to the words of God's Big Story to help us find parts when we look for them and want to study them. Kind of like the address of your house helps your friends find you, using the chapters and verses in the Bible can help us find parts of the Bible that God is using to teach us and change our hearts.
- The Bible divides God's Big Story into two main parts:
    - In the *Old Testament,* God tells us about the world and his plan for it. "We learn that God is perfect and that He created a good world. Bad things happen in the world because people disobey God."[4] But we also learn that God has a Rescue Plan.
    - God told people what he would do in the future. He has always known things would go wrong, so he promised that one day, at just the right time, he would send a Savior. The entire Old Testament points to the Hero of the Bible: Jesus.
    - In the *New Testament,* God tells about Jesus the Hero. He tells us about who Jesus is and how he lived. God also tells us about how he changes our hearts to believe in him as our Savior from sin. Then God sends the Holy Spirit to help us live for him.

- *Perfect:* The Scriptures are perfect. We can trust what the Bible says because the words come from God. The Bible doesn't have any mistakes because God does not lie.
    - Second Timothy 3:16 says, "All Scripture is breathed out by God and profitable for teaching, for reproof, for correction, and for training in righteousness."
- *From God:* God used different men who loved him to write down his Big Story. God the Holy Spirit moved these men to write the exact words God wanted to share with us. The men were different—they included a doctor, a farmer, even a fisherman—but the words came from the same place: the Holy Spirit.

---

[2] Ibid.
[3] Ibid., 15.
[4] Joey Allen, *Big Thoughts for Little Thinkers: The Scripture* (Green Forest, AR: New Leaf Press, 2005), 11.

- Every single part of the Bible is important, even the parts that seem tricky—every bit tells us who God is, and how we can live as part of his Big Story with Jesus as Hero.
- "What the Bible says is what God says; as the Bible speaks to us, God speaks to us."[5]

• After you have believed in Jesus as your Savior from sin, Jesus wants you to keep on listening to his voice in the Bible. For our whole lives, the Holy Spirit keeps on speaking to us through God's words to us in the Bible. We get to actually hear from God—over and over again! God wants to use the Bible every single day to tell us about who he is.

Gospel Link: How does what we know about the Bible connect to the gospel, the good news of God's Rescue Plan through Jesus?

- We learned that in the New Testament, God tells us about Jesus the Hero. He tells us about who Jesus is and how he lived. God also tells us about how he changes people's hearts to believe in Jesus as their Savior from sin. Then God sends the Holy Spirit to help them live for him.
    - In Romans 10:9, it says that "if you confess with your mouth that Jesus is Lord and believe in your heart that God raised him from the dead, you will be saved."
    - If you want to talk more about believing in Jesus as your Rescuer, feel free to talk to your dad or mom, your teacher or Community Group leader, or to read the Bible and talk to Jesus.

APPLICATION

DISCUSSION:

- What are some of the ways that God speaks?
- What do you know about the Bible?
- Who is the Hero of the Bible? How does he connect to you?

SCRIPTURE:

Read:

- Read the story of Moses receiving the Ten Commandments together (Exodus 20; *The Jesus Storybook Bible*, 74–81).

[5] Bruce A. Ware, *Big Truths for Young Hearts: Teaching and Learning the Greatness of God* (Wheaton, IL: Crossway, 2009), 22.

- Discuss:
  - What do God's words teach us about who he is?
  - Why does God talk to Moses?
  - How does this part of the Bible point to Jesus as Hero?

Explore:

- 2 Timothy 3:16: "All Scripture is breathed out by God and profitable for teaching, for reproof, for correction, and for training in righteousness."

PRAYER:

- Pray that Jesus will inspire us to read our Bibles so that we can know him as our Friend and Rescuer.
- Pray through 2 Timothy 3:16.
- Consider keeping a family prayer journal to keep track of evidences of God's grace in your family as God responds to your prayers.

ADDITIONAL RESOURCES:

- Mark Driscoll and Gerry Breshears, "Revelation: God Speaks," in *Doctrine: What Christians Should Believe* (Wheaton, IL: Crossway, 2010), 37–76. See especially pages 50–51 (listing what Scripture says about Scripture) and 72–75 (about interpreting Scripture).
- Sally Lloyd-Jones, "The Story and the Song," in *The Jesus Storybook Bible: Every Story Whispers His Name* (Grand Rapids, MI: Zondervan, 2007), 12–17.
- Bruce A. Ware, "God's Word and God's Own Life as God," in *Big Truths for Young Hearts: Teaching and Learning the Greatness of God* (Wheaton, IL: Crossway, 2009), 17–24.

REVELATION: Lesson 4

PROCLAMATION

BIG IDEA:

God speaks to people who love Jesus through salvation.

FOCUS VOCABULARY:

- **Salvation:** God can change our hearts so that we believe in Jesus as our Savior from sin. We call this way that God speaks to and changes our hearts "salvation."

OBJECTIVES:

- Kids can list ways that God speaks.
- Kids can retell the gospel, and describe personal need for salvation and their response as appropriate.

KEY POINTS:

God speaks in special ways to people who love Jesus.

- God speaks to everyone through his creation and through the way he made us with a conscience.
- Those aren't the only ways God speaks, though! He also speaks in special ways to Christians—people who love Jesus. For example, he speaks to us through the Bible.

God speaks through salvation.

- Salvation is when God changes a person's heart so that they know that they need Jesus as their Savior from sin, and they believe in him as their Savior.
    - We could not see our need for a Rescuer or choose to love Jesus on our own—believing in Jesus and wanting to live for him are gifts from God!
    - It is not enough to simply know that God became a man and died on the cross in our place for our sins. God wants us to know him—that we need him, that we can't be good or keep the rules, that we sin, that we need a Rescuer. And then, that Jesus is the Rescuer! I need Jesus. You need Jesus, too. When you believe that he died on the cross for your sins, then he helps you love him and your whole life changes!

- Knowing and loving Jesus changes everything.
- This thought plus this feeling is God the Holy Spirit speaking especially to me, speaking to my heart. Is he speaking to you?

Gospel Link: How does what we know about salvation connect to the gospel, the good news of God's Rescue Plan through Jesus?

- Salvation is when we believe the gospel. In Romans 10:9, it says that "if you confess with your mouth that Jesus is Lord and believe in your heart that God raised him from the dead, you will be saved."
- If you want to talk more about believing in Jesus as your Rescuer, feel free to talk to your dad or mom, your teacher or Community Group leader, or to read the Bible and talk to Jesus.

APPLICATION

DISCUSSION:

- What are some of the ways that God speaks?
- How does God speak to you?
- What do you know about salvation? How does it connect to you? Have you believed in Jesus as your Savior from sin?

SCRIPTURE: *Review the Scriptures you began exploring last week.*

Read:

- Read the story of Moses receiving the Ten Commandments together (Exodus 20; *The Jesus Storybook Bible,* 74–81).
- Discuss:
  - What do God's words teach us about who he is?
  - Why does God talk to Moses?
  - How does this part of the Bible point to Jesus as Hero?

Explore:

- 2 Timothy 3:16: "All Scripture is breathed out by God and profitable for teaching, for reproof, for correction, and for training in righteousness."

PRAYER:

- Pray that Jesus will inspire us to read our Bibles so that we can know him as our Friend and Rescuer.
- Pray that Jesus will change the heart of each kid to know their need for the Rescuer and to love him.
- Pray through 2 Timothy 3:16. Thank God that all Scripture is from him, and is helpful for teaching, rebuking, correcting, and training in righteousness.

ADDITIONAL RESOURCES:

- Mark Driscoll and Gerry Breshears, "Revelation: God Speaks," in *Doctrine: What Christians Should Believe* (Wheaton, IL: Crossway, 2010), 37–76. See especially pages 50–51 (listing what Scripture says about Scripture) and 72–75 (about interpreting Scripture).
- Sally Lloyd-Jones, "The Story and the Song," in *The Jesus Storybook Bible: Every Story Whispers His Name* (Grand Rapids, MI: Zondervan, 2007), 12–17.
- Bruce A. Ware, "God's Word and God's Own Life as God," in *Big Truths for Young Hearts: Teaching and Learning the Greatness of God* (Wheaton, IL: Crossway, 2009), 17–24.

REVELATION: 4/5/6 Activity 1

God speaks through creation.

God shows us who he is through the things he has made in the world.

For each box, help your child brainstorm something that God has created in each category. While your child sketches, discuss what that piece of creation reveals about who God is. Try using the following series of questions while your child works:

- *(Point to drawing.)* What did God make?
- What does ____ tell you about who God is?
- *(If trouble responding)* Do you think God might be _____? How do you know?

IN THE WATER	IN THE SKY
IN NATURE	IN MY NEIGHBORHOOD

REVELATION: 4/5/6 Activity 2

God wants to speak to us all the time.

God speaks to us through Scripture (the Bible), and by speaking to our hearts.

Color the pictures of times when God wants to speak to you.

While your child works, consider using the following guiding questions:

- *(Point to picture.)* What's going on this picture?
- Does God want to speak to you when you ______?
- *(If trouble responding)* God wants to speak to you *all* the time! That includes when ______.

REVELATION: 7+ Activity 1

Jesus is a Rescuer. When he changes your heart and adopts you as his son or daughter, he keeps on loving you and loving you even when you fail. Your sin makes him sad, but he fully paid for it on the cross and he chooses to forgive you and love you over and over. Then, the more you realize who Jesus is, the more you want to obey him! You obey because he loves you, not to make him love you.

Let's take a look at a man from the Bible and how Jesus responded to him.

1. Read Luke 19:1–7.

In your own words, what is going on here?

2. Now, read Luke 19:8–10.

In your own words, what is going on here? How does Jesus respond to Zacchaeus?

3. Discuss: How does Jesus respond to you? Can you find any passages in the Bible where God speaks to you about how he is a Friend to you in the face of your sin?

REVELATION: 7+ Activity 2

Take a closer look at 2 Timothy 3:16–17 to see what God is telling you about the Bible.

Write the verse below.	What does God say the Bible is good for? (List each one!)	Put in your own words. What could this mean in your own life?
2 Timothy 3:16		
2 Timothy 3:17		

CREATION: Lesson 1

PROCLAMATION

BIG IDEA:

Creation comes from God out of nothing.

FOCUS VOCABULARY:

- **Creation:** "Creation" is a word that describes everything in the whole world. It includes everything we see, hear, touch, taste, and smell. Creation includes people, places, animals, plants, and things.

OBJECTIVES:

- Kids can restate where creation comes from.
- Kids can describe what existed before creation. *(There was nothing but God. Out of nothing, God created everything.)*

KEY POINTS:

"Creation" is a word that describes everything in the whole world.

- Creation includes everything we can see, hear, touch, taste, and smell.
- God made everything.
- God made everything we eat, the clothes we wear, the floor we sit on, our moms, our dads, our favorite places, our playgrounds, the snacks we love—God made *everything!*

Creation comes from God.

- We worship God the Trinity who is one God, three persons. This means that all three persons of the Trinity worked together to make the world. It wasn't just God the Father. Nope! God the Father, God the Son, and God the Holy Spirit were all involved.

God made everything out of nothing.

- "Long, long ago there was no world. . . . There were no people either. There was only God."[6]

[6] *ESV Seek and Find Bible* (Wheaton, IL: Crossway, 2007), 5.

    - "God has always been alive. That means God doesn't have a birthday. No matter how far back in time you go, God was there. He is the one who decided to create our world. Way back then, there was no world at all."[7]
  - Other than God, "there was nothing. Nothing to hear. Nothing to feel. Nothing to see. Only emptiness. And darkness. And . . . nothing but nothing. But God was there. And God had a wonderful Plan. 'I'll take this emptiness,' God said, 'and I'll fill it up! Out of the darkness, I'm going to make light! And out of the nothing, I'm going to make . . . EVERYTHING!'"[8]
  - Let's stop to think a little more about how God made the world. "God spoke. That's all. And whatever he said, it happened."[9]
    - "Let there be light," he said. And it happened! The same with night and day, sky and water, plants and animals, stars . . .
    - In this way, God spoke and created the whole world and everything in it. Not just that, but everything that God created was good.
  - Can you believe that? I have to use stuff to make stuff, but God is different from me. He is powerful. All he has to do is speak!

Gospel Link: How does what we know about creation connect to the gospel, the good news of God's Rescue Plan through Jesus?

  - Creation is when God kicked off his Big Plan for the world—from before the beginning, God had a perfect plan to love his people.
  - God knew that sin would happen. God knew that because of sin, we would be separated from him. He knew that because of sin we can't be good on our own, so he sent a Rescuer: his Son, Jesus!
    - Jesus lived a perfect life, then died a brutal death to take the punishment for all the ways we sin. After three days, he rose again so that if we believe in him as the Savior from sin we can live with him in heaven, telling and singing and shouting the Story of who God is for all of time!
      - In Romans 10:9, it says that "if you confess with your mouth that Jesus is Lord and believe in your heart that God raised him from the dead, you will be saved."
      - If you want to talk more about believing in Jesus as your Rescuer, feel free to talk to your dad or mom, your teacher or Community Group leader, or to read the Bible and talk to Jesus.

---

[7] Marty Machowski, *Long Story Short: Ten-Minute Devotions to Draw Your Family to God* (Greensboro, NC: New Growth Press, 2010), 7.
[8] Lloyd-Jones, *The Jesus Storybook Bible*, 18.
[9] Ibid.

APPLICATION

DISCUSSION:

- Who made everything?
- What are some of your favorite things that God has made?
- How does God's Big Plan connect to you? Have you believed in Jesus as your Savior from sin?

SCRIPTURE:

Read:

- Read the following Scriptures as a family, and brainstorm a list of what the Bible teaches you about creation and who God is in the whole Bible (not Genesis alone):
    - Genesis 1
    - Job 12:10
    - Acts 17:28
    - Colossians 1:15–17
    - Can you find other passages in Scripture that teach you more about creation?

Explore:

- Genesis 1:1: "In the beginning, God created the heavens and the earth."

PRAYER:

- Thank God for making everything out of nothing, and for planning your small part in his Big Story.
- Praise God for the things you are learning about his character: his love, his power, and more.
- Pray through Genesis 1:1.

ADDITIONAL RESOURCES:

- *ESV Seek and Find Bible* (Wheaton, IL: Crossway, 2007), 5.
- Wayne Grudem, "Creation," chap. 15 in *Systematic Theology: An Introduction to Biblical Doctrine* (Grand Rapids, MI: Zondervan, 1994).
- Sally Lloyd-Jones, *The Jesus Storybook Bible: Every Story Whispers His Name* (Grand Rapids, MI: Zondervan, 2007), 18.
- Marty Machowski, *Long Story Short: Ten-Minute Devotions to Draw Your Family to God* (Greensboro, NC: New Growth Press, 2010), 7.
- Bruce A. Ware, *Big Truths for Young Hearts: Teaching and Learning the Greatness of God* (Wheaton, IL: Crossway, 2009), 64.

CREATION: Lesson 2

PROCLAMATION

BIG IDEA:

Creation comes from God, and God takes care of what he makes.

FOCUS VOCABULARY:

- **Creation:** "Creation" is a word that describes everything in the whole world. It includes everything we see, hear, touch, taste, and smell. Creation includes people, places, animals, plants, and things.

OBJECTIVES:

- Kids can restate where creation comes from.
- Kids can restate who is in charge of creation. *(God the Father, God the Son, and God the Holy Spirit.)*

KEY POINTS:

Creation comes from God.

- "Creation" is a word that describes everything in the whole world.
- Creation includes everything we can see, hear, touch, taste, and smell. Because God made all of creation, we know that God made all of these things.
- God made everything we eat, the clothes we wear, the floor we sit on, our moms, our dads, our favorite places, our playgrounds, the snacks we love—God made everything!

God takes care of what he makes.

- God provides for everything he has made. "After creating different things, he doesn't leave them alone. . . . He is involved in providing for and protecting every part of the creation."[10]
- "Why doesn't the moon fall apart? How do the stars stay floating in the sky? . . . [Because] Jesus is holding the whole world together."[11]

---

[10] Ware, *Big Truths for Young Hearts*, 64.
[11] Machowski, *Long Story Short*, 9.

Gospel Link: How does what we know about creation connect to the gospel, the good news of God's Rescue Plan through Jesus?

- Taking care of what he makes doesn't just mean that God provides and protects. No, it also means that before the beginning, God had a good plan for all of creation. Ever since then, God has been following his Big Rescue Plan so that as many people as possible can know Jesus.
  - Just like God the Father, God the Son, and God the Spirit were all involved in creation, they are working together to bring about God's Big Story, and part of God's Big Story happens right here in my heart!
  - God the Father, God the Son, and God the Spirit kicked off God's Rescue Plan in the beginning, and all three continue the plan right here in my heart. They are changing my heart to love Jesus and changing my life to worship him more and more—all as part of God's plan.
    - I worship a God who loves me so much that he lets me be part of his Big Story even though I am worse than I ever dare imagine. Because Jesus died to pay for my sins, God doesn't see my sin when he looks at me. Instead, he chooses to see the righteousness of Jesus. Now that's a Big Story!

APPLICATION

DISCUSSION:

- Who made everything?
- Who takes care of everything?
- How do you fit into God's Big Story? Have you believed in Jesus as your Savior from sin?

SCRIPTURE: *Review the Scriptures you began exploring last week.*

Read:

- Read the following Scriptures as a family, and brainstorm a list of what the Bible teaches you about creation and who God is in the whole Bible (not Genesis alone):
  - Genesis 1
  - Job 12:10
  - Acts 17:28
  - Colossians 1:15–17
  - Can you find other passages in Scripture that teach you more about creation?

Explore:

- Genesis 1:1: "In the beginning, God created the heavens and the earth."

PRAYER:

- Thank God for making everything out of nothing, and for planning your small part in his Big Story.
- Praise God for the things you are learning about his character.
- Pray through Genesis 1:1. Thank God for creating the world and creating you.

ADDITIONAL RESOURCES:

- *ESV Seek and Find Bible* (Wheaton, IL: Crossway, 2007), 5.
- Wayne Grudem, "Creation," chap. 15 in *Systematic Theology: An Introduction to Biblical Doctrine* (Grand Rapids, MI: Zondervan, 1994).
- Sally Lloyd-Jones, *The Jesus Storybook Bible: Every Story Whispers His Name* (Grand Rapids, MI: Zondervan, 2007), 18.
- Marty Machowski, *Long Story Short: Ten-Minute Devotions to Draw Your Family to God* (Greensboro, NC: New Growth Press, 2010), 7.
- Bruce A. Ware, *Big Truths for Young Hearts: Teaching and Learning the Greatness of God* (Wheaton, IL: Crossway, 2009), 64.

CREATION: Lesson 3

PROCLAMATION

BIG IDEA:

God's creation is a gift to us.

FOCUS VOCABULARY:

- **Gift:** A gift is something that one person gives to another person or group of people. The person receiving it does not pay for it or do anything to earn it. It is meant to be enjoyed.

OBJECTIVES:

- Kids can define creation.
- Kids can describe the purpose of creation.

KEY POINTS:

Creation comes from God.

- For six days, out of nothing at all, God made everything. Light and dark. Night and day. Sky and water. Plants and animals. Stars. Everything! But God wasn't done yet . . . At just the right time, when the world was ready, the God who created everything created us—humans!
  - "God saw all [the plants and animals] he had made and he loved them. . . . But God [had] saved the best for last. From the beginning, God had a shining dream in his heart. He would make people to share his Forever Happiness. They would be his children, and the world would be their perfect home."[12]
  - So, "he shaped dust and breathed the breath of life into it, creating Adam. [Then,] from Adam's rib, God created the woman. They were created to be in relationship with each other and with God as living Creator and loving Lord."[13]
  - "God loved them with all of his heart. And they were lovely because he loved them. . . . Their hearts were filled with happiness. And nothing ever made them sad or lonely or sick or afraid."[14]

---

[12] Lloyd-Jones, *The Jesus Storybook Bible*, 25.
[13] Driscoll and Breshears, *Doctrine*, 93.
[14] Lloyd-Jones, *The Jesus Storybook Bible*, 26.

- "'This world is for you,' God said."[15]
- "The most special part of his creation was to form man 'in his own image.' . . . After creating man, God put him in charge of all God's creation and told him to rule over it. Because man was made in God's image he could do things that none of the other animals could do. He could talk with God, worship God, and have a friendship with God."[16]

- And then, creation was finished. God made everything, and God made us. He trusted us with the whole world, and it was very good.

Creation is a gift.

- Did you catch that? Everything comes from God. Even though he doesn't need us, he made the whole world, made us, then gave it all to us as a free gift. We didn't have to do anything to earn it, and we didn't deserve it. That's a big present!
- The gift of creation helps show how big God's love for us is. It's as though "God wrote, 'I love you'—he wrote it in the sky, and on the earth, and under the sea. He wrote his message everywhere! Because God created everything in his world to reflect him like a mirror—to show us what he is like, to help us know him, to make our hearts sing."[17]
    - We get to keep on enjoying creation as a gift in our lives today. "From the bodies we inhabit, the air we breathe, the sun we bask in, the food we eat, the flowers we pick, the water we drink, the ground we walk upon, and the pets we love, to the [things] we enjoy and [places] we visit on vacation, life is filled with good gifts for us to steward and enjoy."[18]

Gospel Link: How does what we know about God's gift of creation connect to the gospel, the good news of God's Rescue Plan through Jesus?

- God has given us an even bigger gift than the things he created. Do you know what it is? From the beginning, God was planning to send the biggest gift of all: Jesus!
- Jesus came on a Rescue Mission to save us from the Forever Sadness of being separated from him by dying for us, giving us his Spirit, and promising to come back one day to finish his Rescue Plan.
- God's Rescue Plan through Jesus is in action right now!
    - In Romans 10:9, it says that "if you confess with your mouth that Jesus is Lord and believe in your heart that God raised him from the dead, you will be saved."
    - If you want to talk more about believing in Jesus as your Rescuer, feel free to talk to your dad or mom, your teacher or Community Group leader, or to read the Bible and talk to Jesus.

---

[15] V. Gilbert Beers, *The Early Reader's Bible* (Grand Rapids, MI: Zondervan, 1995), 4.
[16] Machowski, *Long Story Short*, 10.
[17] Lloyd-Jones, *The Jesus Storybook Bible*, 12.
[18] Driscoll and Breshears, *Doctrine*, 79.

APPLICATION

DISCUSSION:

- Where did Adam and Eve come from? What about the world they lived in?
- What gift did God give to everyone?
- What gift does God give through Jesus?

SCRIPTURE:

Read:

- Read Genesis 1 and 2 as a family.
  - Compare the creation of man and woman with the creation of the heavens and the earth. What is different?
  - Discuss the gifts that God gave to man and woman for his glory.

Explore:

- Isaiah 6:3: "And one called to another and said: 'Holy, holy, holy is the LORD of hosts; the whole earth is full of his glory!'"

PRAYER:

- Thank God for giving creation to us as a gift.
- Thank God for teaching us that all his gifts are created for his glory, and for helping us worship him by thanking him.
- Pray through Isaiah 6:3.

ADDITIONAL RESOURCES:

- *ESV Seek and Find Bible* (Wheaton, IL: Crossway, 2007), 5.
- Wayne Grudem, "Creation," chap. 15 in *Systematic Theology: An Introduction to Biblical Doctrine* (Grand Rapids, MI: Zondervan, 1994).
- Sally Lloyd-Jones, *The Jesus Storybook Bible: Every Story Whispers His Name* (Grand Rapids, MI: Zondervan, 2007), 18.
- Marty Machowski, *Long Story Short: Ten-Minute Devotions to Draw Your Family to God* (Greensboro, NC: New Growth Press, 2010), 7.
- Bruce A. Ware, *Big Truths for Young Hearts: Teaching and Learning the Greatness of God* (Wheaton, IL: Crossway, 2009), 64.

CREATION: Lesson 4

PROCLAMATION

BIG IDEA:

The gift of creation is for God's glory.

FOCUS VOCABULARY:

- **Gift:** A gift is something that one person gives to another person or group of people. The person receiving it does not pay for it or do anything to earn it. It is meant to be enjoyed.
- **God's glory:** The purpose of all creation is to glorify God. Because everything is from God, absolutely everything should be used to worship him.

OBJECTIVE:

- Kids can describe the purpose of creation.

KEY POINTS:

Creation is a gift from God.

- Did you catch that? Everything comes from God. Even though he doesn't need us, he made the whole world, made us, then gave it all to us as a free gift. We didn't have to do anything to earn it, and we didn't deserve it. That's a big present!
- The gift of creation helps show how big God's love for us is. It's as though "God wrote, 'I love you'—he wrote it in the sky, and on the earth, and under the sea. He wrote his message everywhere! Because God created everything in his world to reflect him like a mirror—to show us what he is like, to help us know him, to make our hearts sing."[19]
    - We get to keep on enjoying creation as a gift in our lives today. "From the bodies we inhabit, the air we breathe, the sun we bask in, the food we eat, the flowers we pick, the water we drink, the ground we walk upon, and the pets we love, to the [things] we enjoy and [places] we visit on vacation, life is filled with good gifts for us to steward and enjoy."[20]

---

[19] Lloyd-Jones, *The Jesus Storybook Bible*, 12.
[20] Driscoll and Breshears, *Doctrine*, 79.

The gift of creation is for God's glory.

- God's big free gift to us came with a purpose. Because everything is from God, absolutely everything should be used to worship God—to whisper "Thank you," to tell him "I love you," to shout "You are the Hero of the whole world!"
- We get to thank God for his creation.
  - "When you see the moon, thank God for it. When you see the stars, thank God for them. And thank God for other good things too."[21]
  - Because we have received gifts we don't deserve from our Creator God who loves us, we want to worship him! And when I realize that even the desire to worship him is a gift he's given me, it makes me want to worship him even more! It's too wonderful!

Gospel Link: How does what we know about God's gift of creation connect to the gospel, the good news of God's Rescue Plan through Jesus?

- God has given us an even bigger gift than the things he created. Do you know what it is? From the beginning, God was planning to send the biggest gift of all: Jesus!
- Jesus came on a Rescue Mission to save us from the Forever Sadness of being separated from him by dying for us, giving us his Spirit, and promising to come back one day to finish his Rescue Plan.
- God's Rescue Plan through Jesus is in action right now!
  - In Romans 10:9, it says that "if you confess with your mouth that Jesus is Lord and believe in your heart that God raised him from the dead, you will be saved."
  - If you want to talk more about believing in Jesus as your Rescuer, feel free to talk to your dad or mom, your teacher or Community Group leader, or to read the Bible and talk to Jesus.

APPLICATION

DISCUSSION:

- What gift did God give to everyone?
- How can you thank God for the gift of his creation?
- What gift does God give through Jesus? Have you believed in Jesus as your Savior from sin?

---

[21] Beers, *The Early Reader's Bible*, 9.

SCRIPTURE: *Review the Scriptures you began exploring last week.*

Read:

- Read Genesis 1 and 2 as a family.
  - Compare the creation of man and woman with the creation of the heavens and the earth. What is different?
  - Discuss the gifts that God gave to man and woman for his glory.

Explore:

- Isaiah 6:3: "And one called to another and said: 'Holy, holy, holy is the LORD of hosts; the whole earth is full of his glory!'"

PRAYER:

- Thank God for giving creation to us as a gift.
- Thank God for teaching us that all his gifts are created for his glory, and for helping us worship him by thanking him.
- Pray through Isaiah 6:3, praising him for being holy.

ADDITIONAL RESOURCES:

- *ESV Seek and Find Bible* (Wheaton, IL: Crossway, 2007), 5.
- Wayne Grudem, "Creation," chap. 15 in *Systematic Theology: An Introduction to Biblical Doctrine* (Grand Rapids, MI: Zondervan, 1994).
- Sally Lloyd-Jones, *The Jesus Storybook Bible: Every Story Whispers His Name* (Grand Rapids, MI: Zondervan, 2007), 18.
- Marty Machowski, *Long Story Short: Ten-Minute Devotions to Draw Your Family to God* (Greensboro, NC: New Growth Press, 2010), 7.
- Bruce A. Ware, *Big Truths for Young Hearts: Teaching and Learning the Greatness of God* (Wheaton, IL: Crossway, 2009), 64.

CREATION: 4/5/6 Activity 1

Stop and think about God's Big Story. In the boxes below, sketch three snapshots of God's Big Story: (1) the Rescue Scene, (2) the end of the Story, and (3) another scene you are studying in the Bible as a family.

CREATION: 4/5/6 Activity 2

Sketch at least four things you can thank God for.

While they draw, support your child by asking the following questions:

- *(Point to drawing.)* What gift has God given you?
- How do you thank God for ___?
- *(If struggling)* God gave you ____. Can you thank God for it?

I CAN THANK GOD FOR...

CREATION: 7+ Activity I

Build on your Scripture verse by reading and transcribing the following verses. Dig deeper into how God the Trinity created the world, and his role in it since then. Throughout the Bible (the Old Testament and New Testament), God keeps on telling us that he created the whole world, and his role in it.

Write the verse below.	In your own words, what is this verse saying?	How does this verse add to what you already know about creation?
Ephesians 4:6		
John 1:3		
1 Corinthians 8:6		
Psalm 104:30		

CREATION: 7+ Activity 2

Circle the word GLORY in the verse.	**OT or NT**	**Identify the WHO and/or WHAT in this verse. WHO gets glory? WHAT brings him glory?**	**HOW does this connect to your own life?**
Isaiah 43:6–7: "'I will say to the north, Give up, and to the south, Do not withhold; bring my sons from afar and my daughters from the end of the earth, everyone who is called by my name, whom I created for my glory, whom I formed and made.'"			
Numbers 14:21: "'But truly, as I live, and as all the earth shall be filled with the glory of the LORD . . .'"			
John 12:27–28: "'Now is my soul troubled. And what shall I say? "Father, save me from this hour"? But for this purpose I have come to this hour. Father, glorify your name.' Then a voice came from heaven: 'I have glorified it, and I will glorify it again.'"			
Can you find other verses that speak to you about all of creation as God's gifts for his glory?			

Does God talk about his glory in just part of the Bible, or is it all over both the Old Testament and New Testament? What does that teach you?

IMAGE: Lesson 1

PROCLAMATION

BIG IDEA:

God showed his special love for us by creating men and women in his image.

FOCUS VOCABULARY:

- **Image:** Being made in God's image means that we reflect some of the things that are true about God. God showed that he has special love for people (more than other creatures) because he created us in his image.

OBJECTIVES:

- Kids can define image.
- Kids can identify who images God.

KEY POINTS:

God showed that he has special love for people because he created us in his image.

- Being made in God's image means that we reflect some of the things that are true about God.
    - Imagine looking at yourself in a mirror. Does the mirror reflect some things about you? Can you see your eyes? Your nose? Can you see your smile? Your frown? *(Yes.)* What about what you are thinking? Your voice? *(No.)*
    - In this way, as image bearers, we reflect some things about God, but we are not the same as God. God is God and we are not!
        - In Genesis 1:26, God said, "Let us make man in our image, after our likeness." This means that being images of God has something to do with being *like* God, but not the same as God.
        - When people look at us they should be able to see something of what God is like.
- Every person in the whole world images God all the time no matter what—it's how we were made.

- Because Jesus is God, he reflects God the Father perfectly. As a man, he was the perfect image bearer of God.
- To be like Jesus as best you can (which is only possible with lots of help from the Holy Spirit!) is to reflect God.

Both men and women, boys and girls, are made in God's image.

- Men and women and boys and girls are different in some ways, but they are equally made in God's image. Men and women are of equal value and importance to God.

Gospel Link: How does what we know about image connect to the gospel, the good news of God's Rescue Plan through Jesus?

- Because God has a special love for humans as his image bearers, he made a Rescue Plan for his people.
    - Jesus the Son agreed with the plan from before the world began. Then, he lived, died, and rose to make the plan happen.
    - God knew that we would have dirty hearts because of our sin, so he planned for Jesus to live a perfect life on earth; to die a terrible death to take the punishment we deserve for our dirty sins and to give us clean, new hearts; and to rise again so that we can live forever with him as his friends and family.
        - Romans 10:9 says, "If you confess with your mouth that Jesus is Lord and believe in your heart that God raised him from the dead, you will be saved."
        - If you want to talk more about believing in Jesus as your Rescuer, feel free to talk to your dad or mom, your teacher or Community Group leader, or to read the Bible and talk to Jesus.

APPLICATION

DISCUSSION:

- Are just some people made in the image of God? Who is?
- How are boys and girls like God? How are they different?
- How does God's Rescue Plan connect to you?

SCRIPTURE:

Read:

- Re-read Genesis 1 and 2, and discuss what you learn in the passage about what it means to image God.

Explore:

- Genesis 1:27: "So God created man in his own image, in the image of God he created him; male and female he created them."

PRAYER:

- Thank Jesus for being the perfect image of God and for being our Rescuer.
- Pray that the Holy Spirit will help you to image God more fully.

ADDITIONAL RESOURCES:

- Mark Driscoll and Gerry Breshears, "Image: God Loves," in *Doctrine: What Christians Should Believe* (Wheaton, IL: Crossway, 2010), 138.
- Marty Machowski, *Long Story Short: Ten-Minute Devotions to Draw Your Family to God* (Greensboro, NC: New Growth Press, 2010), 10.
- Bruce A. Ware, *Big Truths for Young Hearts: Teaching and Learning the Greatness of God* (Wheaton, IL: Crossway, 2009), 82.

IMAGE: Lesson 2

PROCLAMATION

BIG IDEA:

God created people in his image, which shows his special love for people more than any other creature.

FOCUS VOCABULARY:

- **Image:** Being made in God's image means that we reflect some of the things that are true about God. God showed that he has special love for people (more than other creatures) because he created us in his image.

OBJECTIVES:

- Kids can define image.
- Kids can identify who images God.
- Kids can restate differences between people and other creatures.

KEY POINTS:

God showed that he has special love for people because he created us in his image.

- Being made in God's image means that we reflect some of the things that are true about God.
    - Imagine looking at yourself in a mirror. Does the mirror reflect some things about you? Can you see your eyes? Your nose? Can you see your smile? Your frown? *(Yes.)* What about what you are thinking? Your voice? *(No.)*
    - In this way, as image bearers, we reflect some things about God, but we are not the same as God. God is God, and we are not!
        - In Genesis 1:26, God said, "Let us make man in our image, after our likeness." This means that being images of God has something to do with being *like* God, but not the same as God.
        - When people look at us they should be able to see something of what God is like.
- Every person in the whole world images God all the time no matter what—it's how we were made.

- Because Jesus is God, he reflects God the Father perfectly. As a man, he was a perfect image bearer of God.
- To be like Jesus as best you can (which is only possible with lots of help from the Holy Spirit!) is to reflect God.

Being made in God's image shows that God created us as special, different from all other creatures.

- Most of the Bible tells about who God is, and about God's relationship with humans who are created for his glory.
  - He created us to be part of his special Rescue Plan.
  - As image bearers, we are more special to God than anything else he created.
- Human beings "are really the greatest part of God's creation." Human beings have been made "to display more of what God is like than anything else does in all of creation."[22]
  - People are "the only part of the creation that can talk with God, worship him, and have a relationship with him. Man can also create things like painting, machines, and music."[23]
  - God even made us in a special way: the rest of creation was made with God's word, but God formed us with his hands and then breathed life into us.

Gospel Link: How does what we know about image connect to the gospel, the good news of God's Rescue Plan through Jesus?

- Because God has a special love for humans as his image bearers, he made a Rescue Plan for his people.
  - Jesus the Son agreed with the plan from before the world began. Then, he lived, died, and rose to make the plan happen.
  - God knew that we would be separated from him because of our sin, so he planned for Jesus to come as Rescuer, to live a perfect life on earth, and to die a terrible death to take the punishment we deserve for our sins.
    - Romans 10:9 says, "If you confess with your mouth that Jesus is Lord and believe in your heart that God raised him from the dead, you will be saved."
    - If you want to talk more about believing in Jesus as your Rescuer, feel free to talk to your dad or mom, your teacher or Community Group leader, or to read the Bible and talk to Jesus.

APPLICATION

[22] Ware, *Big Truths for Young Hearts*, 82.
[23] Machowski, *Long Story Short*, 10.

DISCUSSION:

- Are just some people made in the image of God? Who is?
- How are people different from all other creatures?
- How does God's Rescue Plan connect to you?

SCRIPTURE: *Review the Scriptures you began exploring last week.*

Read:

- Re-read Genesis 1 and 2, and discuss what you learn in the passage about what it means to image God.

Explore:

- Genesis 1:27: "So God created man in his own image, in the image of God he created him; male and female he created them."

PRAYER:

- Thank Jesus for being the perfect image of God.
- If you have believed in Jesus as your Savior from sin, pray that the Holy Spirit will help you to image God more fully.

ADDITIONAL RESOURCES:

- Mark Driscoll and Gerry Breshears, "Image: God Loves," in *Doctrine: What Christians Should Believe* (Wheaton, IL: Crossway, 2010), 138.
- Marty Machowski, *Long Story Short: Ten-Minute Devotions to Draw Your Family to God* (Greensboro, NC: New Growth Press, 2010), 10.
- Bruce A. Ware, *Big Truths for Young Hearts: Teaching and Learning the Greatness of God* (Wheaton, IL: Crossway, 2009), 82.

IMAGE: Lesson 3

PROCLAMATION

BIG IDEA:

Because we are made in God's image, we have qualities that are a little like his.

FOCUS VOCABULARY:

- **Image:** Being made in God's image means that we reflect some of the things that are true about God, but we are not the same as God. God showed that he has special love for people (more than other creatures) because he created us in his image. Being made in God's image also means that we have qualities and responsibilities that are a little like his.

OBJECTIVES:

- Kids can list qualities people have that are a little like God's.
- Kids can restate the purpose of acting out these qualities (with lots of help from the Holy Spirit!).

KEY POINTS:

God created us to have qualities that are a little like his.

- There are some things that are true about God that are not true about us.
    - God is everywhere. God knows everything. God is all powerful. These are examples of things that are true about God that are not true about us.
- Because we are made in God's image, there are some other things that are true about God that can also be partly true about us when the Holy Spirit helps us.
    - After you have believed in Jesus as your Savior from sin, God keeps on making you more holy, forgiving, truthful, beautiful, loving, faithful, and more.
    - Like God the Trinity, the Holy Spirit helps us think big thoughts, ask questions, and learn huge ideas. Animals can't do that! Not only that, but God uses our thinking to change our hearts so we love him more.
        - We have minds and feelings and the ability to choose—all things that God has.

- Like God the Trinity, we can talk to God and to each other.
    - Right after creating Adam and Eve, God talks to them. He didn't do this with anything else he created. God wanted to be able to explain to us who we are and what we should do with our lives.
        - God lets us pray to and praise him, and hear him speaking in words to us.
    - God even lets us have the ability to talk to each other so we can tell people about who Jesus is and what he has done!
- Like God the Trinity, we are made to be in loving relationships, like a family.
    - We get to know God.
    - We get to know ourselves and who God wants us to be.
    - We get to know other people.

We get to live for God's glory by acting out these qualities (with lots of help from the Holy Spirit!).

- To image God the Trinity is to make him visible to the world. When you have believed in Jesus as your Savior from sin, you do this by having the Holy Spirit's help to live with the qualities that are a little like God's.

Gospel Link: How does what we know about image connect to the gospel, the good news of God's Rescue Plan through Jesus?

- We can't live out these qualities on our own—we need help from the Holy Spirit. And because of our sin, we often fail to love others or tell Jesus' Story the way we want to.
    - But the sensational news is that God knows all of this, and every time we sin he wants to tell us the Story of Jesus as Hero all over again. He lovingly tells us who Jesus is. When you have believed in Jesus as your Savior from sin, he helps you confess your sin and receive his grace and forgiveness, then leads you into wonderful worship of him.
        - First John 1:9 says to believers, "If we confess our sins, he is faithful and just to forgive us our sins and to cleanse us from all unrighteousness."

APPLICATION

DISCUSSION:

- What is special about people?
- What are some ways that we are a little like God?
- How does God's Rescue Plan connect to you? Have you believed in Jesus as your Savior from sin?

SCRIPTURE:

Read:

- As a family, explore the concordance of your Bible. Use the concordance to notice characteristics of God, and identify which qualities we have a little bit of.
- Choose some Scriptures from the concordance to study together.

Explore:

- Psalm 73:25–26: "Whom have I in heaven but you? And there is nothing on earth that I desire besides you. My flesh and my heart may fail, but God is the strength of my heart and my portion forever."

PRAYER:

- Thank God for giving us his Word so we know about his plan for the world, including rescuing us through Christ.
- Pray that the Holy Spirit will help us to respond to our love of Jesus by acting out our qualities that are a little like his.
- Thank Jesus that he is our Rescuer, and keeps on rescuing us when we fail.
- Pray through Psalm 73:25–26.

ADDITIONAL RESOURCES:

- Mark Driscoll and Gerry Breshears, "Image: God Loves," in *Doctrine: What Christians Should Believe* (Wheaton, IL: Crossway, 2010), 138.
- Marty Machowski, *Long Story Short: Ten-Minute Devotions to Draw Your Family to God* (Greensboro, NC: New Growth Press, 2010), 10.
- Bruce A. Ware, *Big Truths for Young Hearts: Teaching and Learning the Greatness of God* (Wheaton, IL: Crossway, 2009), 82.

IMAGE: Lesson 4

PROCLAMATION

BIG IDEA:

Because we are made in God's image, we have responsibilities that are a little like his.

FOCUS VOCABULARY:

- **Image:** Being made in God's image means that we reflect some of the things that are true about God, but we are not the same as God. God showed that he has special love for people (more than other creatures) because he created us in his image. Being made in God's image also means that we have qualities and responsibilities that are a little like his.

OBJECTIVES:

- Kids can list responsibilities people have that are a little like God's.
- Kids can restate the purpose of acting out these responsibilities (with lots of help from the Holy Spirit!).

KEY POINTS:

God created us to have responsibilities that are a little like his.

- *Community:* Like God the Father, God the Son, and God the Holy Spirit are Friends who are constantly loving and serving each other, God created us to be friends who love and serve.
- *Dominion:* Like God is sovereign over the whole world—taking care of it—God created us to be in charge of and take care of the world around us.
- *Multiply:* Like God is constantly changing hearts and bringing many sons and daughters into his family through Jesus, God created us to grow up, marry, and bring kids into our families who we pray will use their whole lives to worship Jesus.
- *Mission:* Like God is constantly telling his Big Story to the whole world, God created us to tell the Story of Jesus as Hero to God (in worship), to people in our church (in community), and to our neighbors (on mission).

We get to live for God's glory by acting out these responsibilities (with lots of help from the Holy Spirit!).

- To image God the Trinity is to make him visible to the world. When you have believed in Jesus as your Savior from sin, you do this by having the Holy Spirit's help to live with the qualities and responsibilities that are a little like God's.

Gospel Link: How does what we know about our responsibilities connect to the gospel, the good news of God's Rescue Plan through Jesus?

- We know we can't live out these responsibilities on our own—we need help from the Holy Spirit. And because of our sin, we often fail to love others, take care of the world, or tell Jesus' Story the way we want to.
    - But the sensational news is that God knows all of this, and every time we sin he wants to tell us the Story of Jesus as Hero all over again. He lovingly tells us who Jesus is. When you believe in him as your Savior from sin, he helps you confess your sins and receive his grace and forgiveness, then leads you into wonderful worship of him.
        - Romans 10:9 says, "If you confess with your mouth that Jesus is Lord and believe in your heart that God raised him from the dead, you will be saved."
        - If you want to talk more about believing in Jesus as your Rescuer, feel free to talk to your dad or mom, your teacher or Community Group leader, or to read the Bible and talk to Jesus.

APPLICATION

DISCUSSION:

- What are some things we are created to do that are a little like what God does?
- Tell about a time you imaged God by taking care of something.
- Do you act out your responsibilities perfectly all of the time? How does Jesus respond?

SCRIPTURE: *Review the Scriptures you began exploring last week.*

Read:

- As a family, explore the concordance of your Bible. Use the concordance to notice characteristics of God, and identify which qualities and responsibilities we have a little bit of.
- Choose some Scriptures from the concordance to study together.

Explore:

- Psalm 73:25-26: "Whom have I in heaven but you? And there is nothing on earth that I desire besides you. My flesh and my heart may fail, but God is the strength of my heart and my portion forever."

PRAYER:

- Thank God for giving us his Word so we know about his plan for the world, including rescuing us through Christ.
- If you have believed in Jesus as your Savior from sin, pray that the Holy Spirit will help you to act out your responsibilities that are a little like God's.
- Pray through Psalm 73:25–26, asking that God will help you see him as your strength.

ADDITIONAL RESOURCES:

- Mark Driscoll and Gerry Breshears, "Image: God Loves," in *Doctrine: What Christians Should Believe* (Wheaton, IL: Crossway, 2010), 138.
- Marty Machowski, *Long Story Short: Ten-Minute Devotions to Draw Your Family to God* (Greensboro, NC: New Growth Press, 2010), 10.
- Bruce A. Ware, *Big Truths for Young Hearts: Teaching and Learning the Greatness of God* (Wheaton, IL: Crossway, 2009), 82.

IMAGE: 4/5/6 Activity 1

Circle and color the things that are made in the image of God. Cross out the things that are not made in the image of God.

IMAGE: 4/5/6 Activity 2

When we love Jesus, we respond by obeying him.

In each box, draw a picture of something you do in response to Jesus that is a little like what God does.

To support kids, ask them about their work using the following questions:

- How do you worship God with your actions?
- Does God _____? When you _____, are you being a little like God?
- *(If trouble)* Can you show that you are a little like God by ______?

IMAGE: 7+ Activity 1

Re-read the verses you studied during Community Group, and copy them in the boxes below. Then summarize what they tell you by answering the questions.

Reference	Write the verse.
Colossians 1:15	
Romans 8:29	
2 Corinthians 3:18	
Colossians 3:10	

ADDING IT ALL UP:

Are you a perfect image of God? Use a verse to support your answer.

Are you becoming a better image of God? Who helps you? Use a verse to support your answer.

Who is the perfect image of God? Use a verse to support your answer.

IMAGE: 7+ Activity 2

Write the verse.	What quality does the verse describe?	Describe a time when the Holy Spirit helped you display this quality.	Can you display this quality perfectly all the time? How does God the Trinity respond?
2 Corinthians 1:3			
Romans 2:4			
As a family, find more verses in the Bible that describe qualities God has that we have a little bit, too.			

FALL: Lesson 1

PROCLAMATION

BIG IDEA:

God created a perfect world, but Adam and Eve disobeyed God.

FOCUS VOCABULARY:

- **Perfect:** Exactly right; without a single mistake or shortcoming.
- **Disobey:** To break the rules. To say or do something that you have been told not to by someone in authority over you. It can also be not doing something that you have been told to do by someone in authority over you.

OBJECTIVES:

- Kids can describe creation before the fall.
- Kids can retell how sin began (the fall).

KEY POINTS:

God created a perfect world.

- Adam and Eve had everything they needed, including—most of all—a perfect relationship with God.
    - "When Adam and Eve opened their eyes, the first thing they ever saw was God's face. And when God saw them he was like a new dad. 'You look like me,' he said. 'You're the most beautiful thing I've ever made!' God loved them with all of his heart. . . . And Adam and Eve joined in the song of the stars and the streams and the wind in the trees, the wonderful song of love to the one who made them."[24]
    - God had made a wonderful garden full of fruit trees for Adam and Eve to live in. "But God made a rule: Adam could not eat from one of the trees, the tree of the knowledge of good and evil. He warned Adam that if he ate from that tree he would die."[25]

---

[24] Lloyd-Jones, *The Jesus Storybook Bible*, 26.
[25] Machowski, *Long Story Short*, 13.

- God had given Adam and Eve everything they needed, including friendship with God and perfect directions from him about how to stay safe and happy as they worshiped him.
    - "Their hearts were filled with happiness. And nothing ever made them sad or lonely or sick or afraid. God looked at everything he had made. 'Perfect!' he said. And it was. But all the stars and the mountains and oceans and galaxies and everything were nothing compared to how much God loved his children. He would move heaven and earth to be near them. Always. Whatever happened, whatever it cost him, he would always love them."[26]

Adam and Eve disobeyed God.

- Satan, the enemy of God, tempted Adam and Eve by twisting God's Story.
    - "God had a horrible enemy. His name was Satan. Satan had once been the most beautiful angel, but he didn't want to just be an angel—he wanted to be God. He grew proud and evil and full of hate, and God had to send him out of heaven. Satan was seething with anger and looking for a way to hurt God. He wanted to stop God's plan, stop this love story, right there. So he disguised himself as a snake and waited in the garden."[27]
- Instead of listening to the perfect words God had given them, Adam and Eve listened to the serpent and chose to twist God's Story, too.
    - "As soon as the snake saw his chance, he slithered silently up to Eve. 'Does God really love you?' the serpent whispered. 'If he does, why won't he let you eat the nice, juicy, delicious fruit? Poor you, perhaps God doesn't want you to be happy.' The snake's words hissed into her ears and sunk down deep into her heart, like poison. *Does God love me?* Eve wondered. Suddenly she didn't know anymore. 'Just trust me,' the serpent whispered. 'You don't need God. One small taste, that's all, and you'll be happier than you could ever dream . . . ' Eve picked the fruit and ate some. And Adam ate some, too."[28]

Gospel Link: How does what we know about Adam and Eve connect to the gospel, the good news of God's Rescue Plan through Jesus?

- In the Bible, God tells us about Adam and Eve so that we can really learn about ourselves: just like Adam and Eve, every person everywhere sins.
    - We need God. We need help and forgiveness and a Rescuer. But God knew we would sin from before the beginning, so he made a Rescue Plan. Through Jesus, he forgives people who believe Jesus is the Rescuer and gives them new hearts, bringing them back into his family.
        - If we confess with our mouths and believe in our hearts that Jesus is our Rescuer from sin, we get to live as part of the Forever Family of God.

---

[26] Lloyd-Jones, *The Jesus Storybook Bible*, 26–27.
[27] Ibid., 28.
[28] Ibid., 30.

- If you want to talk more about believing in Jesus as your Rescuer, feel free to talk to your dad or mom, your teacher or Community Group leader, or to read the Bible and talk to Jesus.

APPLICATION

DISCUSSION:

- When God created the garden for Adam and Eve, were there any problems? What was the world like? What was their relationship with God like?
- How did Adam and Eve disobey God?
- How do you fit into God's Rescue Plan?

SCRIPTURE:

Read:

- Read the account of the fall in *The Jesus Storybook Bible* (28–34). What strikes you?
- Read Romans 5 and unpack what you hear in the chapter about sin. Who sins? What is the solution for sin?

Explore:

- Romans 5:12: "Therefore, just as sin came into the world through one man, and death through sin, and so death spread to all men because all sinned."

PRAYER:

- Ask God to help you confess your sins and not hide them like Adam and Eve tried to do.
- Thank God for his Rescue Plan.
- Pray through Romans 5:12.

ADDITIONAL RESOURCES:

- Sally Lloyd-Jones, *The Jesus Storybook Bible: Every Story Whispers His Name* (Grand Rapids, MI: Zondervan, 2007), 26–36.
- Marty Machowski, *Long Story Short: Ten-Minute Devotions to Draw Your Family to God* (Greensboro, NC: New Growth Press, 2010), 13–19.
- Bruce A. Ware, *Big Truths for Young Hearts: Teaching and Learning the Greatness of God* (Wheaton, IL: Crossway, 2009), 92–98.

FALL: Lesson 2

PROCLAMATION

BIG IDEA:

When Adam and Eve disobeyed God, sin began.

FOCUS VOCABULARY:

- **Perfect:** Exactly right; without a single mistake or shortcoming.
- **Disobey:** To break the rules. To say or do something that you have been told not to by someone in authority over you. It can also be not doing something that you have been told to do by someone in authority over you.

OBJECTIVES:

- Kids can retell how sin began.
- Kids can define sin.

KEY POINTS:

Adam and Eve disobeyed God.

- Instead of obeying what God told them to do, Adam and Eve listened to Satan who appeared as a snake to twist God's Story.
    - "As soon as the snake saw his chance, he slithered silently up to Eve. 'Does God really love you?' the serpent whispered. 'If he does, why won't he let you eat the nice, juicy, delicious fruit? Poor you, perhaps God doesn't want you to be happy.' The snake's words hissed into her ears and sunk down deep into her heart, like poison. *Does God love me?* Eve wondered. Suddenly she didn't know anymore. 'Just trust me,' the serpent whispered. 'You don't need God. One small taste, that's all, and you'll be happier than you could ever dream . . . ' Eve picked up the fruit and ate some. And Adam ate some, too."[30]

---

[29] Lloyd-Jones, *The Jesus Storybook Bible,* 30.

Sin began.

- "And a terrible lie came into the world. . . . It would live on in every human heart, whispering to every one of God's children: 'God doesn't love me.'"[30]
- Terrible pain was in God's heart. "His children hadn't just broken the one rule; they had broken God's heart. They had broken their wonderful relationship with him. . . . God's creation would start to unravel, and come undone, and go wrong. From now on, everything would die—even though it was all supposed to last forever. You see, sin had come into God's perfect world. . . . God's children would be always running away from him and hiding in the dark. Their hearts would break now."[31]
- "God was right and the serpent was wrong. Obedience to God always brings blessing, and sin always harms and kills."[32]
- "God told Adam and Eve that if they ate the forbidden fruit they would die. But after they disobeyed, they were still alive. Although it might seem like nothing happened on the outside because they were still alive, something died on the inside. Instead of loving and enjoying God, Adam and Eve became afraid of God and hid. Their friendship with God was broken because they disobeyed. That is why they turned away from God and hid. And they did grow older and, many years later, they did die."[33]

Sin is doing or thinking what God does not want you to do. Sin is also not doing what God wants you to do.

- Eve sinned by doing: she did the thing that God did not want her to do. Adam sinned by not doing: by failing to lovingly lead Eve, he did not do what God wanted.

Gospel Link: How does what we know about Adam and Eve connect to the gospel, the good news of God's Rescue Plan through Jesus?

- In the Bible, God tells us about Adam and Eve so that we can really learn about ourselves: just like Adam and Eve, every person everywhere sins.
    - We need God. We need help and forgiveness and a Rescuer. But God knew we would sin from before the beginning, so he made a Rescue Plan. Through Jesus, he forgives people who believe Jesus is the Rescuer and gives them new hearts, bringing them back into his family.
        - If we confess with our mouths and believe in our hearts that Jesus is our Rescuer from sin, we get to live as part of the Forever Family of God.
        - If you want to talk more about believing in Jesus as your Rescuer, feel free to talk to your dad or mom, your teacher or Community Group leader, or to read the Bible and talk to Jesus.

---

[30] Ibid.
[31] Ibid., 33–34.
[32] Ware, *Big Truths for Young Hearts*, 94.
[33] Machowski, *Long Story Short*, 18.

APPLICATION

DISCUSSION:

- How does Adam and Eve's sin connect to you? Do you sin?
- Tell about a time you did something that God does not want.
- How do you fit into God's Rescue Plan?

SCRIPTURE: *Review the Scriptures you began exploring last week.*

Read:

- Read the account of the fall in *The Jesus Storybook Bible* (28–34). What strikes you?
- Read Romans 5 and unpack what you hear in the chapter about sin. Who sins? What is the solution for sin?

Explore:

- Romans 5:12: "Therefore, just as sin came into the world through one man, and death through sin, and so death spread to all men because all sinned."

PRAYER:

- Ask God to help you confess your sins and not hide them like Adam and Eve tried to do.
- Thank God for his Rescue Plan.
- Pray through Romans 5:12.

ADDITIONAL RESOURCES:

- Sally Lloyd-Jones, *The Jesus Storybook Bible: Every Story Whispers His Name* (Grand Rapids, MI: Zondervan, 2007), 26–36.
- Marty Machowski, *Long Story Short: Ten-Minute Devotions to Draw Your Family to God* (Greensboro, NC: New Growth Press, 2010), 13–19.
- Bruce A. Ware, *Big Truths for Young Hearts: Teaching and Learning the Greatness of God* (Wheaton, IL: Crossway, 2009), 92–98.

FALL: Lesson 3

PROCLAMATION

BIG IDEA:

Because of the fall, we are born as sinners.

FOCUS VOCABULARY:

- **Sin:** Sin is disobeying God. Sin can be doing what God does not want you to do. Sin is also not doing what God wants you to do.

OBJECTIVES:

- Kids can define sin.
- Kids can identify sinners.
- Kids can describe God's response to sin.

KEY POINTS:

Because of the fall, everyone sins.

- "Starting with Adam and Eve, everyone has sinned, except for Jesus. . . . We *all* sin against God and disobey his commands."[34]
- We *all* rebel against God over and over.
  - "Sin always involves thinking we know what is best, not God. Sin always leads us to turn from God and his ways because we think that our ways will end up better for us than God's ways. But this is never true. God's ways are always best for us, and we must resist every temptation to doubt this."[35]
  - "Because we are sinners, we often don't live in holy ways or love others as we should or forgive when we've been wronged or speak the truth instead of lying and so on. Because we are made in the image of God, we should be this way, but we are not."[36]

---

[34] Machowski, *Long Story Short*, 17–18, emphasis added.
[35] Ware, *Big Truths for Young Hearts*, 94.
[36] Ibid., 87.

We are born as sinners.

- Every person in the whole world sins from the time they are born. This includes you. Even babies and little kids sin—they love things other than God more than him, they disobey their parents, and more.
- The punishment that sin deserves is death and the Forever Sadness of separation from God.
- This means that every single person—including me, including you, and including every person you know—needs Jesus as their Savior from sin. From the second you were born, you've been needing Jesus as your Rescuer.

Gospel Link: How does what we know about our sin connect to the gospel, the good news of God's Rescue Plan through Jesus?

- God sent Jesus on a Rescue Mission to save us despite our sin.
- God made a promise to Adam and Eve that he would send God the Son to carry out the Rescue Plan.
- "Before they left the garden, God whispered a promise to Adam and Eve: 'It will not always be so! I will come to rescue you! And when I do, I'm going to do battle against the snake. I'll get rid of the sin and the dark and the sadness you let in here. I'm coming back for you!' And he would. One day, God himself would come."[37]
    - This was the first promise God made that he would send a Savior to save us from our sin—a promise he would repeat many times over the years, and a promise he would keep through Jesus.
- "God loved his children too much to let the story end [with the fall]. Even though he knew he would suffer, God had a plan—a magnificent dream. One day, he would get his children back. One day, he would make the world their perfect home again. And one day, he would wipe away every tear from their eyes. You see, no matter what, in spite of everything, God would love his children—with a Never Stopping, Never Giving Up, Unbreaking, Always and Forever Love."[38]
    - Romans 10:9 says, "If you confess with your mouth that Jesus is Lord and believe in your heart that God raised him from the dead, you will be saved."
    - If you want to talk more about believing in Jesus as your Rescuer, feel free to talk to your dad or mom, your teacher or Community Group leader, or to read the Bible and talk to Jesus.

[37] Lloyd-Jones, *The Jesus Storybook Bible*, 36.
[38] Ibid.

APPLICATION

DISCUSSION:

- What is sin? Who sins?
- When did you start sinning? Do you need Jesus as your Rescuer from sin?
- How does God's Rescue Plan connect to you?

SCRIPTURE:

Read:

- Re-read Genesis 3. Consider focusing on God's promises and provision despite Adam and Eve's sin in the following verses:
    - Verse 15: God's promise that Jesus will come, and that although Satan will hurt him, Jesus will crush Satan and rescue his people from sin.
    - Verse 21: God provides clothes for Adam and Eve.
    - Verse 24: God protects Adam and Eve by guarding the way to the tree of life.

Explore:

- 1 Corinthians 15:22: "For as in Adam all die, so also in Christ shall all be made alive."

PRAYER:

- Thank God for his Rescue Plan, and for sending Jesus as the Rescuer.
- Pray that God will show you your sin and help you to receive grace and worship him over and over.

ADDITIONAL RESOURCES:

- Sally Lloyd-Jones, *The Jesus Storybook Bible: Every Story Whispers His Name* (Grand Rapids, MI: Zondervan, 2007), 26–36.
- Marty Machowski, *Long Story Short: Ten-Minute Devotions to Draw Your Family to God* (Greensboro, NC: New Growth Press, 2010), 13–19.
- Bruce A. Ware, *Big Truths for Young Hearts: Teaching and Learning the Greatness of God* (Wheaton, IL: Crossway, 2009), 92–98.

FALL: Lesson 4

PROCLAMATION

BIG IDEA:

God knew sin would happen, so he made a Rescue Plan through Jesus.

FOCUS VOCABULARY:

- **Sin:** Sin is disobeying God. Sin can be doing what God does not want you to do. Sin is also not doing what God wants you to do.

OBJECTIVES:

- Kids can define sin.
- Kids can describe God's response to sin.

KEY POINTS:

God knew sin would happen.

- "God was not surprised by Adam and Eve's sin. God knew all along that they would sin."[39]
- From before the beginning, God the Father, Jesus the Son, and the Holy Spirit all knew what would happen. So God the Father made a plan, Jesus agreed with the plan then lived the plan, and when we believe in Jesus the Holy Spirit helps us live our part in the plan.

God made a Rescue Plan through Jesus.

- "Even before [sin] happened, God had a wonderful plan to make things right again. God the Father would send his only Son Jesus to earth as a baby. Jesus would grow up as a man like Adam, but instead of disobeying God, Jesus would obey him every day all the time. Because of his perfect life Jesus could take our punishment so we could be forgiven and have peace with God."[40]
- God first let us know about his Rescue Plan when he made a promise to Adam and Eve. He told them that he would send Jesus the Son to carry out his plan.

---

[39] Machowski, *Long Story Short*, 19.
[40] Ibid.

- "God loved his children too much to let the story end [with the fall]."[41]

Gospel Link: How does what we know about our sin connect to the gospel, the good news of God's Rescue Plan through Jesus?

- The gospel, the good news of God's Rescue Plan through Jesus, is good news for us today, too.
- We need God. We need help and forgiveness and a Rescuer. Through Jesus, he forgives people who believe Jesus is the Rescuer and gives them new hearts, bringing them back into his family. This can include you.
  - Romans 10:9 says, "If you confess with your mouth that Jesus is Lord and believe in your heart that God raised him from the dead, you will be saved."
  - If you want to talk more about believing in Jesus as your Rescuer, feel free to talk to your dad or mom, your teacher or Community Group leader, or to read the Bible and talk to Jesus.

APPLICATION

DISCUSSION:

- Did sin surprise God?
- What was God's Rescue Plan?
- How do you fit into God's Rescue Plan?

SCRIPTURE: *Review the Scriptures you began exploring last week.*

Read:

- Re-read Genesis 3. Consider focusing on God's promises and provision despite Adam and Eve's sin in the following verses:
  - Verse 15: God's promise that Jesus will come, and that although Satan will hurt him, Jesus will crush Satan and rescue his people from sin.
  - Verse 21: God provides clothes for Adam and Eve.
  - Verse 24: God protects Adam and Eve by guarding the way to the tree of life.

Explore:

- 1 Corinthians 15:22: "For as in Adam all die, so also in Christ shall all be made alive."

[41] Lloyd-Jones, *The Jesus Storybook Bible*, 36.

PRAYER:

- Thank God for his Rescue Plan, and for sending Jesus the Rescuer.
- Pray that God will help show you your sin and your need for Jesus.

ADDITIONAL RESOURCES:

- Sally Lloyd-Jones, *The Jesus Storybook Bible: Every Story Whispers His Name* (Grand Rapids, MI: Zondervan, 2007), 26–36.
- Marty Machowski, *Long Story Short: Ten-Minute Devotions to Draw Your Family to God* (Greensboro, NC: New Growth Press, 2010), 13–19.
- Bruce A. Ware, *Big Truths for Young Hearts: Teaching and Learning the Greatness of God* (Wheaton, IL: Crossway, 2009), 92–98.

FALL: 4/5/6 Activity 1

We can sin by doing, and we can also sin by not doing.

- In the top box, sketch a time you have done something God didn't want you to do.
- In the bottom box, sketch a time when you didn't do something God wanted you to do.

Support your child by asking the following questions:

- *(Point to picture.)* How did you rebel against God? How does Jesus respond?
- *(If struggling)* God is ____. Does it glorify God when you _____?
- How does Jesus respond?

SOMETIMES I SIN BY DOING THE WRONG THING:

SOMETIMES I SIN BY NOT DOING THE RIGHT THING:

FALL: 4/5/6 Activity 2

Before they left the garden, God gave a promise to Adam and Eve. Draw a picture of what God promised would happen at just the right time.

Support kids while they work by asking the following questions:

- Who did God make a promise to?
- What did he promise?
- Who kept the promise?
- How does God's promise connect to you?

FALL: 7+ Activity 1

In the verse below, circle the word SIN.	What does this verse tell you about WHO sins?	What does this verse tell you about when a person begins to sin?
James 4:17: "So whoever knows the right thing to do and fails to do it, for him it is sin."		
John 8:34: "Jesus answered them, 'Truly, truly, I say to you, everyone who practices sin is a slave to sin.'"		
Romans 3:23: "For all have sinned and fall short of the glory of God."		

FALL: 7+ Activity 2

Let's explore how God makes, keeps, and tells about his promise of Jesus the Rescuer throughout the whole Bible. Read each verse, then answer the five W questions to tell about the Rescue God planned.

Read Isaiah 9:6. WHO would God send?

Read Isaiah 53:1–12. WHAT would he do?

Read Micah 5:2. WHERE would he do it?

Read Malachi 3:1. WHEN would he do it? *(Hint: when was the temple destroyed?)*

Read 2 Corinthians 5:21. WHY would he do it?

COVENANT: Lesson 1

PROCLAMATION

BIG IDEA:

God is a perfect promise keeper.

FOCUS VOCABULARY:

- **Promise:** A promise is something that someone tells another person that they will do in the future. In the Bible, the word "covenant" is often used to describe God's Forever Promises to his people. God's promises are loving and unbreaking, and God keeps his promises.

OBJECTIVE:

- Kids can describe God's promises (loving, unbreaking).

KEY POINTS:

God's promises are loving and unbreaking.

- *Loving:* God loves us with a "Never Stopping, Never Giving Up, Unbreaking, Always and Forever Love."[42] The promises that God makes to us are always for our good, even when they seem hard to understand or far away.
- *Unbreaking:* God makes promises to us the same way he loves us: his promises never stop. He never gives up on them; he does not break them. He keeps them always and forever.

God is a promise keeper.

- Even in the face of sin, God remains God: he keeps on loving us and keeping his promises even though we fail him again and again.
- God keeps on pursuing his people, and he does just what he says he will.
    - Throughout the whole Bible, God responds to our sin by making his perfect, loving promises—and then he keeps them!

[42] Lloyd-Jones, *The Jesus Storybook Bible*, 36.

- The way God keeps his promises tells us lots about him: he speaks, he acts, he loves, he declares his laws, he judges sin, he delivers and provides, and he is present. That sure sounds like a Mighty God and Everlasting Father (Isaiah 9:6).

Gospel Link: How does what we know about God's promises connect to the gospel, the good news of God's Rescue Plan through Jesus?

- The gospel, the good news of God's Rescue Plan through Jesus, is God's biggest promise of all! From the time of Adam and Eve, God promised over and over that he would send Jesus the Son as the Rescuer from sin.
    - Today, God makes and keeps the same promise to us. He knows that we need Jesus. And he promises that if we believe in Jesus as God the Savior from sin, we will be saved. This can include you.
        - Romans 10:9 says, "If you confess with your mouth that Jesus is Lord and believe in your heart that God raised him from the dead, you will be saved."
        - If you want to talk more about believing in Jesus as your Rescuer, feel free to talk to your dad or mom, your teacher or Community Group leader, or to read the Bible and talk to Jesus.

APPLICATION

DISCUSSION:

- What do you know about God's promises?
- Does God keep his promises?
- How does God's promise of Jesus the Savior connect to you?

SCRIPTURE:

Read:

- As a family, focus on Genesis 6–9. Consider:
    - Who makes promises?
    - Who are the promises to?
    - What are the promises?
    - Are the promises kept?
    - How do the promises in Genesis 6–9 connect to your life?

Explore:

- Genesis 9:9: "Behold, I establish my covenant with you and your offspring after you."

PRAYER:

- Thank God for keeping his promises, even when we sin against him.
- Thank God that his promises are loving and unbreaking.

ADDITIONAL RESOURCES:

- Sally Lloyd-Jones, *The Jesus Storybook Bible: Every Story Whispers His Name* (Grand Rapids, MI: Zondervan, 2007), 36–47, 56–60.
- Marty Machowski, *Long Story Short: Ten-Minute Devotions to Draw Your Family to God* (Greensboro, NC: New Growth Press, 2010), 44–49.

COVENANT: Lesson 2

PROCLAMATION

BIG IDEA:

We are promise breakers who need to be rescued, and God rescues.

FOCUS VOCABULARY:

- **Promise:** A promise is something that someone tells another person that they will do in the future. In the Bible, the word "covenant" is often used to describe God's Forever Promises to his people. God's promises are loving and unbreaking, and God keeps his promises.

OBJECTIVES:

- Kids can describe God's promises (loving, unbreaking).
- Kids can give at least one example of a promise that God made in the Old Testament.

KEY POINTS:

We are promise breakers who need to be rescued.

- What began in the garden has continued in every story since: we fail to obey God and we sin; God loves and saves. We are unfaithful; God is faithful. We are unreliable; God is reliable.
    - As image bearers, we make lots of promises. But as sinners, we break lots of them. We cannot keep our promises perfectly, and sometimes we make them for selfish reasons that do not glorify God. We need Jesus the Rescuer. Every single person in the world—including you—needs Jesus.

God rescues.

- Over and over throughout the Bible, God gives us stories of times when his people failed to obey God and sinned, and God responded by making and keeping promises to take care of them. People sinned; God rescued.
- One example is the story of Noah. God knew Noah needed to be rescued, so, in love, he made a promise.

- "Everyone everywhere had forgotten about God and were only doing bad things all the time. God's heart was filled with pain when he saw what had happened to the world he loved."[43]
- Sin made God sad and angry—he knew he would have to do something to stop it, so he had planned a storm. "The storm was going to wash away all the hate and sadness and everything that had gone wrong, and make the world clean again."[44]
- God chose to protect a man named Noah and his family so that God's people could continue. God made a promise to protect Noah, but Noah would have to trust God and do exactly what God told him.
    - And so, Noah did what God told him and built a boat called an ark to protect himself and his family during the storm. God gave Noah faith in his plan, and Noah obeyed. Then, just like God promised he would do, he kept Noah and his family safe in the storm.
    - "The first thing Noah did was to thank God for rescuing them, just as he had promised. And the first thing God did was make another promise. 'I won't ever destroy the world again.' And like a warrior who puts away his bow and arrow at the end of a great battle, God said, 'See, I have hung up my bow in the clouds.' And there, in the clouds—just where the storm meets the sun—was a beautiful bow made of light. It was a new beginning in God's world."[45]

Gospel Link: How does what we know about God's promises connect to the gospel, the good news of God's Rescue Plan through Jesus?

- Noah and his family needed to be rescued before the flood, and they still needed the Rescuer after the flood. I need the Rescuer just like Noah did.
    - God does amazing things for us: he speaks to us, he makes loving promises to us, and he blesses us. But our hearts are so sinful that even though we've received all these amazing things from God, we continue to sin against God.
    - But before the beginning, before Noah or you or me, God knew that sin would happen so he made a Rescue Plan. He sent Jesus the Son to take the penalty for our sin and to defeat death. If you believe in him as your Savior from sin, God promises to make you part of his Forever Family—and God always keeps his promises!
        - Romans 10:9 says, "If you confess with your mouth that Jesus is Lord and believe in your heart that God raised him from the dead, you will be saved."
        - If you want to talk more about believing in Jesus as your Rescuer, feel free to talk to your dad or mom, your teacher or Community Group leader, or to read the Bible and talk to Jesus.

---

[43] Lloyd-Jones, *The Jesus Storybook Bible*, 38.
[44] Ibid., 40.
[45] Ibid., 46–47.

APPLICATION

DISCUSSION:

- Do people keep all of their promises? Do you?
- Did God keep his promise to Noah to keep him safe? Does God keep all his promises?
- How does God's promise of Jesus the Savior connect to you?

SCRIPTURE: *Review the Scriptures you began exploring last week.*

Read:

- As a family, focus on Genesis 6–9. Consider:
    - Who makes promises?
    - Who are the promises to?
    - What are the promises?
    - Are the promises kept?
    - How do the promises in Genesis 6–9 connect to your life?

Explore:

- Genesis 9:9: "Behold, I establish my covenant with you and your offspring after you."

PRAYER:

- Thank God for keeping his promises, even when we sin against him.
- Thank God that his promises are loving and unbreaking.

ADDITIONAL RESOURCES:

- Sally Lloyd-Jones, *The Jesus Storybook Bible: Every Story Whispers His Name* (Grand Rapids, MI: Zondervan, 2007), 36–47, 56–60.
- Marty Machowski, *Long Story Short: Ten-Minute Devotions to Draw Your Family to God* (Greensboro, NC: New Growth Press, 2010), 44–49.

COVENANT: Lesson 3

PROCLAMATION

BIG IDEA:

God makes promises throughout the Bible that respond to our sin and need for a Rescuer.

FOCUS VOCABULARY:

- **Promise:** A promise is something that someone tells another person that they will do in the future. In the Bible, the word "covenant" is often used to describe God's Forever Promises to his people. God's promises are loving and unbreaking, and God keeps his promises.

OBJECTIVES:

- Kids can describe God's promises.
- Kids can give examples of promises God made in the Old Testament and how God kept them.

KEY POINTS:

God makes promises throughout the Bible.

- Every promise is loving and unbreaking.
- He makes promises to people in the Old Testament and in the New Testament, and he keeps every one.
- In the Bible, he also makes promises to you and me—we can be sure he'll keep those, too! He's keeping them right now as he loves us and teaches us more about him.

Each promise is in response to our sin and need for a Rescuer.

- In every promise (both God's promises to other people in the Bible and his promises to us), God's people still sin, but God continues loving them and keeps his promise.
- Over and over in the Bible and in our own lives, we see that God's people fail and need Jesus, and that every time, God is a loving promise keeper who makes good on his plan to rescue.

- God shows us this over-and-over story throughout the Bible: we are sinners who need to be rescued, and God rescues.

Gospel Link: How does what we know about God's promises connect to the gospel, the good news of God's Rescue Plan through Jesus?

- Throughout his whole Story, God had been promising to send Jesus as the Rescuer to act out his Forever Promise. Even from hundreds of years before Jesus was born, God has been using his people to tell the world about the Rescuer who was coming.
- Then, in the New Testament, Jesus made a promise called the new covenant. It's a promise that he keeps right here in my own heart if I have believed in him as the Savior from sin.
    - Romans 10:9 says, "If you confess with your mouth that Jesus is Lord and believe in your heart that God raised him from the dead, you will be saved."
    - If you want to talk more about believing in Jesus as your Rescuer, feel free to talk to your dad or mom, your teacher or Community Group leader, or to read the Bible and talk to Jesus.

APPLICATION

DISCUSSION:

- What do you know about God's promises in the Bible?
- How does God respond to our sin and need for a Rescuer?
- How does God's Forever Promise in Jesus connect to you?

SCRIPTURE:

Read:

- Review God's covenant with Abraham. (See Genesis 12:1–9; 15; and 17.)
- Explore God's covenant with Moses: Moses fails. God saves. Repeat. (See Exodus.)
- Explore God's covenant with David: David fails. God saves. Repeat. (See 2 Samuel 7.)
- Explore Jeremiah's prophecy about God's Forever Promise. (See Jeremiah 31.)

Explore:

- Genesis 17:7: "And I will establish my covenant between me and you and your offspring after you throughout their generations for an everlasting covenant, to be God to you and to your offspring after you."

PRAYER:

- Thank God that his promises are loving and unbreaking.
- Pray that the Holy Spirit will show you ways you sin and break God's law, then help you apply the gospel and celebrate God's grace and forgiveness through Jesus.

ADDITIONAL RESOURCES:

- Sally Lloyd-Jones, *The Jesus Storybook Bible: Every Story Whispers His Name* (Grand Rapids, MI: Zondervan, 2007), 36–47, 56–60.
- Marty Machowski, *Long Story Short: Ten-Minute Devotions to Draw Your Family to God* (Greensboro, NC: New Growth Press, 2010), 44–49.

COVENANT: Lesson 4

PROCLAMATION

BIG IDEA:

God makes promises throughout the Bible that point to God's Forever Promise in Jesus.

FOCUS VOCABULARY:

- **Promise:** A promise is something that someone tells another person that they will do in the future. In the Bible, the word "covenant" is often used to describe God's Forever Promises to his people. God's promises are loving and unbreaking, and God keeps his promises.

OBJECTIVES:

- Kids can describe God's promises.
- Kids can give examples of promises God made in the Old Testament and how God kept them.
- Kids can make connections between Old Testament promises and Jesus.

KEY POINTS:

God makes promises throughout the Bible.

- Today we'll look at an example from the Old Testament. We'll look at the promises that God made to Abraham, and how God responded to Abraham's sin.
- God made a promise to Abraham:
    - "God told Abraham his Secret Rescue Plan. 'Abraham, I will make your family very big,' God promised. 'Until one day, your family will come to number more than even all the stars in the sky.' Abraham looked up at the dark night sky, thick with stars. 'You will be my special family, my people, and through you everyone on earth will be blessed!' It was an incredible promise—God was going to rescue the world through Abraham's family! One of his great-great-great-grandchildren would be the Child, the Promised One, the Rescuer."[46]

---

[46] Lloyd-Jones, *The Jesus Storybook Bible*, 58–59.

Each promise is in response to our sin and need for a Rescuer.

- Abraham was glad to hear God's promise. But it didn't come true right away—while he was waiting, Abraham showed his sin and need for a Rescuer.
    - God had promised that Abraham's family would number greater than the stars in the sky, but there was a problem. For years and years, Abraham and his wife didn't have any children! They twisted God's promise and didn't believe that God would do it, so Abraham sinned. Instead of trusting God to be his Rescuer, Abraham tried to keep God's promise himself. He had a baby with a woman named Hagar instead of his wife—this was not the way God planned to bring about his family!
        - But did God break his promise to Abraham even though Abraham had sinned? No! God is a promise keeper.
        - Later, at just the right time, God gave Abraham and his wife Sarah a son named Isaac, and through him, God continued to bring about the family he had promised.

Each promise points to God's Forever Promise in Jesus.

- God's promise didn't depend on whether Abraham sinned; it depended only on God.
    - God treats us in the exact same way: even though we sin and deserve death, when we believe in Jesus as our Savior from sin, he forgives and rescues us.
        - Every promise in the Old Testament points to God's Forever Promise in Jesus.
        - God will keep his promise to send Jesus back one day, and he will continue keeping his promise to be our all-the-time Rescuer in the in-between time if we believe in him as our Savior from sin.

Gospel Link: How does what we know about God's promises connect to the gospel, the good news of God's Rescue Plan through Jesus?

- Throughout his whole Story, God had been promising to send Jesus as the Rescuer to act out his Forever Promise. Even from hundreds of years before Jesus was born, God has been using his people to tell the world about the Rescuer who was coming.
- Then, in the New Testament, Jesus made a promise called the new covenant. It's a promise that he keeps right here in my own heart if I have believed in him as the Savior from sin.
    - Romans 10:9 says, "If you confess with your mouth that Jesus is Lord and believe in your heart that God raised him from the dead, you will be saved."
    - If you want to talk more about believing in Jesus as your Rescuer, feel free to talk to your dad or mom, your teacher or Community Group leader, or to read the Bible and talk to Jesus.

APPLICATION

DISCUSSION:

- What did God promise to Abraham?
- Did Abraham trust God? What did Abraham do?
- Did God's promise depend on whether Abraham sinned? Why?
- How does God's Forever Promise in Jesus connect to you?

SCRIPTURE: *Review the Scriptures you began exploring last week.*

Read:

- Review God's covenant with Abraham. (See Genesis 12:1–9; 15; and 17.)
- Explore God's covenant with Moses: Moses fails. God saves. Repeat. (See Exodus.)
- Explore God's covenant with David: David fails. God saves. Repeat. (See 2 Samuel 7.)
- Explore Jeremiah's prophecy about God's Forever Promise. (See Jeremiah 31.)

Explore:

- Genesis 17:7: "And I will establish my covenant between me and you and your offspring after you throughout their generations for an everlasting covenant, to be God to you and to your offspring after you."

PRAYER:

- Thank God that his promises are loving and unbreaking.
- Pray that the Holy Spirit will show you ways you sin and break God's law, then help you apply the gospel and celebrate God's grace and forgiveness through Jesus.

ADDITIONAL RESOURCES:

- Sally Lloyd-Jones, *The Jesus Storybook Bible: Every Story Whispers His Name* (Grand Rapids, MI: Zondervan, 2007), 36–47, 56–60.
- Marty Machowski, *Long Story Short: Ten-Minute Devotions to Draw Your Family to God* (Greensboro, NC: New Growth Press, 2010), 44–49.

COVENANT: 4/5/6 Activity 1

Everyone in the world needs Jesus all of the time.

- In each box below, sketch someone who needs Jesus. Brainstorm people in your own life! Write down the name of each person.

Support your child while they work by asking the following questions:

- Who needs Jesus?
- *(Point to picture.)* Does this person need Jesus?
- Do you need Jesus? Why?

____________ NEEDS JESUS

____________ NEEDS JESUS

____________ NEEDS JESUS

____________ NEEDS JESUS

COVENANT: 4/5/6 Activity 2

Circle and color the people that God wants to hear about his Forever Promise.

Support kids while they work by asking the following questions:

- Who does God want to hear about his Forever Promise?
- *(Point to picture.)* Does God want this person to hear his Forever Promise?
- Who in your life does God want to tell about his Forever Promise?

COVENANT: 7+ Activity 1

Noah is mentioned multiple times in the Old Testament and New Testament. Explore some of the passages where he is mentioned to see what God teaches you about who he is and who you are.

Circle the word NOAH in the verse.	**What does this verse tell you about who God is?**	**What does this verse tell you about who you are?**
Luke 3:36: ". . . the son of Cainan, the son of Arphaxad, the son of Shem, the son of Noah, the son of Lamech . . ."		
Luke 17:26–27: "'Just as it was in the days of Noah, so will it be in the days of the Son of Man. They were eating and drinking and marrying and being given in marriage, until the day when Noah entered the ark, and the flood came and destroyed them all.'"		
2 Peter 2:4–10: "For if God did not spare angels when they sinned, but cast them into hell and committed them to chains of gloomy darkness to be kept until the judgment; if he did not spare the ancient world, but preserved Noah, a herald of righteousness, with seven others, when he brought a flood upon the world of the ungodly; if by turning the cities of Sodom and Gomorrah to ashes he condemned them to extinction, making them an example of what is going to happen to the ungodly; and if he rescued righteous Lot, greatly distressed by the sensual conduct of the wicked (for as that righteous man lived among them day after day, he was tormenting his righteous soul over their lawless deeds that he saw and heard); then the Lord knows how to rescue the godly from trials, and to keep the unrighteous under punishment until the day of judgment, and especially those who indulge in the lust of defiling passion and despise authority. Bold and willful, they do not tremble as they blaspheme the glorious ones."		

COVENANT: 7+ Activity 2

We learn more about God's promises in Jeremiah. Explore the following passages from Jeremiah to see what you hear about who God is and who you are.

Circle any words that refer to God's promises in the verses.	What do these verses teach you about who God is?	What do these verses teach you about who you are?
Jeremiah 31:3: "'The LORD appeared to him from far away. I have loved you with an everlasting love; therefore I have continued my faithfulness to you.'"		
Jeremiah 31:31: "'Behold, the days are coming, declares the LORD, when I will make a new covenant with the house of Israel and the house of Judah.'"		
Jeremiah 31:33: "'For this is the covenant that I will make with the house of Israel after those days, declares the LORD: I will put my law within them, and I will write it on their hearts. And I will be their God, and they shall be my people.'"		
Jeremiah 31:34: "'And no longer shall each one teach his neighbor and each his brother, saying, "Know the LORD," for they shall all know me, from the least of them to the greatest, declares the LORD. For I will forgive their iniquity, and I will remember their sin no more.'"		

Want to dig deeper? Explore the new covenant by reading the following verses and discussing as a family:

- Luke 22:20
- 1 Corinthians 11:25
- 2 Corinthians 3:6
- Hebrews 8, 9, and 12

INCARNATION: Lesson 1

PROCLAMATION

BIG IDEA:

Jesus the Son is eternal, and in the middle of God's Big Story, Jesus came to the earth.

FOCUS VOCABULARY:

- **Eternal:** Always, always, always! Eternal refers to always in the past, always in the world we know, and always in the future. Jesus the Son has always existed, exists now, and will exist forever.

OBJECTIVES:

- Kids can define eternal.
- Kids can describe Jesus before, during, and after the incarnation.

KEY POINTS:

Jesus the Son is eternal.

- You've probably heard the most about the time Jesus spent living as both God and man on the earth. But did you know that Jesus has no beginning? That's right! Jesus is eternal.
  - Jesus has always existed as the second person of the Trinity—yes, he existed long, long before he was born as a baby. He even existed from before the world was made!
    - The book of John tells us that Jesus created the world. John says, "He was in the world, and the world was made through him."[47]
  - Just like Jesus has no beginning, he has no end. Even though he doesn't live on the earth right now, he exists today and will continue to exist forever and ever!
  - "Jesus is different from any other human ever born. His life never began. He is God the Son and he has no beginning and no end."[48]

---

[47] John 1:10.

[48] Starr Meade, *Mighty Acts of God: A Family Bible Story Book* (Wheaton, IL: Crossway, 2010), 146.

In the middle of God's Big Story, Jesus came to the earth.

- "God planned the exact moment when Jesus would come into the world to save us from our sins. . . . God had our salvation all planned out even before he made the world."[49]
  - God tells us about his plan in Galatians. Paul, the author, says, "But when the fullness of time had come, God sent forth his Son."[50]
- What God had been promising to his people from the beginning started to come true at the birth of Jesus. "Jesus, God's forever king, had been born!"[51]
  - In the Bible, we see that from the beginning, God had been telling his people that he would send Jesus the Rescuer.
    - God told Adam and Eve before they left the garden.
    - He told a prophet named Isaiah. Seven hundred years before Jesus was even born, he said, "Therefore the Lord himself will give you a sign. Behold, the virgin shall conceive and bear a son, and shall call his name Immanuel."[52]
    - All over the Old Testament, we can find clues and promises God gave his people to tell them that Jesus was coming.
    - And at just the right moment, "In Bethlehem, God the Son, who had always lived, was born as a human baby."[53]

Gospel Link: How does what we know about Jesus on the earth connect to the gospel, the good news of God's Rescue Plan through Jesus?

- Jesus had to come to the earth to live out God's Rescue Plan—it was the way that God would save his people. "He lived a perfectly holy life without ever sinning," then he "carried our sins for us on the cross and took our punishment." But "death could not win over him. Jesus came back to life on the third day so that some day we can rise and be with him in heaven."[54]
  - In Acts, a book in the New Testament of the Bible, God tells us, "Believe in the Lord Jesus, and you will be saved."[55]
    - When God changes your heart and you believe in Jesus the God-man as the Savior from sin, he rescues you from the punishment you deserve and makes you part of his Forever Family.
    - If you want to talk more about Jesus as your Rescuer, feel free to talk to your dad or mom, your teacher or Community Group leader, or to read the Bible and talk to Jesus.

---

[49]Marty Machowski, *The Gospel Story Bible: Discovering Jesus in the Old and New Testaments* (Greensboro, NC: New Growth Press, 2011), 161.
[50]Gal. 4:4.
[51]David R. Helm, *The Big Picture Story Bible* (Wheaton, IL: Crossway, 2004), 268.
[52]Isa. 7:14.
[53]Meade, *Mighty Acts of God*, 146.
[54]Machowski, *The Gospel Story Bible*, 158.
[55]Acts 16:31.

APPLICATION

DISCUSSION:

- Did Jesus exist before he was born as a baby? Does he have a beginning or an end?
- Why did Jesus come to the earth?
- How did Jesus live out God's Rescue Plan?

SCRIPTURE:

Read:

- Work through Isaiah 52–53 as a family this week. While you read, consider:
  - What did Isaiah predict about Jesus?
  - Where do we see these predictions come true in the New Testament?

Explore:

- John 1:14: "And the Word became flesh and dwelt among us, and we have seen his glory, glory as of the only Son from the Father, full of grace and truth."

PRAYER:

- Thank God for sending Jesus to live out his Rescue Plan.
- Pray that God will pursue the hearts of the kids in your family to believe in Jesus as the Savior from sin.
- Pray that God will continue to teach you and your kids about who he is.

ADDITIONAL RESOURCES:

- Sergio Cariello, illus., *The Action Bible: God's Redemptive Story,* ed. Doug Mauss (Colorado Springs, CO: David C. Cook, 2010). See especially "Birth of a Savior" (532–537), "Tough Lessons" (586–591), "Faith at First Sight" (592–594), "Palm Sunday" (612–614), and "On Trial!" (627–630).
- David R. Helm, *The Big Picture Story Bible* (Wheaton, IL: Crossway, 2004), 268.
- Sally Lloyd-Jones, *The Jesus Storybook Bible: Every Story Whispers His Name* (Grand Rapids, MI: Zondervan, 2007), 179–190.
- Marty Machowski, *The Gospel Story Bible: Discovering Jesus in the Old and New Testaments* (Greensboro, NC: New Growth Press, 2011), 158–161.
- Starr Meade, *Mighty Acts of God: A Family Bible Story Book* (Wheaton, IL: Crossway, 2010), 146–147.
- Bruce A. Ware, *Big Truths for Young Hearts: Teaching and Learning the Greatness of God* (Wheaton, IL: Crossway, 2009), 111.

INCARNATION: Lesson 2

PROCLAMATION

BIG IDEA:

During his life on the earth, Jesus was fully God and fully man.

FOCUS VOCABULARY:

- **God:** Jesus is fully God. He is a person of God the Trinity. Along with God the Father and God the Holy Spirit, Jesus is fully and equally God.
- **Man:** Jesus is fully man. Jesus had to come as a man so that he could die—the payment for our sins. Because God is eternal, he can't die. As a result, Jesus had to live as both God *and* man. His death and resurrection are the way God the Trinity planned to rescue his creation.

OBJECTIVES:

- Kids can restate what it means that Jesus is fully God.
- Kids can restate what it means that Jesus is fully man.
- Kids can describe Jesus' role in God's Rescue Plan.

KEY POINTS:

During his life on the earth, Jesus was fully God.

- Jesus was not just a little bit God. Jesus was really, truly, all-the-way God.
  - In Jesus, "the God who made the universe with just a word, the one who could do anything at all—was making himself small. And coming down . . . as a baby."[56]
    - People "had heard about this Promised Child and now he was here. Heaven's Son. The Maker of the Stars. A baby sleeping in his mother's arms."[57]
  - When he was born, "Mary and Joseph named him Jesus, 'Emmanuel'—which means 'God has come to live with us.' Because, of course, he had."[58]

---

[56]Sally Lloyd-Jones, *The Jesus Storybook Bible*, 179.
[57]Ibid., 190.
[58]Ibid., 182.

- Jesus is really God. Even when living as both God and man, Jesus was loving, patient, all-powerful, obedient, and much more.

During his life on the earth, Jesus was fully man.

- In order to live out God's Rescue Plan, in addition to being fully God, Jesus also needed to be fully man.
    - "[Jesus] had always been involved in leading, protecting, and providing for his people. Now he was coming to save and to redeem them. To do all that, he would need to obey all God's laws in their place, and he could only do that if he was a human being himself. He would also need to die in the place of God's people, to take the punishment they deserved for their sins, and he could only do that if he was a human being."[59]
    - "If Jesus was not fully God, he could not be our Savior (just as he also could not be our Savior if he were not fully man)."[60]
- Being a man means that Jesus could die, but what else does it mean? It means that Jesus the God-man had lots in common with us:
    - He was born as a baby.
    - He had brothers and sisters.
    - He grew.
    - He got tired, hungry, and thirsty.
    - He slept.
    - He had a job as a carpenter.
    - He went to parties.
    - He had feelings.
    - He prayed.
    - He worshiped God.
    - He obeyed God the Father.[61]

Gospel Link: How does what we know about Jesus on the earth connect to the gospel, the good news of God's Rescue Plan through Jesus?

- Because Jesus was both God and man, he could be our Rescuer. "As a man, Jesus carried our sins for us on the cross and took our punishment. As God, he lived a perfectly holy life without ever sinning. And because he was God, he grew up to heal the sick and raise the dead. Death could not win over him. Jesus came back to life on the third day so that some day we can rise and be with him in heaven."[62]

---

[59] Meade, *Mighty Acts of God*, 147.
[60] Ware, *Big Truths for Young Hearts*, 111.
[61] See Driscoll and Breshears, *Doctrine*, 228–229.
[62] Machowski, *The Gospel Story Bible*, 158.

- In Acts, a book in the New Testament of the Bible, God tells us, "Believe in the Lord Jesus, and you will be saved."[63]
    - When God changes your heart and you believe in Jesus the God-man as the Savior from sin, he rescues you and makes you part of his Forever Family.

APPLICATION

DISCUSSION:

- Was Jesus just a little bit God? Or was he really, truly, all-the-way God?
- Because Jesus was fully man, what are some of the things that are true about him? How was his life like yours?
- How did Jesus live out God's Rescue Plan?

SCRIPTURE: *Review the Scriptures you began exploring last week.*

Read:

- Work through Isaiah 52–53 as a family this week. While you read, consider:
    - What did Isaiah predict about Jesus?
    - Where do we see these predictions come true in the New Testament?

Explore:

- John 1:14: "And the Word became flesh and dwelt among us, and we have seen his glory, glory as of the only Son from the Father, full of grace and truth."

PRAYER:

- Thank God for sending Jesus to live out his Rescue Plan.
- Pray that God will pursue the hearts of the kids in your family to believe in Jesus as the Savior from sin.
- Pray that God will continue to teach you and your kids about who he is.

[63] Acts 16:31.

ADDITIONAL RESOURCES:

- Sergio Cariello, illus., *The Action Bible: God's Redemptive Story,* ed. Doug Mauss (Colorado Springs, CO: David C. Cook, 2010). See especially "Birth of a Savior" (532–537), "Tough Lessons" (586–591), "Faith at First Sight" (592–594), "Palm Sunday" (612–614), and "On Trial!" (627–630).
- David R. Helm, *The Big Picture Story Bible* (Wheaton, IL: Crossway, 2004), 268.
- Sally Lloyd-Jones, *The Jesus Storybook Bible: Every Story Whispers His Name* (Grand Rapids, MI: Zondervan, 2007), 179–190.
- Marty Machowski, *The Gospel Story Bible: Discovering Jesus in the Old and New Testaments* (Greensboro, NC: New Growth Press, 2011), 158–161.
- Starr Meade, *Mighty Acts of God: A Family Bible Story Book* (Wheaton, IL: Crossway, 2010), 146–147.
- Bruce A. Ware, *Big Truths for Young Hearts: Teaching and Learning the Greatness of God* (Wheaton, IL: Crossway, 2009), 111.

INCARNATION: Lesson 3

PROCLAMATION

BIG IDEA:

Jesus lived in a way that shows us a glimpse of what God is like: he is sinless and powerful.

FOCUS VOCABULARY:

- **Sinless:** Completely without sin. Not ever sinning. Not even once. Not even a little bit! Jesus was the only man who could ever live like this.

OBJECTIVES:

- Kids can describe characteristics of God.
- Kids can give examples of how Jesus showed the characteristics of God during his life on this earth.

KEY POINTS:

Jesus lived in a way that shows us a glimpse of what God is like.

- Because Jesus is God, the way he lived on the earth as both God and man shows us a picture of what God is like.
    - Jesus' actions show us small glimpses of really big truths about God. Jesus treating a stranger kindly is a small glimpse of how God is *perfectly* and *totally* kind. That's a big truth!

Jesus is sinless.

- Over and over, Jesus did what we could not do. He kept from sinning. He lived his entire life obeying God's law perfectly all the time. In his life, he showed that God is without sin.
    - He obeyed God's rules and directions perfectly every single time. He didn't break the rules, not even once!
    - Hebrews 4:15 tells us that Jesus "in every respect has been tempted as we are, yet without sin."

- Stop and think about that: Jesus never sinned. Not even once. "He kept God's law perfectly, even as a child. . . . Can you imagine that?"[64]
- Jesus is not just kind of sinless. He is not sinless just some of the time. No! Because Jesus is God, he is *perfectly* and *totally* sinless. That's a big truth!

Jesus is powerful.

- Many times during his life, Jesus did things that showed that God is powerful. He did lots of things that showed that he was so strong and had such power over creation that he *must* be God!
    - "Jesus didn't boast about who he was. He didn't go around telling everyone he was God."[65] Instead, he did things over and over that *showed* he is God.
        - The disciples worshiped Jesus as God in part because of the things they had seen him do. "They had seen Jesus' miracle of the fishes and the loaves; they had watched him command the wind and the waves and heal the sick. . . . They had seen him walk on water. Jesus was more than a prophet, a great teacher, and an ordinary man. Jesus was God, and he deserved to be worshiped."[66]
        - "Jesus helped and healed many people. . . . He made blind people see. He made deaf people hear. He made lame people walk. Jesus was making the sad things come untrue. He was mending God's broken world."[67]
        - Jesus even made a dead man named Lazarus come back to life. *The Big Picture Story Bible* tells it well:
            - "Lazarus came out. He was alive. A dead man was now alive again. Jesus showed the people that God's Spirit had power to bring new life. Many people believed in Jesus on that day. They believed: Here is the one who will rescue God's people. . . . Here is the one who even rules over death and can bring God's blessing to all the peoples of the earth."[68]
        - Jesus, as God, is King over everything in the world. "His miracles demonstrate that he can command anything—disease, fish, storms, demons, even death—and all things obey him."[69]
            - Over and over, Jesus' miracles showed that God is *perfectly* and *totally* powerful!
- Jesus is not just kind of powerful. He is not powerful just some of the time. No! Because Jesus is God, he is *perfectly* and *totally* powerful. That's a big truth!

Gospel Link: How does what we know about Jesus' sinless and powerful life connect to the gospel, the good news of God's Rescue Plan through Jesus?

---

[64] Machowski, *The Gospel Story Bible*, 163.
[65] Ibid., 201.
[66] Ibid.
[67] Lloyd-Jones, *The Jesus Storybook Bible*, 220.
[68] Helm, *The Big Picture Story Bible*, 352–355.
[69] Meade, *Mighty Acts of God*, 177.

- Jesus had to live a sinless life in order to complete God's Rescue Plan. "He lived a perfectly holy life without ever sinning," then he "carried our sins for us on the cross and took our punishment." But "death could not win over him. Jesus came back to life on the third day so that some day we can rise and be with him in heaven."[70]
    - In Acts, a book in the New Testament of the Bible, God tells us, "Believe in the Lord Jesus, and you will be saved."[71]
        - When God changes your heart and you believe in Jesus the God-man as the Savior from sin, he rescues you from the punishment you deserve and makes you part of his Forever Family.
        - If you want to talk more about Jesus as your Rescuer, feel free to talk to your dad or mom, your teacher or Community Group leader, or to read the Bible and talk to Jesus.

APPLICATION

DISCUSSION:

- Is God just kind of sinless? Is he sinless just some of the time?
- How is Jesus different from you? Are you sinless?
- Is God powerful? How do you know?

SCRIPTURE:

Read:

- As a family, read selections from the book of Mark and identify verses that teach you about who Jesus is. How did his life as both God and man on this earth show God's character?

Explore:

- Hebrews 4:15: "For we do not have a high priest who is unable to sympathize with our weaknesses, but one who in every respect has been tempted as we are, yet without sin."

PRAYER:

- Thank Jesus for helping his children to become more and more like him.
- Thank Jesus for living a sinless life so that he could pay the cost for your sin and give you eternal life if you believe in him as your Savior from sin.
- Pray that the kids in your family will see their lives as a part of Jesus' loving Rescue Plan.

[70] Machowski, *The Gospel Story Bible*, 158.
[71] Acts 16:31.

ADDITIONAL RESOURCES:

- Mark Driscoll and Gerry Breshears, *Doctrine: What Christians Should Believe* (Wheaton, IL: Crossway, 2010), 238.
- David R. Helm, *The Big Picture Story Bible* (Wheaton, IL: Crossway, 2004), 352–355.
- Sally Lloyd-Jones, *The Jesus Storybook Bible: Every Story Whispers His Name* (Grand Rapids, MI: Zondervan, 2007), 220–228.
- Marty Machowski, *The Gospel Story Bible: Discovering Jesus in the Old and New Testaments* (Greensboro, NC: New Growth Press, 2011), 163–201.
- Starr Meade, *Mighty Acts of God: A Family Bible Story Book* (Wheaton, IL: Crossway, 2010), 155–177.

INCARNATION: Lesson 4

PROCLAMATION

BIG IDEA:

Jesus lived in a way that shows us a glimpse of what God is like: he is patient and loving.

FOCUS VOCABULARY:

- **Patient:** Patient here refers to the idea that Jesus kept going without giving up, even when it was very hard. In order to live out God's Rescue Plan, Jesus had to patiently endure many things. Over and over, he obeyed God and patiently kept going even though what he was facing was difficult.

OBJECTIVES:

- Kids can describe characteristics of God.
- Kids can give examples of how Jesus showed the characteristics of God during his life on this earth.

KEY POINTS:

Jesus lived in a way that shows us a glimpse of what God is like.

- Because Jesus is God, the way he lived on the earth as both God and man shows us a picture of what God is like.
  - Jesus' actions show us small glimpses of really big truths about God. Jesus treating a stranger kindly is a small glimpse of how God is *perfectly* and *totally* kind. That's a big truth!

Jesus is patient.

- In order to live out God's Rescue Plan, Jesus had to patiently endure lots of hard things. Jesus never sinned, but he had many temptations and chances to sin. Over and over, he obeyed God and patiently kept going even though what he was facing was hard.
  - Even though Jesus never sinned, he still experienced weakness, pain, and sadness. Even though these things were hard, Jesus never sinned. He kept on obeying God to live out his plan.

- After he was baptized, Jesus went out into the desert and was tempted by Satan. Satan wanted Jesus to disobey God and sin.
    - *The Jesus Storybook Bible* tells it well:
        - "'No!' Jesus said to the liar. 'I will do what God says.' And from that moment on, nothing would ever be the same. Jesus wasn't like Adam. Jesus was a new kind of man. He would not believe the terrible lie that the enemy spoke. Jesus knew God loved him. And he would trust God. No matter what. It was just as God had promised to Adam and Eve all those years before. Jesus had come to do battle against the snake's work. He would get rid of the sin and the darkness and the tears. And he would suffer—but he would win."[72]

- Jesus "came into this world to feel what we feel and face what we face while" still not sinning.[73] This required a lot of patience.
    - Jesus really was "a new kind of king. Though he was the Prince of Heaven, he had become poor. Though he was the Mighty God, he had become a helpless baby. This King hadn't come to be the boss. He had come to be a servant."[74]
    - This shows us that Jesus is not just kind of patient. He is not patient just some of the time. No! Because Jesus is God, he is *perfectly* and *totally* patient. That's a big truth!

Jesus is loving.

- To live out God's Rescue Plan, Jesus did the most loving thing anyone has ever done.
    - "Before the foundation of the world," Jesus the Son and God the Father "both knew what would have to happen. To rescue God's children, Jesus would have to die. There was no other way. It was the reason he had come."[75]
    - Jesus loved God the Father and his people so much that he "would obey his Father to the point of death, even death on the cross."[76]
- Jesus is not just kind of loving. He is not loving just some of the time. No! Because Jesus is God, he is *perfectly* and *totally* loving. That's a big truth!
    - When Jesus lived a sinless life and "died for our sins and rose from the grave three days later, he made a way for everyone who believes in him to be forgiven and go to heaven. Jesus took the punishment we deserved for our sin. Now we can have peace with God instead of punishment. That is really good news!"[77] And that is *really* loving.

Gospel Link: How does what we know about Jesus' patient and loving life connect to the gospel, the good news of God's Rescue Plan through Jesus?

- Jesus' death on the cross to pay the penalty for all people's sins was the most loving thing anyone has ever done. He had to do it to act out God's Rescue Plan.

---

[72] Lloyd-Jones, *The Jesus Storybook Bible*, 209.
[73] Driscoll and Breshears, *Doctrine*, 238.
[74] Lloyd-Jones, *The Jesus Storybook Bible*, 198.
[75] Ibid., 208.
[76] Ware, *Big Truths for Young Hearts*, 112.
[77] Machowski, *The Gospel Story Bible*, 176.

- "He lived a perfectly holy life without ever sinning," then he "carried our sins for us on the cross and took our punishment." But "death could not win over him. Jesus came back to life on the third day so that some day we can rise and be with him in heaven."[78]
  - In Acts, a book in the New Testament of the Bible, God tells us, "Believe in the Lord Jesus, and you will be saved."[79]
    - When God changes your heart and you believe in Jesus the God-man as the Savior from sin, he rescues you from the punishment you deserve and makes you part of his Forever Family.
    - If you want to talk more about Jesus as your Rescuer, feel free to talk to your dad or mom, your teacher or Community Group leader, or to read the Bible and talk to Jesus.

APPLICATION

DISCUSSION:

- Is God just kind of loving? Is he loving just a little bit, just some of the time?
- Was Jesus more patient than you are? How do you know?
- Was Jesus more loving than you are? How do you know?
- Are you part of Jesus' loving Rescue Plan? How do you know?

SCRIPTURE: *Review the Scriptures you began exploring last week.*

Read:

- As a family, read selections from the book of Mark and identify verses that teach you about who Jesus is. How did his life as both God and man on this earth show God's character?

Explore:

- Hebrews 4:15: "For we do not have a high priest who is unable to sympathize with our weaknesses, but one who in every respect has been tempted as we are, yet without sin."

PRAYER:

- Thank Jesus for helping his children to become more and more like him.
- Thank Jesus for living a sinless life so that he could pay the cost for your sin and give you eternal life if you believe in him as your Savior from sin.
- Pray that the kids in your family will see their lives as a part of Jesus' loving Rescue Plan.

---

[78] Ibid., 158.
[79] Acts 16:31.

ADDITIONAL RESOURCES:

- Mark Driscoll and Gerry Breshears, *Doctrine: What Christians Should Believe* (Wheaton, IL: Crossway, 2010), 238.
- David R. Helm, *The Big Picture Story Bible* (Wheaton, IL: Crossway, 2004), 352–355.
- Sally Lloyd-Jones, *The Jesus Storybook Bible: Every Story Whispers His Name* (Grand Rapids, MI: Zondervan, 2007), 220–228.
- Marty Machowski, *The Gospel Story Bible: Discovering Jesus in the Old and New Testaments* (Greensboro, NC: New Growth Press, 2011), 163–201.
- Starr Meade, *Mighty Acts of God: A Family Bible Story Book* (Wheaton, IL: Crossway, 2010), 155–177.

INCARNATION: 4/5/6 Activity 1

Jesus is eternal. This means that Jesus has always existed in the past, exists now, and will continue to exist forever. Circle and color the times when Jesus has existed. Hint: *always!*

INCARNATION: 4/5/6 Activity 2

When we love Jesus and believe that he is the Savior from sin, he changes our hearts and our lives so that we become more and more like him. We cannot be patient or loving on our own, but through the Holy Spirit, Jesus helps us to become more patient and more loving as we grow in faith.

- In the box with the circle, draw an example of a time when someone in your family was patient.
- In the box with the square, draw an example of a time when someone in your family was loving.

PATIENT

LOVING

Thank Jesus that he helps you and others to be patient and loving!

INCARNATION: 7+ Activity 1

Jesus is eternal. This means that Jesus has always existed in the past, exists now, and will continue to exist forever. Before Jesus was born on the earth, God gave his people many clues and promises that Jesus would come as both God and man. Explore some of these clues and promises in the Scriptures below.

Scripture	What does this verse predict about Jesus' life as both God and man?	Did this prediction come true? How do you know?
Micah 5:2: "But you, O Bethlehem Ephrathah, who are too little to be among the clans of Judah, from you shall come forth for me one who is to be ruler in Israel, whose coming forth is from of old, from ancient days."		
Malachi 3:1: "Behold, I send my messenger, and he will prepare the way before me. And the Lord whom you seek will suddenly come to his temple; and the messenger of the covenant in whom you delight, behold, he is coming, says the LORD of hosts."		
Isaiah 53:9: "And they made his grave with the wicked and with a rich man in his death, although he had done no violence, and there was no deceit in his mouth."		

INCARNATION: 7+ Activity 2

Scripture	In your own words, what is happening in this verse?	What does this teach you about what God is like? God is _________.
Mark 2:5: "And when Jesus saw their faith, he said to the paralytic, 'Son, your sins are forgiven.'"		
Mark 2:8–12: "And immediately Jesus, perceiving in his spirit that they thus questioned within themselves, said to them, 'Why do you question these things in your hearts? Which is easier, to say to the paralytic, "Your sins are forgiven," or to say, "Rise, take up your bed and walk"? But that you may know that the Son of Man has authority on earth to forgive sins'—he said to the paralytic—'I say to you, rise, pick up your bed, and go home.' And he rose and immediately picked up his bed and went out before them all, so that they were all amazed and glorified God, saying, 'We never saw anything like this!'"		
Mark 2:16–17: "And the scribes of the Pharisees, when they saw that he was eating with sinners and tax collectors, said to his disciples, 'Why does he eat with tax collectors and sinners?' And when Jesus heard it, he said to them, 'Those who are well have no need of a physician, but those who are sick. I came not to call the righteous, but sinners.'"		
Choose another New Testament verse that tells you about who Jesus is. Write the verse here.		

INRI

CROSS: Lesson 1

PROCLAMATION

BIG IDEA:

Jesus knew what he would have to do to live out God's Rescue Plan before it happened.

FOCUS VOCABULARY:

- **Cross:** The thing that the Roman soldiers used to torture and kill Jesus. When we see the cross in church or somewhere else, we often think of God's Big Story, especially how Jesus rose again and how we can live as his family when we believe he is the Savior from sin. But the cross itself is actually the thing that was used to torture and kill him.

OBJECTIVES:

- Kids can retell the events of the crucifixion.
- Kids can explain what it means that Jesus won over sin.

KEY POINTS:

Jesus knew what he would have to do before it happened.

- From before the beginning of the world, Jesus knew about God's Rescue Plan and agreed to live the plan by coming to the earth as both God and man.
- Jesus shows us that he was in on the plan many times in the Bible.
    - Jesus spoke many times to his friends (the disciples) and to other people about what would happen to him. He spoke openly about his coming death. He knew about it and wanted to obey God the Father by living out the Rescue Plan.[80]
    - *The Jesus Storybook Bible* explains it well:
        - "[Jesus] knew it was time for him to die. They had planned it long ago, he and his Father. Jesus was going to take the punishment for all the wrong things anybody had ever done, or would ever do. 'Papa! Father!' Jesus cried. And he fell to the ground. 'Is there any other way to get your children back? To heal their hearts? To get rid of the poison?' But Jesus knew—there was no other way. All the poison of

[80]Driscoll and Breshears, *Doctrine*, 248.

sin was going to have to go into his own heart. God was going to pour into Jesus' heart all the sadness and brokenness in people's hearts. He was going to pour into Jesus' body all the sickness in people's bodies. God was going to have to blame his son for everything that had gone wrong. It would crush Jesus."[81]

- Even though he knew he would be crushed and it would hurt very, very badly, Jesus obeyed. "Jesus stood up. He woke his friends. 'Now is the time,' he said gently. 'Everything that was written about me—what God has been telling his people all through the long years—it's all coming true.' . . . But it would be all right. It was God's Plan. 'It was for this reason that I was born into the world,' Jesus said."[82]

Jesus lived out God's Rescue Plan.

- When Jesus was having his last meal with his friends, the disciples, he explained to them that he was living God's Plan for the world. Let's read together from *The Jesus Storybook Bible*:
    - "Then Jesus picked up some bread and broke it. He gave it to his friends. He picked up a cup of wine and thanked God for it. He poured it out and shared it. 'My body is like this bread. It will break,' Jesus told them. 'This cup of wine is like my blood. It will pour out. But this is how God will rescue the whole world. My life will break and God's broken world will mend. My heart will tear apart—and your hearts will heal. Just as the Passover lamb died, so now I will die instead of you. My blood will wash away all of your sins. And you'll be clean on the inside—in your hearts. So whenever you eat and drink, remember,' Jesus said, 'I've rescued you!'"[83]
- Right before he died, Jesus said in a loud voice, "It is finished."[84]
    - "When Jesus said, 'It is finished,' he was saying that the punishment was over, the penalty had been paid, and God's anger over the sins of those who believe in his Son Jesus was all gone."[85]

Gospel Link: Today we have been learning about God's Rescue Plan through Jesus. This Rescue Plan connects to everyone—including *you*.

- In Acts, a book in the New Testament of the Bible, God tells us, "Believe in the Lord Jesus, and you will be saved."[86]
    - When God changes your heart and you believe in Jesus the God-man as the Savior from sin, he rescues you from the punishment you deserve and makes you part of his Forever Family. Have you believed in Jesus as your Savior from sin?
    - If you want to talk more about Jesus as your Rescuer, feel free to talk to your dad or mom, your teacher or Community Group leader, or to read the Bible and talk to Jesus.

---

[81]Lloyd-Jones, *The Jesus Storybook Bible*, 294.
[82]Ibid., 299–301.
[83]Ibid., 292.
[84]John 19:30.
[85]Machowski, *The Gospel Story Bible*, 232.
[86]Acts 16:31.

APPLICATION

DISCUSSION:

- Was Jesus surprised by the things that happened to him? How do you know?
- How did Jesus live out God's Rescue Plan?
- How does God's Rescue Plan connect to you?

SCRIPTURE:

Read:

- Read Luke 22–23 as a family. Discuss how Jesus lived out God's Rescue Plan.

Explore:

- 2 Corinthians 5:21: "For our sake he made him to be sin who knew no sin, so that in him we might become the righteousness of God."

PRAYER:

- Thank Jesus for living out God's Recue Plan.
- Pray that the kids in your family will believe in Jesus as the Savior from sin.
- Pray that the Holy Spirit will help you to understand the cross better and better.

ADDITIONAL RESOURCES:

- Sergio Cariello, illus., *The Action Bible: God's Redemptive Story*, ed. Doug Mauss (Colorado Springs, CO: David C. Cook, 2010). See especially "Death Sentence" (631-634) and "Crucified!" (635-640).
- Mark Driscoll and Gerry Breshears, *Doctrine: What Christians Should Believe* (Wheaton, IL: Crossway, 2010), 248.
- David R. Helm, *The Big Picture Story Bible* (Wheaton, IL: Crossway, 2004), 276.
- Sally Lloyd-Jones, *The Jesus Storybook Bible: Every Story Whispers His Name* (Grand Rapids, MI: Zondervan, 2007), 294–301.
- Marty Machowski, *The Gospel Story Bible: Discovering Jesus in the Old and New Testaments* (Greensboro, NC: New Growth Press, 2011), 226–232.

INRI

CROSS: Lesson 2

PROCLAMATION

BIG IDEA:

To live out God's Rescue Plan, Jesus suffered and died.

FOCUS VOCABULARY:

- **Suffer:** To experience really painful things—things that hurt *a lot*.

OBJECTIVES:

- Kids can retell the events of the crucifixion.
- Kids can describe Jesus' suffering on the cross.

KEY POINTS:

Jesus suffered.

- Before he got to the cross, Jesus was tortured and his body was hurt in many ways.
    - Jesus was whipped and beaten until his body bled and bled.
    - He had to carry the cross up a big hill on his bare back and shoulders, right in the middle of the cuts and blood that were already there. Think about the last time you scraped your knee. You probably got to cover your scrape with a Band-Aid that helped protect it. Jesus didn't get to put anything on his cuts and scrapes to make them feel better. Instead, the soldiers put the big, heavy cross right on top of them. Can you imagine how much it must have hurt?
        - The cross weighed more than one hundred pounds, so it must have hurt *a lot*. It was so heavy and painful that he collapsed and couldn't carry it alone.
- After being tortured, Jesus was nailed to the cross. Touch your palm. Now imagine a nail being hammered right through the middle. Ouch! That is exactly what happened to Jesus. Through his hands and feet, he was nailed up on the cross.
    - After Jesus was nailed to the cross, he didn't die right away. He hung there in horrible pain for hours and hours.

- Not only was Jesus' body in terrible pain, but in his mind and heart he was suffering too.
  - There were many people watching him while he suffered and died. Some of those people made fun of him, yelling at him and saying mean things to him as he suffered.
- "It is important to remember that [Jesus'] suffering was all part of God's plan. Hundreds of years earlier, [a prophet named] Isaiah wrote about Jesus' arrest, saying that even though he would be treated cruelly, Jesus would not fight back or say anything to stop the people arresting him (Isa. 53:7–8). Jesus could have called down angels from heaven to recue him, but he didn't. He let the soldiers take him without fighting so he could die on the cross for our sins."[87]
  - "Jesus could have just climbed down. Actually, he could have just said a word and made it all stop. Like when he healed that little girl. And stilled the storm. And fed 5,000 people. But Jesus stayed. You see, they didn't understand. It wasn't the nails that kept Jesus there. It was love."[88]

Jesus died.

- At last, Jesus died. "He was buried in a tomb. A big stone was rolled in front of the entrance, and the people all went home."[89]
- Let's take a moment to think about what this means. Jesus died. All the way dead. His heart stopped beating. He stopped breathing. He was truly dead. This seems like a sad ending at first, but God has revealed in his Big Story that this death is not the end. In fact, it is right in the middle of the most extraordinary part of the Story.

Gospel Link: Today we have been learning about God's Rescue Plan through Jesus. This Rescue Plan connects to everyone—including *you*.

- In Acts, a book in the New Testament of the Bible, God tells us, "Believe in the Lord Jesus, and you will be saved."[90]
  - When God changes your heart and you believe in Jesus the God-man as the Savior from sin, he rescues you from the punishment you deserve and makes you part of his Forever Family. Have you believed in Jesus as your Savior from sin?
  - If you want to talk more about Jesus as your Rescuer, feel free to talk to your dad or mom, your teacher or Community Group leader, or to read the Bible and talk to Jesus.

---

[87]Machowski, *The Gospel Story Bible*, 226.
[88]Lloyd-Jones, *The Jesus Storybook Bible*, 304.
[89]Helm, *The Big Picture Story Bible*, 376.
[90]Acts 16:31.

APPLICATION

DISCUSSION:

- How did Jesus suffer? List some of the ways he was hurt.
- Did Jesus really die?
- How does God's Rescue Plan connect to you?

SCRIPTURE: *Review the Scriptures you began exploring last week.*

Read:

- Read Luke 22–23 as a family. Discuss how Jesus lived out God's Rescue Plan.

Explore:

- 2 Corinthians 5:21: "For our sake he made him to be sin who knew no sin, so that in him we might become the righteousness of God."

PRAYER:

- Thank Jesus for living out God's Rescue Plan.
- Pray that the kids in your family will believe in Jesus as the Savior from sin.
- Pray that the Holy Spirit will help you to understand the cross better and better.

ADDITIONAL RESOURCES:

- Sergio Cariello, illus., *The Action Bible: God's Redemptive Story,* ed. Doug Mauss (Colorado Springs, CO: David C. Cook, 2010). See especially "Death Sentence" (631-634) and "Crucified!" (635-640).
- Mark Driscoll and Gerry Breshears, *Doctrine: What Christians Should Believe* (Wheaton, IL: Crossway, 2010), 248.
- David R. Helm, *The Big Picture Story Bible* (Wheaton, IL: Crossway, 2004), 276.
- Sally Lloyd-Jones, *The Jesus Storybook Bible: Every Story Whispers His Name* (Grand Rapids, MI: Zondervan, 2007), 294-301.
- Marty Machowski, *The Gospel Story Bible: Discovering Jesus in the Old and New Testaments* (Greensboro, NC: New Growth Press, 2011), 226-232.

INRI

CROSS: Lesson 3

PROCLAMATION

BIG IDEA:

On the cross, Jesus paid for sins.

FOCUS VOCABULARY:

- **Cross:** The thing that the Roman soldiers used to torture and kill Jesus. When we see the cross in church or somewhere else, we often think of God's Big Story, especially how Jesus rose again and how we can live as his family when we believe he is the Savior from sin. But the cross itself is actually the thing that was used to torture and kill him.

OBJECTIVE:

- Kids can describe how, through the cross, Jesus paid for all the sins of the world.

KEY POINTS:

Jesus died on the cross.

- Jesus died. All the way dead. His heart stopped beating. He stopped breathing. He was truly dead. This seems like a sad ending at first, but God has revealed in his Big Story that this death is not the end. In fact, it is right in the middle of the most extraordinary part of the Story, and it happened for a magnificent reason.

On the cross, Jesus paid for sins.

- God the Father must always punish sin.
    - Because God is holy, that means he is perfect. He must punish sin. That's why Jesus had to pay by dying—sin deserves punishment.
    - The Bible says in Romans 6:23, "For the wages of sin is death, but the free gift of God is eternal life in Christ Jesus our Lord."
    - Sin is things we do that break God's laws.
    - Every person other than Jesus (including you) has sinned against God, and because of sin deserves death and life forever in hell.

- But that's not where God ends his Big Story. No! You deserve death and hell, but Jesus the Son took the punishment for all your sins when he died on the cross.
    - Jesus died because of our sins. "It was *our* sins but *his* death."[91]
        - Because he died on the cross to take our punishment, Jesus stands between us and God the Father. He suffered and took the punishment we actually deserve.

Gospel Link: How does what we know about Jesus' death on the cross connect to the gospel, the good news of God's Rescue Plan through Jesus?

- God's Rescue Plan to bring people into his Forever Family was only possible because Jesus died. Sin deserves punishment, so Jesus had to die to pay the penalty of our sins. Isn't it amazing that he did something so hard to bring back his people?
    - Jesus' death also connects to *you*.
        - In Acts, a book in the New Testament of the Bible, God tells us, "Believe in the Lord Jesus, and you will be saved."[92]
        - When God changes your heart and you believe in Jesus the God-man as the Savior from sin, he rescues you from the punishment you deserve and makes you part of his Forever Family. Have you believed in Jesus as your Savior from sin?
        - If you want to talk more about Jesus as your Rescuer, feel free to talk to your dad or mom, your teacher or Community Group leader, or to read the Bible and talk to Jesus.

APPLICATION

DISCUSSION:

- Did Jesus really die? Why?
- Why does God have to punish sin?
- How does Jesus' death connect to you?

SCRIPTURE:

Read:

- As a family, re-read Luke 22–23. Discuss how Jesus died and why Jesus died.

Explore:

- Philippians 2:8: "And being found in human form, he humbled himself by becoming obedient to the point of death, even death on a cross."

---

[91]Driscoll and Breshears, *Doctrine*, 253.
[92]Acts 16:31.

PRAYER:

- Thank Jesus for living out God's Rescue Plan.
- Pray that the kids in your family will believe that Jesus is the Savior from sin.
- Pray that God will help us to understand the cross more and more, and to tell other people about it.

ADDITIONAL RESOURCES:

- Mark Driscoll and Gerry Breshears, *Doctrine: What Christians Should Believe* (Wheaton, IL: Crossway, 2010), 253–258.
- Marty Machowski, *The Gospel Story Bible: Discovering Jesus in the Old and New Testaments* (Greensboro, NC: New Growth Press, 2011), 231.
- Starr Meade, *Mighty Acts of God: A Family Bible Story Book* (Wheaton, IL: Crossway, 2010), 237.

INRI

CROSS: Lesson 4

PROCLAMATION

BIG IDEA:

On the cross, Jesus gave new life.

FOCUS VOCABULARY:

- **Cross:** The thing that the Roman soldiers used to torture and kill Jesus. When we see the cross in church or somewhere else, we often think of God's Big Story, especially how Jesus rose again and how we can live as his family when we believe he is the Savior from sin. But the cross itself is actually the thing that was used to torture and kill him.

OBJECTIVE:

- Kids can describe how, through the cross, Jesus gives new life.

KEY POINTS:

Jesus died on the cross.

- Jesus died. All the way dead. His heart stopped beating. He stopped breathing. He was truly dead. This seems like a sad ending at first, but God has revealed in his Big Story that this death is not the end. In fact, it is right in the middle of the most extraordinary part of the Story, and it happened for a magnificent reason.

On the cross, Jesus gave new life.

- When God changes your heart so you believe in Jesus, you get an amazing new relationship with God. You go from deserving death to receiving new life.
    - *From death:* "We all started out as God's enemies in our sin."[93]
        - "None of us deserves love, grace, or mercy from God."[94]
    - *To new life:* "But Jesus' death on the cross brings us back into a good relationship with God."[95] If we believe, when God looks at us, he sees Jesus' perfect obedience instead of our sin.

---

[93] Machowski, *The Gospel Story Bible*, 231.
[94] Driscoll and Breshears, *Doctrine*, 259.
[95] Machowski, *The Gospel Story Bible*, 231.

        - "Because of the cross, God's justice has been completely satisfied, and God is free to shower his people with the blessings of righteousness."[96]
        - "Jesus came to make the way in which God the Judge could righteously punish sin, and still bless his people as he had promised."[97]
            - Jesus is so amazingly loving that he not only lived out God's Rescue Plan by suffering and dying on the cross to take our sins, he *also* gives us new hearts and new lives full of the blessings and promises God has been telling us about since the beginning. This gift is for you when you believe in Jesus as the Savior from sin.
    - Jesus has not only paid for our sins, but also has:
        - Redeemed us to eternal life with God.
        - Promised to give us new bodies that will live forever without being hurt or tired.
        - Promised that he will return and make everything sad come untrue.
        - Given us family status as God's very own sons and daughters. John 1:12 says, "But to all who did recieve him, who believed in his name, he gave the right to become children of God."
    - Do you believe that all these things are true about God's Big Story? Do you believe that Jesus is the Savior from sin? Have you received him?
        - "Jesus taught these things because it is so easy to pretend to be good on the outside when we are really sinful on the inside. The only real way to cover up our sin is to cover it with the blood of Jesus, who died on the cross to take our sin away. For when we trust in Jesus, he covers our sin with his perfect record of obedience. Then he changes our desire to impress others to a desire to live for God—on the inside and the outside."[98]

Gospel Link: How does what we know about Jesus' death on the cross connect to the gospel, the good news of God's Rescue Plan through Jesus?

- God's Rescue Plan to bring people into his Forever Family was only possible because Jesus died. Sin deserves punishment, so Jesus had to die to pay the penalty of our sins. Isn't it amazing that he did something so hard to bring back his people?
    - Jesus' death also connects to *you*.
        - In Acts, a book in the New Testament of the Bible, God tells us, "Believe in the Lord Jesus, and you will be saved."[99]
        - When God changes your heart and you believe in Jesus the God-man as the Savior from sin, he rescues you from the punishment you deserve and makes you part of his Forever Family. Have you believed in Jesus as your Savior from sin?
        - If you want to talk more about Jesus as your Rescuer, feel free to talk to your dad or mom, your teacher or Community Group leader, or to read the Bible and talk to Jesus.

---

[96] Meade, *Mighty Acts of God*, 237.
[97] Ibid.
[98] Machowski, *The Gospel Story Bible*, 187.
[99] Acts 16:31.

APPLICATION

DISCUSSION:

- Did Jesus really die? Why?
- What does Jesus' death on the cross pay for? What else does it do?
- How does Jesus' death connect to you?

SCRIPTURE: *Review the Scriptures you began exploring last week.*

Read:

- As a family, re-read Luke 22–23. Discuss how Jesus died and why Jesus died.

Explore:

- Philippians 2:8: "And being found in human form, he humbled himself by becoming obedient to the point of death, even death on a cross."

PRAYER:

- Thank Jesus for living out God's Rescue Plan.
- Pray that the kids in your family will believe that Jesus is the Savior from sin.
- Pray that God will help us to understand the cross more and more, and to tell other people about it.

ADDITIONAL RESOURCES:

- Mark Driscoll and Gerry Breshears, *Doctrine: What Christians Should Believe* (Wheaton, IL: Crossway, 2010), 253–258.
- Marty Machowski, *The Gospel Story Bible: Discovering Jesus in the Old and New Testaments* (Greensboro, NC: New Growth Press, 2011), 231.
- Starr Meade, *Mighty Acts of God: A Family Bible Story Book* (Wheaton, IL: Crossway, 2010), 237.

CROSS: 4/5/6 Activity 1

Listen to the story of the cross from *The Jesus Storybook Bible (302–308)*. While you listen, sketch a picture of the scene that you are hearing about.

CROSS: 4/5/6 Activity 2

Color the picture of Jesus' death on the cross.

While you color, discuss how Jesus died and why he died.

CROSS: 7+ Activity 1

Scripture	In your own words, what is happening in this verse?	What does this verse teach you about God's Rescue Plan?
Luke 23:1–3: "Then the whole company of them arose and brought him before Pilate. And they began to accuse him, saying, 'We found this man misleading our nation and forbidding us to give tribute to Caesar, and saying that he himself is Christ, a king.' And Pilate asked him, 'Are you the King of the Jews?' And he answered him, 'You have said so.'"		
Luke 23:13–16: "Pilate then called together the chief priests and the rulers and the people, and said to them, 'You brought me this man as one who was misleading the people. And after examining him before you, behold, I did not find this man guilty of any of your charges against him. Neither did Herod, for he sent him back to us. Look, nothing deserving death has been done by him. I will therefore punish and release him.'"		
Luke 23:22–25: "A third time he said to them, 'Why, what evil has he done? I have found in him no guilt deserving death. I will therefore punish and release him.' But they were urgent, demanding with loud cries that he should be crucified. And their voices prevailed. So Pilate decided that their demand should be granted. He released the man who had been thrown into prison for insurrection and murder, for whom they asked, but he delivered Jesus over to their will."		

CROSS: 7+ Activity 2

Scripture	In your own words, what is going on in this verse?	What does this verse teach you about who Jesus is?
Luke 23:44–46: "It was now about the sixth hour, and there was darkness over the whole land until the ninth hour, while the sun's light failed. And the curtain of the temple was torn in two. Then Jesus, calling out with a loud voice, said, 'Father, into your hands I commit my spirit!' And having said this he breathed his last."		
Hebrews 12:2: ". . . looking to Jesus, the founder and perfecter of our faith, who for the joy that was set before him endured the cross, despising the shame, and is seated at the right hand of the throne of God."		
Ephesians 2:13: "But now in Christ Jesus you who once were far off have been brought near by the blood of Christ."		
Choose another New Testament verse about the cross. Write the verse here.		

RESURRECTION: Lesson 1

PROCLAMATION

BIG IDEA:

Jesus defeated death to live again.

FOCUS VOCABULARY:

- **Defeat:** To beat or win against something.

OBJECTIVES:

- Kids can retell the events of the resurrection.
- Kids can connect the story of the resurrection to their own hearts and lives.

KEY POINTS:

Jesus defeated death.

- Last week we learned that on the cross, Jesus died. Really died. All the way dead. No breathing, no heartbeat. But that wasn't the end of the story. No, we are right in the middle of God's Rescue Plan! Because Jesus didn't stay dead. He defeated death by rising again!
    - "He won the greatest victory of all, over death, when on the third day he rose from the dead!"[100]
    - First Corinthians 15:3–4 says, "Christ died for our sins in accordance with the Scriptures, that he was buried, that he was raised on the third day in accordance with the Scriptures."
    - "If Jesus had not risen, he would have been a good man who had died, but nothing more. When he rose from the dead, Jesus demonstrated that he was really God, and his death was worth enough to pay for the sins of his people. Not only that, but since Jesus rose from the dead, death has been conquered."[101]

---

[100] Machowski, *The Gospel Story Bible*, 202.
[101] Meade, *Mighty Acts of God*, 240.

- When Jesus beat death and rose again, he showed once and for all what he had been showing his whole life on this earth: that he really is God, and that he is the Forever King that God the Father promised as our Rescuer from before the beginning!

Jesus is alive.

- Jesus rose from the dead with a real body—not just any body, though. It wasn't the old body he had before—it was a new body, perfect and strong! It was a body that would never get sick or tired. It was a body that sin could not hurt. And Jesus will continue to live in his new, better-than-before body forever.

Gospel Link: How does the fact that Jesus is alive connect to the gospel, the good news of God's Rescue Plan through Jesus?

- God's Rescue Plan for his people wouldn't have been possible unless Jesus defeated death to be alive again. Because Jesus is alive again, we know that he conquered sin and that if we believe in him as the Savior from sin, we are forgiven and can live forever as part of his family.
    - Jesus' life connects to *you*.
        - In Acts, a book in the New Testament of the Bible, God tells us, "Believe in the Lord Jesus, and you will be saved."[102]
        - When God changes your heart and you believe in Jesus the God-man as the Savior from sin, he rescues you from the punishment you deserve and makes you part of his Forever Family. Have you believed in Jesus as your Savior from sin?
        - If you want to talk more about Jesus as your Rescuer, feel free to talk to your dad or mom, your teacher or Community Group leader, or to read the Bible and talk to Jesus.

APPLICATION

DISCUSSION:

- Did Jesus stay dead? What happened?
- Does Jesus have a body? What is his body like?
- How does Jesus' life connect to you?

SCRIPTURE:

Read:

- Read Luke 24 as a family and discuss the events of the resurrection.

---

[102]Acts 16:31.

Explore:

- John 11:25–26: "Jesus said to her, 'I am the resurrection and the life. Whoever believes in me, though he die, yet shall he live, and everyone who lives and believes in me shall never die. Do you believe this?'"

PRAYER:

- Thank God for his Rescue Plan.
- Thank God for giving us a record of the events of Jesus' life, death, and resurrection in Scripture.
- Pray that God will continue to teach us about who he is through his Word.

ADDITIONAL RESOURCES:

- Sergio Cariello, illus., *The Action Bible: God's Redemptive Story,* ed. Doug Mauss (Colorado Springs, CO: David C. Cook, 2010). See especially "The Sealed Tomb" (641–644) and "The Last Command" (645–650).
- David R. Helm, *The Big Picture Story Bible* (Wheaton, IL: Crossway, 2004), 392–395.
- Sally Lloyd-Jones, *The Jesus Storybook Bible: Every Story Whispers His Name* (Grand Rapids, MI: Zondervan, 2007), 321–324.
- Marty Machowski, *The Gospel Story Bible: Discovering Jesus in the Old and New Testaments* (Greensboro, NC: New Growth Press, 2011), 202.
- Starr Meade, *Mighty Acts of God: A Family Bible Story Book* (Wheaton, IL: Crossway, 2010), 240.

RESURRECTION: Lesson 2

PROCLAMATION

BIG IDEA:

Real people saw Jesus defeat death, and they tell us the story in the New Testament.

FOCUS VOCABULARY:

- **Defeat:** To beat or win against something.
- **New Testament:** The Bible, God's words for us, is divided into two main parts. The first part is called the Old Testament, and it tells about how God has taken care of his people from before the beginning. The Old Testament also promises—many times and in many ways—that Jesus is coming. The New Testament is the second part, and it tells the story of God's Rescue Plan through Jesus, and how people continue to live to tell others about Jesus until he returns to make everything new again.

OBJECTIVES:

- Kids can identify evidence of the resurrection in Scripture.
- Kids can connect the story of the resurrection to their own hearts and lives.

KEY POINTS:

Real people saw Jesus defeat death.

- Jesus appeared in his brand-new body for the first time three days after he died.
- For forty days, Jesus appeared to many different people, including his friends, the disciples.
    - He visited, talked with, and continued to teach them.
        - When Jesus first appeared to his friends, the disciples, they were sure surprised! "Some of Jesus' followers were meeting together. They were afraid, so they had locked the doors. Suddenly Jesus came and stood among them! At first his followers were frightened, but then their fear turned to joy. The sadness they had felt was gone. Their hearts were glad again. Jesus was alive. Jesus really was alive. Jesus was risen from the dead. The Son had risen! It was a brand-new day."[103]

[103]Helm, *The Big Picture Story Bible*, 392–395.

- Here's how *The Jesus Storybook Bible* tells it:
  - "'I'm really here!' Jesus said. And he really was. Peter's heart leaped with joy and he fell into Jesus' arms, hugging and kissing him. The others followed. They felt their hearts would burst from the happiness. The friends ate together and chatted happily. And every now and then, they'd just gaze at Jesus, and have to touch him to be sure they weren't dreaming. Jesus had a real body but this body was better. It had come through death and couldn't get sick or be killed again. This body would live forever. Jesus had come back with a brand-new body. Not only were sad things coming untrue, the friends realized, they were becoming new again."[104]
- In the Bible, in Luke 24:36–43, we read, "As they were talking about these things, Jesus himself stood among them, and said to them, 'Peace to you!' But they were startled and frightened and thought they saw a spirit. And he said to them, 'Why are you troubled, and why do doubts arise in your hearts? See my hands and my feet, that it is I myself. Touch me, and see. For a spirit does not have flesh and bones as you see that I have.' And when he had said this, he showed them his hands and his feet. And while they still disbelieved for joy and were marveling, he said to them, 'Have you anything here to eat?' They gave him a piece of broiled fish, and he took it and ate before them."
  - A person without a real body sure wouldn't be able to eat fish for dinner—the disciples knew that Jesus was really alive again!

- After forty days, Jesus' friends, the disciples, saw another amazing thing happen: "Jesus rose up into the bright air, higher and higher. They shaded their eyes and watched him go, until a cloud hid Jesus so they couldn't seem him anymore. They stood looking up into the sky like that for a long time. Suddenly two shining men appeared. 'What are you doing?' they asked. 'Jesus has gone up to heaven. But one day he will come back. In the same way you saw him leave. From heaven. And from the sky.' Jesus' friends went back to Jerusalem with a strange gladness in their hearts. And something Jesus said that stuck in their minds: 'Even though you won't be able to see me anymore, I will never leave you. No! Not ever! I will be with you. Yes! Always and forever!'"[105]

Real people tell us the story in the New Testament.

- Jesus' resurrection shows that God's promises that he'd been telling his people throughout the Old Testament were coming true. It shows us that everything God has promised really will come true, even the things about our very own hearts!
- God wants *everyone* to know the story of how Jesus the Rescuer defeated death and is alive again, so he inspired people who saw Jesus to write down what they saw. Today, we can read what they wrote in the New Testament of the Bible!
  - The books of Matthew, Mark, Luke, and John tell us stories about Jesus' life.

---

[104] Lloyd-Jones, *The Jesus Storybook Bible*, 321.
[105] Ibid., 324.

        - Then, all the other books of the New Testament tell us about men and women who continued to live for Jesus after he left. They told people all over the world about his Rescue Plan, knowing that one day he would return again.
    - God has used the Bible to tell his Rescue Plan to you: even though you sin and deserve death, Jesus obeyed God and lived as both God and man, then died to take the punishment for *your* sins. After three days, he conquered death and rose again, living forever in a better-than-before body with his Father and his people.
        - When God changes your heart to believe in Jesus as the Savior from sin, you know that you are part of his Big Story and that all his promises will come true, both in the world and in your very own heart.

Gospel Link: How does the fact that Jesus is alive connect to the gospel, the good news of God's Rescue Plan through Jesus?

- God's Rescue Plan for his people wouldn't have been possible unless Jesus defeated death to be alive again. Because Jesus is alive again, we know that he conquered sin and that if we believe in him as the Savior from sin, we are forgiven and can live forever as part of his family.
    - Jesus' life connects to *you*.
        - In Acts, a book in the New Testament of the Bible, God tells us, "Believe in the Lord Jesus, and you will be saved."[106]
        - When God changes your heart and you believe in Jesus the God-man as the Savior from sin, he rescues you from the punishment you deserve and makes you part of his Forever Family. Have you believed in Jesus as your Savior from sin?
        - If you want to talk more about Jesus as your Rescuer, feel free to talk to your dad or mom, your teacher or Community Group leader, or to read the Bible and talk to Jesus.

APPLICATION

DISCUSSION:

- Was Jesus really alive again? How do you know?
- What is God's Rescue Plan?
- How does Jesus' life connect to you?

[106] Acts 16:31.

SCRIPTURE: *Review the Scriptures you began exploring last week.*

Read:

- Read Luke 24 as a family and discuss the events of the resurrection.

Explore:

- John 11:25–26: "Jesus said to her, 'I am the resurrection and the life. Whoever believes in me, though he die, yet shall he live, and everyone who lives and believes in me shall never die. Do you believe this?'"

PRAYER:

- Thank God for his Rescue Plan.
- Thank God for giving us a record of the events of Jesus' life, death, and resurrection in Scripture.
- Pray that God will continue to teach us about who he is through his Word.

ADDITIONAL RESOURCES:

- Sergio Cariello, illus., *The Action Bible: God's Redemptive Story,* ed. Doug Mauss (Colorado Springs, CO: David C. Cook, 2010). See especially "The Sealed Tomb" (641–644) and "The Last Command" (645–650).
- David R. Helm, *The Big Picture Story Bible* (Wheaton, IL: Crossway, 2004), 392–395.
- Sally Lloyd-Jones, *The Jesus Storybook Bible: Every Story Whispers His Name* (Grand Rapids, MI: Zondervan, 2007), 321–324.
- Marty Machowski, *The Gospel Story Bible: Discovering Jesus in the Old and New Testaments* (Greensboro, NC: New Growth Press, 2011), 202.
- Starr Meade, *Mighty Acts of God: A Family Bible Story Book* (Wheaton, IL: Crossway, 2010), 240.

RESURRECTION: Lesson 3

PROCLAMATION

BIG IDEA:

Knowing that Jesus is alive changed God's people in the New Testament.

FOCUS VOCABULARY:

- **Change:** To change means that something starts out one way, then becomes another way. A thing is not the same after it has changed.
- **New Testament:** The Bible, God's words for us, is divided into two main parts. The first part is called the Old Testament, and it tells about how God has taken care of his people from before the beginning. The Old Testament also promises—many times and in many ways—that Jesus is coming. The New Testament is the second part, and it tells the story of God's Rescue Plan through Jesus, and how people continue to live to tell others about Jesus until he returns to make everything new again.

OBJECTIVE:

- Kids can describe ways that Jesus' resurrection changed people in the New Testament.

KEY POINTS:

Jesus is alive.

- Jesus rose from the dead with a real body—not just any body, though. It wasn't the old body he had before—it was a new body, perfect and strong! It was a body that would never get sick or tired. It was a body that sin could not hurt. And Jesus will continue to live in his new, better-than-before body forever.

Knowing that Jesus is alive changed people in the New Testament.

- Seeing Jesus rise was such a big deal that people changed the day they met at church! For thousands of years, Jews had attended church on Saturdays. Suddenly, they began worshiping on Sundays in order to remember the day that Jesus rose.[107]
- After Jesus went up to heaven, his friends, the disciples, kept on obeying him by telling people about him. Jesus sent God the Holy Spirit to fill his people, and many of them

[107] Driscoll and Breshears, *Doctrine*, 293.

became even *more* excited about sharing the story of Jesus the Rescuer than they had been before.

- Peter, one of Jesus' disciples, went from denying Jesus three times on the day Jesus died, to preaching about him and seeing thousands of people believe in Jesus in a single day! Seeing that Jesus is alive changed Peter *a lot*.
- *The Gospel Story Bible* says it like this: "What a difference the Holy Spirit made in Peter's life! He went from being afraid of a servant girl at Jesus' arrest to fearlessly challenging the men who helped put Jesus to death! . . . We can see that Peter certainly received that power as he talked about the good news of Jesus' life, death, and resurrection to the crowd. Peter's fear was gone, replaced by courage from the Holy Spirit to tell everyone about Jesus."[108]

Gospel Link: How does the fact that Jesus is alive connect to the gospel, the good news of God's Rescue Plan through Jesus?

- God's Rescue Plan for his people wouldn't have been possible unless Jesus defeated death to be alive again. Because Jesus is alive again, we know that he conquered sin and that if we believe in him as the Savior from sin, we are forgiven and can live forever as part of his family.
    - Jesus' life connects to *you*.
        - In Acts, a book in the New Testament of the Bible, God tells us, "Believe in the Lord Jesus, and you will be saved."[109]
        - When God changes your heart and you believe in Jesus the God-man as the Savior from sin, he rescues you from the punishment you deserve and makes you part of his Forever Family. Have you believed in Jesus as your Savior from sin?
        - If you want to talk more about Jesus as your Rescuer, feel free to talk to your dad or mom, your teacher or Community Group leader, or to read the Bible and talk to Jesus.

APPLICATION

DISCUSSION:

- Is Jesus alive today? What is his body like?
- What changed after Jesus rose? What changed in the church? In the disciples?
- How does Jesus' life connect to you?

[108]Machowski, *The Gospel Story Bible*, 247.
[109]Acts 16:31.

SCRIPTURE:

Read:

- As a family, read and compare Luke 22 and Acts 2. Consider how witnessing the resurrection and receiving the Holy Spirit changed Peter.

Explore:

- Revelation 21:5: "And he who was seated on the throne said, 'Behold, I am making all things new.' Also he said, 'Write this down, for these words are trustworthy and true.'"

PRAYER:

- Thank Jesus for living out God's Rescue Plan.
- Thank God for revealing in the Bible that he keeps his promises.
- Thank God for his promise that the resurrection is something for all people who believe: that he will make all things new.

ADDITIONAL RESOURCES:

- Mark Driscoll and Gerry Breshears, *Doctrine: What Christians Should Believe* (Wheaton, IL: Crossway, 2010), 293–303.
- Marty Machowski, *The Gospel Story Bible: Discovering Jesus in the Old and New Testaments* (Greensboro, NC: New Growth Press, 2011), 212–247.
- Starr Meade, *Mighty Acts of God: A Family Bible Story Book* (Wheaton, IL: Crossway, 2010), 210.

RESURRECTION: Lesson 4

PROCLAMATION

BIG IDEA:

Knowing that Jesus is alive can change us today.

FOCUS VOCABULARY:

- **Change:** To change means that something starts out one way, then becomes another way. A thing is not the same after it has changed.

OBJECTIVES:

- Kids can describe ways that Jesus' resurrection changes people today.
- Kids can evaluate whether and how Jesus has changed their own heart.

KEY POINTS:

Jesus is alive.

- Jesus rose from the dead with a real body—not just any body, though. It wasn't the old body he had before—it was a new body, perfect and strong! It was a body that would never get sick or tired. It was a body that sin could not hurt. And Jesus will continue to live in his new, better-than-before body forever.

Knowing that Jesus is alive can change people today.

- Whether from the Bible or from another person, when we hear the story of Jesus the Rescuer and believe in him as the Savior from sin, a lot changes. Our heart changes and we agree with God that we're sinners and he is the only Savior. Then our whole life begins to change because we want to live for God, not for our sin. And even what happens when we die changes.
    - If we believe in Jesus, when we die, our bodies go into the ground and our souls go to be with God. But that's not the end. One day, at just the right time, Jesus will return to the earth and make all things new—better than before—including our bodies! Just like Jesus had a brand-new body when he rose, one day we will live together with God as his family in our own better-than-before bodies that cannot get hurt or sick.

- Yes, "When Jesus comes again, he will raise the bodies of his people, he will make those bodies perfect, and he will unite them to their spirits to live with him forever."[110]
- What an amazing thing! Just like Jesus' better-than-before body was in perfect health, our bodies will be too. When Jesus returns, everyone who has believed in him as the Savior from sin will have bodies that never go through pain or get hurt or die.[111]

- *The Gospel Story Bible* helps us understand. It tells the story from the Bible of when Jesus rose a man named Lazarus from the dead: "When Jesus raised Lazarus from the dead, it gave us a picture of what Jesus does for anyone who trusts in him. Because of sin, death comes to everyone, but Jesus conquered death and sin when he died on the cross. And just as he raised Lazarus, Jesus himself rose again, winning a battle over death forever for everyone who believes."[112]

Gospel Link: How does the fact that Jesus is alive connect to the gospel, the good news of God's Rescue Plan through Jesus?

- God's Rescue Plan for his people wouldn't have been possible unless Jesus defeated death to be alive again. Because Jesus is alive again, we know that he conquered sin and that if we believe in him as the Savior from sin, we are forgiven and can live forever as part of his family.

  - Jesus' life connects to *you.*
    - In Acts, a book in the New Testament of the Bible, God tells us, "Believe in the Lord Jesus, and you will be saved."[113]
    - When God changes your heart and you believe in Jesus the God-man as the Savior from sin, he rescues you from the punishment you deserve and makes you part of his Forever Family. Have you believed in Jesus as your Savior from sin?
    - If you want to talk more about Jesus as your Rescuer, feel free to talk to your dad or mom, your teacher or Community Group leader, or to read the Bible and talk to Jesus.

---

[110] Meade, *Mighty Acts of God*, 210.
[111] Driscoll and Breshears, *Doctrine*, 303.
[112] Machowski, *The Gospel Story Bible*, 212.
[113] Acts 16:31.

APPLICATION

DISCUSSION:

- Is Jesus alive today? What is his body like?
- If you believe in Jesus, what will happen to you after you die? Will you have a body again someday?
- How does Jesus' life connect to you?

SCRIPTURE: *Review the Scriptures you began exploring last week.*

Read:

- As a family, read and compare Luke 22 and Acts 2. Consider how witnessing the resurrection and receiving the Holy Spirit changed Peter.

Explore:

- Revelation 21:5: "And he who was seated on the throne said, 'Behold, I am making all things new.' Also he said, 'Write this down, for these words are trustworthy and true.'"

PRAYER:

- Thank Jesus for living out God's Rescue Plan.
- Thank God for revealing in the Bible that he keeps his promises.
- Thank God for his promise that the resurrection is something for all people who believe: that he will make all things new.

ADDITIONAL RESOURCES:

- Mark Driscoll and Gerry Breshears, *Doctrine: What Christians Should Believe* (Wheaton, IL: Crossway, 2010), 293–303.
- Marty Machowski, *The Gospel Story Bible: Discovering Jesus in the Old and New Testaments* (Greensboro, NC: New Growth Press, 2011), 212–247.
- Starr Meade, *Mighty Acts of God: A Family Bible Story Book* (Wheaton, IL: Crossway, 2010), 210.

RESURRECTION: 4/5/6 Activity 1

Draw pictures showing the sequence of some of the events of the resurrection. If you need help getting ideas, check out an illustrated children's Bible like *The Jesus Storybook Bible, The Big Picture Story Bible*, or *The Gospel Story Bible*.

Draw Jesus appearing to the disciples for the first time in his new body.

Draw something Jesus did while he was on the earth in his better-than-before body.

Draw Jesus rising up to heaven.

RESURRECTION: 4/5/6 Activity 2

Knowing Jesus changes people. Think of someone who changed a lot when they believed in Jesus. You can think of someone you know from your own life, or someone you've read about in the Bible, like Peter.

Discuss and sketch their life before they were changed by Jesus, and after.

BEFORE:

AFTER:

RESURRECTION: 7+ Activity 1

Read Matthew 28 and then complete the table below.

Focus on:	In your own words, what is happening in these verses?	What do these verses tell you about Jesus?
Matthew 28:1–10		
Matthew 28:11–15		
Matthew 28:16–20		

RESURRECTION: 7+ Activity 2

Knowing and believing God's Rescue Plan changes people: first God changes their hearts so they believe, then bit by bit he changes their lives. Consider how believing in Jesus changed Zacchaeus by reading the following Scriptures.

Scripture	Does this verse describe Zacchaeus before or after he believed?	What is Zacchaeus like in this verse? What is he doing? Thinking?
Luke 19:2: "And behold, there was a man named Zacchaeus. He was a chief tax collector and was rich."		
Luke 19:8–10: "And Zacchaeus stood and said to the Lord, 'Behold, Lord, the half of my goods I give to the poor. And if I have defrauded anyone of anything, I restore it fourfold.' And Jesus said to him, 'Today salvation has come to this house, since he also is a son of Abraham. For the Son of Man came to seek and to save the lost.'"		

Can you find other examples in Scripture of people who were changed by Jesus?

Describe them below.

CHURCH: Lesson 1

PROCLAMATION

BIG IDEA:

The church is all people who believe in Jesus as the Savior from sin (all over the world and right where you live).

FOCUS VOCABULARY:

- **Church:** All people who love Jesus and believe in him as the Savior from sin. The church is not a building. It is God's people, not a place. Sometimes God's people meet in what we call "church buildings," but the people themselves are the church.

OBJECTIVES:

- Kids can define church.
- Kids can distinguish between church and church building.
- Kids can describe the universal church (the church all over the world).
- Kids can describe the local church (the church right where you live).

KEY POINTS:

The church is all people who believe in Jesus as the Savior from sin.

- The church is a group of people, not a place.
    - This might seem confusing at first. After all, we've all heard people say, "It's time to go to church," or "I'll see you at church." That makes you think that the church is the building we're in right now. But it's not! The word "church" is really talking about all the people who love Jesus and believe in him as the Savior from sin.

The church includes people who love Jesus all over the world.

- The church includes "all God's people in all times and places."[114]
    - The church includes people who followed Jesus that you read about in the Bible.
    - The church includes people who love Jesus right where you live.

---

[114]Driscoll and Breshears, *Doctrine*, 307.

- The church includes people who love Jesus in other cities and other states.
- The church includes people who love Jesus in other countries all over the world.
- The church includes people who love Jesus on every continent!

- Jesus is in charge of the whole church all over the world. He changes the hearts of every person who believes in him as their Savior from sin, making them part of the church. He leads all the leaders and teachers and parents in the church. He leads all the kids, too![115]

The church includes people who love Jesus right where you live.

- Sometimes, when we talk about the church right where you live, we call it the "local church." "Local" just means "nearby."
    - The local church usually meets once a week in a building together. Some people call this "going to church." Maybe they should really say they are "going to be with the church" since the church is God's people, not the place where they meet.
    - People in the local church do important things together:[116]
        - They help each other follow Jesus.
        - They listen to a leader called a pastor or elder teach them from the Bible about God's Big Story.
        - They get baptized to tell the world that they know that God loves them, and that they love Jesus.
            - Baptism helps us remind ourselves how Jesus brought us from death to life, and how he washed away our sins.
        - They take Communion together.
            - At Communion, we eat a meal together to remember that Jesus died for us.
        - They love each other and take care of each other, because Jesus takes care of his people.

Gospel Link: How does what we know about the church connect to the gospel, the good news of God's Rescue Plan through Jesus?

- The church is made up of all people who have believed that Jesus is the Savior from sin. This means that, as part of God's Rescue Plan through Jesus, they have been saved from the punishment they deserve for sin.
    - Jesus' life connects to *you*.
        - In Acts, a book in the New Testament of the Bible, God tells us, "Believe in the Lord Jesus, and you will be saved."[117]
        - When God changes your heart and you believe in Jesus the God-man as the Savior from sin, he rescues you from the punishment you deserve and makes you part of his Forever Family. Have you believed in Jesus as your Savior from sin?

---

[115] Ibid., 315.
[116] Ibid., 309–311.
[117] Acts 16:31.

- If you want to talk more about Jesus as your Rescuer, feel free to talk to your dad or mom, your teacher or Community Group leader, or to read the Bible and talk to Jesus.

APPLICATION

DISCUSSION:

- Is the church a building? What is the church?
- Who is part of the church? Is the church just in the city where you live?
- What do you know about the church right where you live? What are some of the things the people of the church do together?
- How does God's Rescue Plan connect to you?

SCRIPTURE:

Read:

- Read selections from Acts 1–6 as a family this week. Notice what the church does together, and how they respond to their faith in Jesus.

Explore:

- Ephesians 5:25b: "Christ loved the church and gave himself up for her."

PRAYER:

- Pray for your local church—the people who love Jesus that you worship with at your church building.
- Pray for people who participate in your local church but do not yet believe in Jesus as the Savior from sin. Pray that their hearts will be transformed.
- Pray for the kids in your family. Pray that God will reveal ways that they can help and love others in their local church.

ADDITIONAL RESOURCES:

- Mark Driscoll and Gerry Breshears, *Doctrine: What Christians Should Believe* (Wheaton, IL: Crossway, 2010), 307–315.
- Sally Lloyd-Jones, *The Jesus Storybook Bible: Every Story Whispers His Name* (Grand Rapids, MI: Zondervan, 2007), 210.

CHURCH: Lesson 2

PROCLAMATION

BIG IDEA:

The church is all people who believe in Jesus as the Savior from sin, and the church is always growing.

FOCUS VOCABULARY:

- **Church:** All people who love Jesus and believe in him as the Savior from sin. The church is not a building. It is God's people, not a place. Sometimes God's people meet in what we call "church buildings," but the people themselves are the church.

OBJECTIVES:

- Kids can define church.
- Kids can distinguish between church and church building.

KEY POINTS:

The church is all people who believe in Jesus as the Savior from sin.

- The church is a group of people, not a place.
    - This might seem confusing at first. After all, we've all heard people say, "It's time to go to church," or "I'll see you at church." That makes you think that the church is the building we're in right now. But it's not! The word "church" is really talking about all the people who love Jesus and believe in him as the Savior from sin.

The church is always growing.

- The church started when Jesus lived on this earth as both God and man. He is the Head Pastor of the church, and his friends, the disciples, were some of the first people to join the church.
    - They became part of the church when Jesus changed their hearts to believe in him as God and the Savior from sin. They followed him, and their whole lives changed.
- After Jesus' life on this earth, people all around Jerusalem continued to see Jesus at work as he changed people to love and follow him. When they saw this, many more people believed. The church kept growing and growing!

- A handful of Jesus' followers have become, two thousand years later, billions of people all over the world. And the church will keep on growing until Jesus returns.
- The church doesn't grow into a bigger building, because the church is not a building. No! The church—the group of all people who have believed in Jesus as the Savior from sin—grows every time someone believes.

Gospel Link: How does what we know about the church connect to the gospel, the good news of God's Rescue Plan through Jesus?

- The church is made up of all people who have believed that Jesus is the Savior from sin. This means that, as part of God's Rescue Plan through Jesus, they have been saved from the punishment they deserve for sin.
    - Jesus' life connects to *you.*
        - In Acts, a book in the New Testament of the Bible, God tells us, "Believe in the Lord Jesus, and you will be saved."[118]
        - When God changes your heart and you believe in Jesus the God-man as the Savior from sin, he rescues you from the punishment you deserve and makes you part of his Forever Family. Have you believed in Jesus as your Savior from sin?
        - If you want to talk more about Jesus as your Rescuer, feel free to talk to your dad or mom, your teacher or Community Group leader, or to read the Bible and talk to Jesus.

APPLICATION

DISCUSSION:

- Is the church a building? What is the church?
- Are you part of the church? How do you know?
- How does God's Rescue Plan connect to the church? To you?

SCRIPTURE: *Review the Scriptures you began exploring last week.*

Read:

- Read selections from Acts 1–6 as a family this week. Notice what the church does together, and how they respond to their faith in Jesus.

Explore:

- Ephesians 5:25b: "Christ loved the church and gave himself up for her."

[118] Acts 16:31.

PRAYER:

- Pray for your local church—the people who love Jesus that you worship with at your church building.
- Pray for people who participate in your local church but do not yet believe in Jesus as the Savior from sin. Pray that their hearts will be transformed.
- Pray for the kids in your family. Pray that God will reveal ways that they can help and love others in their local church.

ADDITIONAL RESOURCES:

- Mark Driscoll and Gerry Breshears, *Doctrine: What Christians Should Believe* (Wheaton, IL: Crossway, 2010), 307–315.
- Sally Lloyd-Jones, *The Jesus Storybook Bible: Every Story Whispers His Name* (Grand Rapids, MI: Zondervan, 2007), 210.

CHURCH: Lesson 3

PROCLAMATION

BIG IDEA:

Jesus gave the church a special mission.

FOCUS VOCABULARY:

- **Mission:** A mission is like a special job or purpose. Jesus' special purpose for the church is to live for him, and to tell as many people as possible the story of Jesus the Rescuer.

OBJECTIVE:

- Kids can restate the Great Commission.

KEY POINTS:

Jesus gave the church a special mission.

- A mission is like a special job or purpose. Jesus' special mission is the thing that he wants all his people to do for their whole life.
    - Lots of people you know or have heard about have missions. A teacher's mission is to help kids learn. Spiderman's mission is to fight crime. A baseball player's mission is to win the game.
    - Did you know that Jesus has a special mission for people who believe in him as the Savior from sin? Let's find out what it is!
- Jesus' special mission for those who have believed in him as their Savior from sin is to tell people about his Big Story—people right here in our neighborhoods, and people all the way around the world.
    - "Jesus gave his followers a command we now call the Great Commission. He said, 'Go and tell people from every nation about me, so they can believe and become my disciples too. Baptize those who believe in the name of the Father and of the Son and of the Holy Spirit. Teach them everything I have taught you. And be sure of this: I will always be with you.' The disciples followed those instructions for the rest of their lives."[119]

---

[119] Machowski, *The Gospel Story Bible*, 240.

- *The Jesus Storybook Bible* says it like this:
    - "When at last they reached the top of the highest hill near Jerusalem, Jesus turned to them and said, 'Go everywhere and tell everyone the happy news! Tell them I love them so much that I died for them. It's the Truth that overcomes the terrible lie. God loves his children. Yes, he really does! . . . Now everyone can come home to God,' Jesus said. 'Death is not the end of you. You can live forever with your Father in heaven because I have rescued the whole world!'"[120]
        - Jesus didn't expect his people to do this special work on their own, though. No—he sent "a special gift to help them do that work."[121] Who do you think the gift was? It was God the Holy Spirit!

Gospel Link: How does what we know about the special mission of the church connect to the gospel, the good news of God's Rescue Plan through Jesus?

- God uses the church, people who believe in him as the Savior from sin, to tell others the gospel. Then, when they have heard the gospel, God changes their hearts to believe it is true—to believe in Jesus as the Savior from sin.
    - Have you heard the gospel from someone at your local church? Have you believed in Jesus as the Savior from sin?
    - In Acts, a book in the New Testament of the Bible, God tells us, "Believe in the Lord Jesus, and you will be saved."[122]
        - When God changes your heart and you believe in Jesus the God-man as the Savior from sin, he rescues you from the punishment you deserve and makes you part of his Forever Family.
        - If you want to talk more about Jesus as your Rescuer, feel free to talk to your dad or mom, your teacher or Community Group leader, or to read the Bible and talk to Jesus.

APPLICATION

DISCUSSION:

- What is the special mission of the church?
- How does God's Rescue Plan connect to you?

[120] Lloyd-Jones, *The Jesus Storybook Bible*, 322–323.
[121] Helm, *The Big Picture Story Bible*, 414.
[122] Acts 16:31.

SCRIPTURE:

Read:

- Read Matthew 28 as a family and explore the context and content of the Great Commission.

Explore:

- Matthew 28:19–20: "'Go therefore and make disciples of all nations, baptizing them in the name of the Father and of the Son and of the Holy Spirit, teaching them to observe all that I have commanded you. And behold, I am with you always, to the end of the age.'"

PRAYER:

- Thank Jesus for letting people who believe in him as the Savior from sin be part of his work in the world by telling people about him.
- Pray for the kids in your family. Pray that Jesus will give them a desire to be part of his mission, and ideas of how to do it.
- Pray for your neighbors. Pray that Jesus will help you live in a way that tells your neighbors his Big Story.

ADDITIONAL RESOURCES:

- David R. Helm, *The Big Picture Story Bible* (Wheaton, IL: Crossway, 2004), 414–428.
- Sally Lloyd-Jones, *The Jesus Storybook Bible: Every Story Whispers His Name* (Grand Rapids, MI: Zondervan, 2007), 323–332.
- Marty Machowski, *The Gospel Story Bible: Discovering Jesus in the Old and New Testaments* (Greensboro, NC: New Growth Press, 2011), 240–249.

CHURCH: Lesson 4

PROCLAMATION

BIG IDEA:

Jesus' followers started the church's special mission in the New Testament, and we get to continue it today.

FOCUS VOCABULARY:

- **Mission:** A mission is like a special job or purpose. Jesus' special purpose for the church is to live for him, and to tell as many people as possible the story of Jesus the Rescuer.

OBJECTIVES:

- Kids can describe mission in the early church.
- Kids can describe mission in the church today.

KEY POINTS:

Jesus' followers started the church's special mission in the New Testament.

- When Jesus went up to be with his Father, he sent the Holy Spirit to fill his people. With the Holy Spirit fueling them, Jesus' followers started to carry out the special mission he gave them.
    - They told people around them about Jesus with words.
        - For example, one of Jesus' friends named Peter told lots of people about Jesus by preaching. "[Peter] told them of the prophets who had said God would send his Spirit. He told them to repent and to believe in God's forever king. This news entered into their hearts. Many confessed their sins and believed."[123]
    - They told people from other places about Jesus.
        - "Because of Jesus, people from every tribe, language, and nation can worship the Lord together."[124]

[123] Helm, *The Big Picture Story Bible*, 423.
[124] Machowski, *The Gospel Story Bible*, 240.

- As more and more people heard about Jesus, "women and men, boys and girls, young and old from many different nations, decided to follow Jesus as their king."[125]
- "The wonderful news of Jesus spread. Like sparks from a fire. To villages. Towns. Cities. Every day, more and more people believed. And so it was that the family of God's children, his special people, grew."[126]

We get to continue the mission today.

- "Did you know that Jesus is still calling people to become fishers of men? Today, when we hear about Jesus' amazing life and how he died on the cross, the Holy Spirit helps us to see our sin. . . . God calls us to leave our sinful lives behind and follow Jesus. God changes our hearts so that we want to tell others about Jesus. That is how we become fishers of men. When we believe, our job is to 'cast the net' of the gospel to 'catch' as many unbelievers as we can and bring them in to follow Jesus."[127]
    - Jesus wants us to believe in our hearts—and then to share with others—that Jesus lived a perfect life, died to pay for the sins of the whole world (including me most of all!), and rose again to live forever with God.
- Did you know that we couldn't believe or share this on our own? Not at all. It's Jesus who gives us the special mission, and it's Jesus who accomplishes the mission by changing hearts. Isn't it amazing that he lets us be involved in his special work of bringing his people back into his family?

Gospel Link: How does what we know about the special mission of the church connect to the gospel, the good news of God's Rescue Plan through Jesus?

- God uses the church, people who believe in him as the Savior from sin, to tell others the gospel. Then, when they have heard the gospel, God changes their hearts to believe it is true—to believe in Jesus as the Savior from sin.
    - Have you heard the gospel from someone at your local church? Have you believed in Jesus as the Savior from sin?
    - In Acts, a book in the New Testament of the Bible, God tells us, "Believe in the Lord Jesus, and you will be saved."[128]
        - When God changes your heart and you believe in Jesus the God-man as the Savior from sin, he rescues you from the punishment you deserve and makes you part of his Forever Family.
        - If you want to talk more about Jesus as your Rescuer, feel free to talk to your dad or mom, your teacher or Community Group leader, or to read the Bible and talk to Jesus.

---

[125] Helm, *The Big Picture Story Bible*, 428.
[126] Lloyd-Jones, *The Jesus Storybook Bible*, 332.
[127] Machowski, *The Gospel Story Bible*, 179.
[128] Acts 16:31.

APPLICATION

DISCUSSION:

- What are some of the things God's people did in the New Testament to carry out Jesus' special mission?
- Are you part of Jesus' special mission today? How?
- How does God's Rescue Plan connect to you?

SCRIPTURE: *Review the Scriptures you began exploring last week.*

Read:

- Read Matthew 28 as a family and explore the context and content of the Great Commission.

Explore:

- Matthew 28:19–20: "'Go therefore and make disciples of all nations, baptizing them in the name of the Father and of the Son and of the Holy Spirit, teaching them to observe all that I have commanded you. And behold, I am with you always, to the end of the age.'"

PRAYER:

- Thank Jesus for letting people who believe in him as the Savior from sin be part of his work in the world by telling people about him.
- Pray for the kids in your family. Pray that Jesus will give them a desire to be part of his mission, and ideas of how to do it.
- Pray for your neighbors. Pray that Jesus will help you live in a way that tells your neighbors his Big Story.

ADDITIONAL RESOURCES:

- David R. Helm, *The Big Picture Story Bible* (Wheaton, IL: Crossway, 2004), 414–428.
- Sally Lloyd-Jones, *The Jesus Storybook Bible: Every Story Whispers His Name* (Grand Rapids, MI: Zondervan, 2007), 323–332.
- Marty Machowski, *The Gospel Story Bible: Discovering Jesus in the Old and New Testaments* (Greensboro, NC: New Growth Press, 2011), 240–249.

CHURCH: 4/5/6 Activity 1

Circle and color the pictures of things that people in the local church do together.

CHURCH: 4/5/6 Activity 2

Jesus wants people to believe in him and be part of his special mission today. Look at the pictures and ask yourself, "Is this something someone who loves Jesus could do to carry out Jesus' special mission to tell people about him?" If it is, circle and color the picture. If it isn't, cross it out.

CHURCH: 7+ Activity I

Scripture	What does this passage teach you about the church?
Acts 5:12–16: "Now many signs and wonders were regularly done among the people by the hands of the apostles. And they were all together in Solomon's Portico. None of the rest dared join them, but the people held them in high esteem. And more than ever believers were added to the Lord, multitudes of both men and women, so that they even carried out the sick into the streets and laid them on cots and mats, that as Peter came by at least his shadow might fall on some of them. The people also gathered from the towns around Jerusalem, bringing the sick and those afflicted with unclean spirits, and they were all healed."	
Acts 6:7: "And the word of God continued to increase, and the number of the disciples multiplied greatly in Jerusalem, and a great many of the priests became obedient to the faith."	
Acts 10:44–48: "While Peter was still saying these things, the Holy Spirit fell on all who heard the word. And the believers from among the circumcised who had come with Peter were amazed, because the gift of the Holy Spirit was poured out even on the Gentiles. For they were hearing them speaking in tongues and extolling God. Then Peter declared, 'Can anyone withhold water for baptizing these people, who have received the Holy Spirit just as we have?' And he commanded them to be baptized in the name of Jesus Christ. Then they asked him to remain for some days."	

CHURCH: 7+ Activity 2

Scripture	Are God's people helping carry out their special mission in this verse?	Why do you think so?
Acts 5:12–16: "Now many signs and wonders were regularly done among the people by the hands of the apostles. And they were all together in Solomon's Portico. None of the rest dared join them, but the people held them in high esteem. And more than ever believers were added to the Lord, multitudes of both men and women, so that they even carried out the sick into the streets and laid them on cots and mats, that as Peter came by at least his shadow might fall on some of them. The people also gathered from the towns around Jerusalem, bringing the sick and those afflicted with unclean spirits, and they were all healed."		
Acts 10:44–48: "While Peter was still saying these things, the Holy Spirit fell on all who heard the word. And the believers from among the circumcised who had come with Peter were amazed, because the gift of the Holy Spirit was poured out even on the Gentiles. For they were hearing them speaking in tongues and extolling God. Then Peter declared, 'Can anyone withhold water for baptizing these people, who have received the Holy Spirit just as we have?' And he commanded them to be baptized in the name of Jesus Christ. Then they asked him to remain for some days."		

WORSHIP, Lesson 1

PROCLAMATION

BIG IDEA:

Every person worships all of the time.

FOCUS VOCABULARY:

- **Worship:** To worship is to really, really love something and to live for it. We serve and pour ourselves out for the person or thing we worship. What we do and the way we do it shows who or what we worship.

OBJECTIVES:

- Kids can define worship.
- Kids can restate when people worship (all of the time).

KEY POINTS:

Every person worships.

- To worship is to really, really love something and to live for it. We serve and pour ourselves out for the person or thing we worship. What we do and the way we do it shows who or what we worship.
- God created all people as worshipers. We are designed to love and worship God in everything that we do, and the way we do it.
  - "What you do and the way you do it express your desire to serve *something.*"[129]
- When we hear the word "worship," sometimes we think of singing or praying with other Christians at church. This can be worship of God if we are loving Jesus and living for him while we're doing it, but it is not the only kind of worship.
  - Sometimes, together with God's people at our church building, we worship God by listening to and reading God's Word, taking Communion, seeing baptisms, praying, singing, helping other people, or giving money to the church. These things are not worship of God because they are the "right thing to do" at the church building. No! Worship is from the heart.

---

[129] Tripp, *Instruments in the Redeemer's Hands*, 44.

    - For example, if you eat food with thankfulness to God in your heart, it's worship.
    - After all, we show who or what we are worshiping by both what we do, and the way we do it!

Every person worships all of the time.

- Because God designed all people as worshipers, we have been worshiping someone or something from the very second we were born.
- We are worshiping someone or something every second of every single day. We are never *not* worshiping.
- Whoa! That's a lot of worship! It might seem hard to believe since you might not even realize that you're worshiping something—it might just seem like you're playing a game with a friend or eating lunch. But even while you do those normal things, you are either loving and living for Jesus, or loving and living for something else.
    - All people are designed to love and worship Jesus all the time. Learning about this is exciting because we can think more and more to ourselves, "What am I really loving right now?" The more the Holy Spirit helps you to reflect on this, the more you will grow in your worship of Jesus if you have believed in him as your Savior from sin.

Gospel Link: How does what we know about worship connect to the gospel, the good news of God's Rescue Plan through Jesus?

- God's Rescue Plan makes it possible for people to worship God. Because Jesus lived a perfect life as God and man, died to pay the penalty for our sin, and conquered death by rising to live forever with God, we can be part of the Forever Family of God—worshiping him forever—if we believe in Jesus as the Savior from sin. Have you believed in Jesus as the Savior from sin?
    - In Acts, a book in the New Testament of the Bible, God tells us, "Believe in the Lord Jesus, and you will be saved."[130]
        - If you want to talk more about Jesus as your Rescuer, feel free to talk to your dad or mom, your teacher or Community Group leader, or to read the Bible and talk to Jesus.

APPLICATION

DISCUSSION:

- Do you worship?
- Is there ever a time when you are *not* worshiping?
- How does God's Rescue Plan connect to worship? To you?

[130] Acts 16:31.

SCRIPTURE:

Read:

- Read the Exodus account of the golden calf (Exodus 32), and discuss what worship means.

Explore:

- John 4:23: "'But the hour is coming, and is now here, when the true worshipers will worship the Father in spirit and truth, for the Father is seeking such people to worship him.'"

PRAYER:

- Thank God for giving us his Word to tell us what we were created for.
- Thank Jesus for his Rescue Plan so we can be part of God's family if we believe in Jesus as the Savior from sin.

ADDITIONAL RESOURCES:

- Paul David Tripp, *Instruments in the Redeemer's Hands: People in Need of Change Helping People in Need of Change* (Phillipsburg, NJ: P&R Publishing, 2002), 44.

WORSHIP: Lesson 2

PROCLAMATION

BIG IDEA:

Every person worships God or something else.

FOCUS VOCABULARY:

- **Worship:** To worship is to really, really love something and to live for it. We serve and pour ourselves out for the person or thing we worship. What we do and the way we do it shows who or what we worship.

OBJECTIVES:

- Kids can describe what it means to worship God.
- Kids can list examples of worshiping things other than God.

KEY POINTS:

Every person worships God or something else.

- We were created to worship God all of the time—to love him and live for him even in the normal everyday things like eating breakfast or reading a book. But because of sin, we don't always do this. Sometimes we love and live for people or things other than God. This is sin.
- When we make something more important than God in our minds and our hearts, we are worshiping it. Because of sin, we all do this. We were created to worship and never stop worshiping, so sometimes as sinners we worship the wrong thing.
  - Sometimes it is a thing you want, like a new toy or special treat. When something takes over your thoughts and your feelings, and you feel like you just have to have it, you are worshiping something other than God.
  - Does this sound familiar? Can you think of a time when you worshiped something other than God? Maybe you had a tantrum or got really mad because you didn't get what you wanted.

Knowing that we sometimes worship something other than God shows that we need Jesus.

- We all worship something other than God some of the time. This is sin. But there is good news! There is a Rescuer who lived and died to pay for this sin. His name is Jesus.
- When God changes our hearts so we believe in him as the Savior from sin, he sends the Holy Spirit to change our hearts so we can worship him. He helps us worship him more and more as our lives continue.
- Once you know and love Jesus, when you realize that you are worshiping something other than him (sin!), you get to tell him you're sorry, and receive his forgiveness over and over again. First John 1:9 says, "If we confess our sins, he is faithful and just to forgive us our sins and to cleanse us from all unrighteousness." What a loving God to forgive us so many times!

Gospel Link: How does what we know about worship connect to the gospel, the good news of God's Rescue Plan through Jesus?

- God's Rescue Plan makes it possible for people to worship God. Because Jesus lived a perfect life as God and man, died to pay the penalty for our sin, and conquered death by rising to live forever with God, we can be part of the Forever Family of God—worshiping him forever—if we believe in Jesus as the Savior from sin. Have you believed in Jesus as the Savior from sin?
    - In Acts, a book in the New Testament of the Bible, God tells us, "Believe in the Lord Jesus, and you will be saved."[131]
        - If you want to talk more about Jesus as your Rescuer, feel free to talk to your dad or mom, your teacher or Community Group leader, or to read the Bible and talk to Jesus.

APPLICATION

DISCUSSION:

- What have you worshiped other than God? Share an example.
- Do you need Jesus? How do you know?
- How does God's Rescue Plan connect to worship? To you?

SCRIPTURE: *Review the Scriptures you began exploring last week.*

Read:

- Read the Exodus account of the golden calf (Exodus 32), and discuss what worship means.

[131]Acts 16:31.

Explore:

- John 4:23: "'But the hour is coming, and is now here, when the true worshipers will worship the Father in spirit and truth, for the Father is seeking such people to worship him.'"

PRAYER:

- Thank God for giving us his Word to tell us what we were created for.
- Thank Jesus for his Rescue Plan so we can be part of God's family if we believe in Jesus as the Savior from sin.

ADDITIONAL RESOURCES:

- Paul David Tripp, *Instruments in the Redeemer's Hands: People in Need of Change Helping People in Need of Change* (Phillipsburg, NJ: P&R Publishing, 2002), 44.

WORSHIP: Lesson 3

PROCLAMATION

BIG IDEA:

When Jesus changes your heart to love him, he changes your whole life bit by bit.

FOCUS VOCABULARY:

- **Worship:** To worship is to really, really love something and to live for it. We serve and pour ourselves out for the person or thing we worship. What we do and the way we do it shows who or what we worship.

OBJECTIVES:

- Kids can describe how Jesus changes hearts.
- Kids can describe how worship changes once you have believed in Jesus as the Savior from sin.

KEY POINTS:

Jesus changes hearts to love him.

- "Jesus can do something no one else can do—he can change a heart. Jesus can change the hardest heart and make it love and desire what God loves and desires."[132]
  - This is a *big* deal! Changing hearts isn't a small job—it's something only Jesus can do.
    - "That's because every human is born a sinner and an enemy to Christ. People don't want Jesus to rule over them. Not only are people unwilling, but they are also unable to obey. But that doesn't stop King Jesus. When he commands people to follow him, he gives them the desire and ability to obey. He can do this because he can change hearts and can give new life."[133]
  - "Isn't it amazing how God's power changes people? All of us are born selfish sinners who want to keep what we have for ourselves. Even little children don't like to share their toys. But . . . God could change even the hearts of the people who crucified Jesus! Did you know that God's Spirit works in us the same way today? First, God

---

[132] Meade, *Mighty Acts of God*, 222.
[133] Ibid., 167.

helps us to see how sinful we are. Then he helps us believe that Jesus died for us to take away our sins. When we believe, we are changed by God's Spirit. Our hearts fill with the joy of being forgiven."[134]

If you have believed in Jesus as the Savior from sin, he changes your whole life bit by bit.

- When Jesus changes your heart to love him and believe in him as the Savior from sin, he makes you brand new inside.
    - "Did you know that amazing changes take place in people's lives when they become Christians? They might still look the same on the outside, but inside a whole lot is different. That's why the Holy Spirit inspired Paul to describe a Christian as a 'new creation,' where the old is gone and the new has come. Every person starts out as a sinner inside—that's the old part Paul is talking about. We don't follow God or do what he wants us to do. Instead, we are slaves to sin and we can't change on our own. But . . . when God makes us a new creation, he brings us back to life, forgives our sin, and gives us Christ's righteousness so we are brand new inside. Then, day by day, God changes us on the outside too! We still sin, but we can confess our sin and God forgives us. Then we get back up and try again! Instead of living for sin, we start living for God.[135]
- When Jesus changes your heart so you believe in him as the Savior from sin, lots of things in your life change.
    - Bit by bit, Jesus changes what we want. We don't just want things for ourselves. More and more, we want what Jesus wants.[136]
    - Jesus gives us new feelings. The things that make Jesus sad make us sad, and the things that make Jesus happy make us happy.
    - Jesus gives us a new family. We want to be with his people and to love and help them however we can.
    - Jesus gives us a new mission. We want to live for him by doing the special job of telling other people about him.

Gospel Link: How does what we know about worship connect to the gospel, the good news of God's Rescue Plan through Jesus?

- God's Rescue Plan makes it possible for people to worship God. Because Jesus lived a perfect life as God and man, died to pay the penalty for our sin, and conquered death by rising to live forever with God, we can be part of the Forever Family of God—worshiping him forever—if we believe in Jesus as the Savior from sin. Have you believed in Jesus as the Savior from sin?
    - In Acts, a book in the New Testament of the Bible, God tells us, "Believe in the Lord Jesus, and you will be saved."[137]

---

[134] Machowski, *The Gospel Story Bible*, 249.
[135] Ibid., 269.
[136] Driscoll and Breshears, *Doctrine*, 364.
[137] Acts 16:31.

- If you want to talk more about Jesus as your Rescuer, feel free to talk to your dad or mom, your teacher or Community Group leader, or to read the Bible and talk to Jesus.

APPLICATION

DISCUSSION:

- What does it mean that Jesus changes hearts? What is different than before?
- What are some of the things that change when you believe in Jesus?
- How does God's Rescue Plan connect to you?

SCRIPTURE:

Read:

- As a family, read the story of Saul's conversion in the Bible (Acts 9:1–31) or in an illustrated children's Bible. Discuss how Jesus changed his heart, then changed his worship and bit by bit changed his whole life.
- As a family, read the story of Zacchaeus' conversion in the Bible (Luke 19:1–10) or in an illustrated children's Bible. Discuss how Jesus changed his heart, then changed his worship and bit by bit changed his whole life.

Explore:

- 2 Corinthians 5:17: "Therefore, if anyone is in Christ, he is a new creation. The old has passed away; behold, the new has come."

PRAYER:

- Thank God for sending Jesus to live out his Rescue Plan so that we can be part of his family if we believe in Jesus as the Savior from sin.
- Thank God for telling us about examples like Paul and Zacchaeus in the Bible, showing us that Jesus changes hearts and then bit by bit changes whole lives.
- Pray that Jesus will transform the worship of the kids in your family.

ADDITIONAL RESOURCES:

- Mark Driscoll and Gerry Breshears, *Doctrine: What Christians Should Believe* (Wheaton, IL: Crossway, 2010), 364.
- Sally Lloyd-Jones, *The Jesus Storybook Bible: Every Story Whispers His Name* (Grand Rapids, MI: Zondervan, 2007), 338.
- Marty Machowski, *The Gospel Story Bible: Discovering Jesus in the Old and New Testaments* (Greensboro, NC: New Growth Press, 2011), 257.
- Starr Meade, *Mighty Acts of God: A Family Bible Story Book* (Wheaton, IL: Crossway, 2010), 167–222, 263–264.

WORSHIP: Lesson 4

PROCLAMATION

BIG IDEA:

In the New Testament, we see examples of how Jesus changes hearts and lives.

FOCUS VOCABULARY:

- **Worship:** To worship is to really, really love something and to live for it. We serve and pour ourselves out for the person or thing we worship. What we do and the way we do it shows who or what we worship.

OBJECTIVES:

- Kids can describe how Jesus changes hearts.
- Kids can describe how worship changes once you have believed in Jesus as the Savior from sin.

KEY POINTS:

Jesus changes hearts and lives.

- "Jesus can do something no one else can do—he can change a heart. Jesus can change the hardest heart and make it love and desire what God loves and desires."[138]
- He changes hearts so that people believe in Jesus as the Savior from sin. Then, he changes their whole lives bit by bit.

In the New Testament, Paul's life is an example of how Jesus changes hearts and lives.

- In the Bible, God gives us many examples of people who got new hearts that love Jesus, and then shows us how their whole lives changed, including who or what they worshiped. One great example is a man named Paul. That's what we call him now, anyway. He wasn't always called Paul . . .
    - *Before his heart was changed:* Earlier in his life, his name was Saul, and at the time he was alive he was the worst of Jesus' many enemies. "Saul went from house to house in Jerusalem, looking for Christians to drag to trial and to prison. When the council would vote on what to do with them, Saul always voted for death. At last, most

[138] Meade, *Mighty Acts of God*, 222.

Christians had left Jerusalem, but Saul was not content. He wanted them stamped out completely, so he headed off for Damascus, in Syria, to find more Christians to arrest."[139]

- *Jesus changes Saul's heart:* "On the way, though, Jesus stopped him with a bright light from heaven that blinded him. Because Saul was such an active rebel against the Lord Jesus, wouldn't you expect him to be killed on the spot as judgment for his actions? But Jesus has such power that . . . instead of killing his ardent enemy, Jesus turned him into a devoted servant."[140] Jesus changed Saul's heart to love and live for him (to worship him!), then changed everything in Saul's life, from his name to the things that he wanted to do.
    - "Suddenly Saul . . . saw everything differently. He wasn't mean anymore. He even changed his name from Saul to Paul, which means 'small' and 'humble'—the very opposite of proud."[141]
- *After his heart was changed:* "Instead of capturing Christians to take them to jail, Saul began to preach the gospel to anyone who would listen. . . . Did you know that Saul is the same person as the apostle Paul? After he became a Christian, Saul used the name Paul. And just as Jesus foretold, the Lord used Paul to spread the gospel . . . all over the world. Saul's conversion shows us that God can save anyone, no matter how sinful. Saul had planned to destroy the church but he was no match for Jesus. No one can stop the spread of the gospel."[142]
    - "But if you had known Paul—or Saul, as he was called then—when he was a young man, you would never have expected him to do those things. God expected it, though. God knew it would happen. That's because before Saul had been born, before Saul had even begun to grow inside his mother, before the world had even been created, God had appointed Saul to a very specific task. He had chosen him to be his servant."[143]
- Paul's worship sure changed a lot! He went from living for the death and end of all Christians, to living for Jesus and telling as many people as possible about him. Jesus changes hearts, and then he changes who we worship and our whole lives!

Gospel Link: How does what we know about worship connect to the gospel, the good news of God's Rescue Plan through Jesus?

- God's Rescue Plan makes it possible for people to worship God. Because Jesus lived a perfect life as God and man, died to pay the penalty for our sin, and conquered death by rising to live forever with God, we can be part of the Forever Family of God—worshiping him forever—if we believe in Jesus as the Savior from sin.
    - In Acts, a book in the New Testament of the Bible, God tells us, "Believe in the Lord Jesus, and you will be saved."[144]

---

[139]Meade, *Mighty Acts of God*, 263.
[140]Ibid., 264.
[141]Lloyd-Jones, *The Jesus Storybook Bible*, 338.
[142]Machowski, *The Gospel Story Bible*, 257.
[143]Meade, *Mighty Acts of God*, 263.
[144]Acts 16:31.

- If you want to talk more about Jesus as your Rescuer, feel free to talk to your dad or mom, your teacher or Community Group leader, or to read the Bible and talk to Jesus.

APPLICATION

DISCUSSION:

- What is something Jesus does that no one else can do?
- Has the truth that Jesus is the Savior from sin changed your life? How are the changes in your life the same as or different from the changes in Paul's life?
- How does God's Rescue Plan connect to you?

SCRIPTURE: *Review the Scriptures you began exploring last week.*

Read:

- As a family, read the story of Saul's conversion in the Bible (Acts 9:1–31) or in an illustrated children's Bible. Discuss how Jesus changed his heart, then changed his worship and bit by bit changed his whole life.
- As a family, read the story of Zacchaeus' conversion in the Bible (Luke 19:1–10) or in an illustrated children's Bible. Discuss how Jesus changed his heart, then changed his worship and bit by bit changed his whole life.

Explore:

- 2 Corinthians 5:17: "Therefore, if anyone is in Christ, he is a new creation. The old has passed away; behold, the new has come."

PRAYER:

- Thank God for sending Jesus to live out his Rescue Plan so that we can be part of his family if we believe in Jesus as the Savior from sin.
- Thank God for telling us about examples like Paul and Zacchaeus in the Bible, showing us that Jesus changes hearts and then bit by bit changes whole lives.
- Pray that Jesus will transform the worship of the kids in your family.

ADDITIONAL RESOURCES:

- Mark Driscoll and Gerry Breshears, *Doctrine: What Christians Should Believe* (Wheaton, IL: Crossway, 2010), 364.
- Sally Lloyd-Jones, *The Jesus Storybook Bible: Every Story Whispers His Name* (Grand Rapids, MI: Zondervan, 2007), 338.
- Marty Machowski, *The Gospel Story Bible: Discovering Jesus in the Old and New Testaments* (Greensboro, NC: New Growth Press, 2011), 257.
- Starr Meade, *Mighty Acts of God: A Family Bible Story Book* (Wheaton, IL: Crossway, 2010), 167–222, 263–264.

WORSHIP: 4/5/6 Activity 1

In the Bible, God gives us many examples of times when his people were worshiping him. He also gives examples of times his people worshiped someone or something other than him. Color and discuss the pictures. Circle the examples of worshiping God. Cross out the examples of worshiping someone or something else.

THE FALL (EVE BELIEVES THE SERPENT'S LIE)

GOD'S PEOPLE WORSHIP THE GOLDEN CALF

PETER PREACHES ABOUT JESUS TO THOUSANDS OF PEOPLE

WORSHIP: 4/5/6 Activity 2

Read the story of Zacchaeus in the Bible (Luke 19:1–10) or in an illustrated children's Bible like *The Jesus Storybook Bible*, *The Big Picture Story Bible*, or *The Gospel Story Bible*. Then complete the activity below.

Jesus changed Zacchaeus' heart to love and live for him (to worship him!), then changed everything in his life, from his desires to the things that he did. In the boxes provided, sketch Zacchaeus' life before and after he believed in Jesus.

BEFORE:

AFTER:

WORSHIP: 7+ Activity 1

In the Bible, God gives us many examples of times when his people were worshiping him. He also gives examples of times his people worshiped someone or something other than him. Examine the following passages from Scripture to determine what people were worshiping, and how the gospel of Jesus applies.

Scripture	**Who or what were people worshiping?**	**How does the gospel of Jesus apply here?**
Deuteronomy 9:16: "'And I looked, and behold, you had sinned against the LORD your God. You had made yourselves a golden calf. You had turned aside quickly from the way that the LORD had commanded you.'"		
Judges 3:7: "And the people of Israel did what was evil in the sight of the LORD. They forgot the LORD their God and served the Baals and the Asheroth."		
1 Samuel 1:3: "Now this man used to go up year by year from his city to worship and to sacrifice to the LORD of hosts at Shiloh, where the two sons of Eli, Hophni and Phinehas, were priests of the LORD."		
Can you find another example of people worshiping? Write the verse here.		

WORSHIP: 7+ Activity 2

Scripture	What is going on in this verse?	What is Zacchaeus like? What is he doing? What does he want? What does he really, really love and live for?
Luke 19:2: "And behold, there was a man named Zacchaeus. He was a chief tax collector and was rich."		
Luke 19:3–4: "And he was seeking to see who Jesus was, but on account of the crowd he could not, because he was small in stature. So he ran on ahead and climbed up into a sycamore tree to see him, for he was about to pass that way."		
Luke 19:5–6: "And when Jesus came to the place, he looked up and said to him, 'Zacchaeus, hurry and come down, for I must stay at your house today.' So he hurried and came down and received him joyfully."		
Luke 19:8–10: "And Zacchaeus stood and said to the Lord, 'Behold, Lord, the half of my goods I give to the poor. And if I have defrauded anyone of anything, I restore it fourfold.' And Jesus said to him, 'Today salvation has come to this house, since he also is a son of Abraham. For the Son of Man came to seek and to save the lost.'"		

STEWARDSHIP: Lesson 1

PROCLAMATION

BIG IDEA:

God is the owner of everything, and God stewards everything.

FOCUS VOCABULARY:

- **Steward:** To take care of something.

OBJECTIVES:

- Kids can define stewardship.
- Kids can identify the owner of everything.

KEY POINTS:

God owns everything.

- God made everything out of nothing, and God takes care of what he makes. Because God made and is in charge of everything in the world, he is also the real owner of everything.
    - Have you ever looked at a toy or a book or something special to you and said, "That's mine"? You're not quite telling the whole story. While it may be a gift God has given to you to enjoy and take care of for a while, God is really the one in charge of it. God is the real owner of everything.
    - Everyone and everything belongs to God.[145]
        - The air we breathe belongs to God.
        - The food we eat belongs to God.
        - The clothes we wear belong to God.
        - The toys we play with belong to God.
        - The friends we love belong to God.
    - Yes, *everything* belongs to God. He sure gives us lots of good gifts, doesn't he?

[145] Driscoll and Breshears, *Doctrine*, 373.

God stewards everything.

- "To steward" means to take care of something. You can steward something that belongs to you, and you can also steward something that someone has given to you to take special care of for a little while.
- God is the owner of everything, and he takes care of everything. This means that God is a steward.

Gospel Link: How does what we know about stewardship connect to the gospel, the good news of God's Rescue Plan through Jesus?

- God's Rescue Plan shows us that God is the best steward of all. He promised to take care of his people by sending Jesus the Rescuer even though we disobeyed him by sinning.
- Because Jesus lived a perfect life as God and man, died to pay the penalty for our sin, and conquered death by rising to live forever with God, we can be part of the Forever Family of God—worshiping him forever—if we believe in Jesus as the Savior from sin.
    - In Acts, a book in the New Testament of the Bible, God tells us, "Believe in the Lord Jesus, and you will be saved."[146]
        - If you want to talk more about Jesus as your Rescuer, feel free to talk to your dad or mom, your teacher or Community Group leader, or to read the Bible and talk to Jesus.

APPLICATION

DISCUSSION:

- Who owns everything?
- What does God take care of?
- How does God's Rescue Plan connect to you?

SCRIPTURE:

Read:

- Read 2 Chronicles 2–4 as a family this week and discuss ways in which Solomon was a steward of the gifts that God gave him.

Explore:

- 1 Peter 4:10: "As each has received a gift, use it to serve one another, as good stewards of God's varied grace."

[146] Acts 16:31.

PRAYER:

- Thank God for the gifts he has given you.
- If you have believed in Jesus as the Savior from sin, pray that the Holy Spirit will help you to be a better steward in response to Jesus, who is the best steward of all.

ADDITIONAL RESOURCES:

- Mark Driscoll and Gerry Breshears, *Doctrine: What Christians Should Believe* (Wheaton, IL: Crossway, 2010), 373.
- Marty Machowski, *The Gospel Story Bible: Discovering Jesus in the Old and New Testaments* (Greensboro, NC: New Growth Press, 2011), 188.

STEWARDSHIP: Lesson 2

PROCLAMATION

BIG IDEA:

We get to steward what God gives us by taking care of it.

FOCUS VOCABULARY:

- **Steward:** To take care of something.

OBJECTIVES:

- Kids can define stewardship.
- Kids can describe how Jesus is the best steward of all.

KEY POINTS:

We get to be stewards.

- "To steward" means to take care of something. You can steward something that belongs to you, and you can also steward something that someone has given to you to take special care of for a little while.
    - Since God is the owner of everything, everything that you have is a gift that God has given to you to take special care of for a little while.
    - The things that you steward (or take care of) are both for you to enjoy and for you to use to love and help other people.
- When you think about the fact that everything you have is a gift from God for you to take special care of, it makes you want to treat things really well.
    - We have talked about how worshiping God is really, really loving him and living for him. Did you know that taking special care of the things that he has given you is a way you can worship him?
        - When you care for the things God has given to you to steward because you love Jesus in your heart, you are worshiping!

Jesus is the best steward of all.

- By living out God's Rescue Plan, Jesus was the best steward of all. Living as both God and man on this earth, Jesus showed how to take care of what God had given him during his life. But at the same time, he was taking perfect care of all people at all times by being the Savior from sin.

- "We might think food and clothing are our most important needs, but we have a bigger need: we all need to be forgiven for our sins. Jesus died on the cross so we can be forgiven. He took care of our biggest need. . . . God was willing to give up his only Son to take our sins away."[147]

Gospel Link: How does what we know about stewardship connect to the gospel, the good news of God's Rescue Plan through Jesus?

- God's Rescue Plan shows us that God is the best steward of all. He promised to take care of his people by sending Jesus the Rescuer even though we disobeyed him by sinning.
- Because Jesus lived a perfect life as God and man, died to pay the penalty for our sin, and conquered death by rising to live forever with God, we can be part of the Forever Family of God—worshiping him forever—if we believe in Jesus as the Savior from sin.
  - In Acts, a book in the New Testament of the Bible, God tells us, "Believe in the Lord Jesus, and you will be saved."[148]
    - If you want to talk more about Jesus as your Rescuer, feel free to talk to your dad or mom, your teacher or Community Group leader, or to read the Bible and talk to Jesus.

APPLICATION

DISCUSSION:

- What does it mean to steward something? Why should you steward?
- How was Jesus the best steward of all?
- How does God's Rescue Plan connect to you?

SCRIPTURE: *Review the Scriptures you began exploring last week.*

Read:

- Read 2 Chronicles 2–4 as a family this week and discuss ways in which Solomon was a steward of the gifts that God gave him.

Explore:

- 1 Peter 4:10: "As each has received a gift, use it to serve one another, as good stewards of God's varied grace."

[147] Machowski, *The Gospel Story Bible*, 188.
[148] Acts 16:31.

PRAYER:

- Thank God for the gifts he has given you.
- If you have believed in Jesus as the Savior from sin, pray that the Holy Spirit will help you to be a better steward in response to Jesus, who is the best steward of all.

ADDITIONAL RESOURCES:

- Mark Driscoll and Gerry Breshears, *Doctrine: What Christians Should Believe* (Wheaton, IL: Crossway, 2010), 373.
- Marty Machowski, *The Gospel Story Bible: Discovering Jesus in the Old and New Testaments* (Greensboro, NC: New Growth Press, 2011), 188.

STEWARDSHIP: Lesson 3

PROCLAMATION

BIG IDEA:

We get to steward our time because it is a gift from God.

FOCUS VOCABULARY:

- **Steward:** To take care of something.

OBJECTIVES:

- Kids can describe what it means to steward their time.
- Kids can connect good stewardship to Jesus, who is the best steward of all.

KEY POINTS:

We get to steward our time.

- God gives us some gifts over and over every single day. Do you know one of the gifts that God gives us most often? It's time! Every second that passes is a second that God has given us to take good care of for his glory.
  - Let's count for ten seconds. *(Count backwards from ten.)* That's ten seconds God gave us right there! And he is giving us time constantly.
  - Because God made time and gives it to us as a free gift for his glory, we get to take good care of it. What do you think it could mean to take good care of your time?
  - When people who love Jesus take care of their time by doing what God tells them to do with their time, they are worshiping him.
- We can steward our time with work.
  - The Bible says a lot about work: God made us to work, work hard, enjoy our work, get food and clothes with our work, and more.[149]
  - Sometimes work can be having a job. For example, your dad might have a job so he can take care of your family. He works, but while he works he worships God in his heart by really, really loving him and living for him.

[149] Driscoll and Breshears, *Doctrine*, 380.

- Sometimes work can be volunteering at church or helping someone. Your teachers and Community Group leaders are all working by volunteering. By helping you and playing with you because they love Jesus in their hearts, they are worshiping God.

- We can steward our time with rest.
  - Even God enjoyed a day of rest (called a Sabbath day) after he finished creating the world. He rested and saw that everything was good.
  - Jesus rested, too. While he lived on this earth as both God and man, he often went away to be on his own to rest and talk to God by praying.

Knowing Jesus, the best steward of all, makes us want to take care of things well.

- Taking care of our time is only worship if we are really, really loving Jesus and living for him while we do it. If we are doing it to be good or to get a compliment from someone else, we are not worshiping Jesus.
  - Every day, we get it wrong. We do things for ourselves and disobey God because we sin.
  - But every day, seeing our sin also shows us that we need Jesus. When the Holy Spirit helps us see our sin, we get to tell Jesus that we are sorry and ask him to forgive us. First John 1:9 says, "If we confess our sins, he is faithful and just to forgive us our sins and to cleanse us from all unrighteousness."
  - Over and over, when we realize that he loves and forgives us every time, we get to remember that Jesus is the Forever Rescuer. We receive his grace and we *celebrate!* Because that's good news!

Gospel Link: How does what we know about stewardship connect to the gospel, the good news of God's Rescue Plan through Jesus?

- God's Rescue Plan shows us that God is the best steward of all. He promised to take care of his people by sending Jesus the Rescuer even though we disobeyed him by sinning.
- Because Jesus lived a perfect life as God and man, died to pay the penalty for our sin, and conquered death by rising to live forever with God, we can be part of the Forever Family of God—worshiping him forever—if we believe in Jesus as the Savior from sin.
  - In Acts, a book in the New Testament of the Bible, God tells us, "Believe in the Lord Jesus, and you will be saved."[150]
    - If you want to talk more about Jesus as your Rescuer, feel free to talk to your dad or mom, your teacher or Community Group leader, or to read the Bible and talk to Jesus.

[150] Acts 16:31.

APPLICATION

DISCUSSION:

- How can you worship God by taking care of your time? How can you use your time well by working? By resting?
- Describe a time when you did not take good care of your time. How does Jesus respond?
- How does God's Rescue Plan connect to you?

SCRIPTURE:

Read:

- Read 2 Corinthians 9:6–15 as a family and discuss the ways that your family stewards your treasure.

Explore:

- 2 Corinthians 9:9: "As it is written, 'He has distributed freely, he has given to the poor; his righteousness endures forever.'"

PRAYER:

- Thank Jesus for being the best steward of all so that we can be part of his family if we believe.
- Pray that Jesus will help you and your family to steward your time in worship of who he is.

ADDITIONAL RESOURCES:

- Mark Driscoll and Gerry Breshears, *Doctrine: What Christians Should Believe* (Wheaton, IL: Crossway, 2010), 380.
- Marty Machowski, *The Gospel Story Bible: Discovering Jesus in the Old and New Testaments* (Greensboro, NC: New Growth Press, 2011), 270.

STEWARDSHIP: Lesson 4

PROCLAMATION

BIG IDEA:

We get to steward our talent and treasure because they are gifts from God.

FOCUS VOCABULARY:

- **Talent:** The things that you are really good at; the things that God made you especially able to do.
- **Treasure:** Your money and other things you have that are really special to you.

OBJECTIVES:

- Kids can describe what it means to steward their talent.
- Kids can describe what it means to steward their treasure.
- Kids can connect good stewardship to Jesus, who is the best steward of all.

KEY POINTS:

We get to steward our talent.

- God gives each person special gifts. He gives each of us things that we really love to do or are especially good at. These things are called talents.
- We take care of our talents by using them in ways that show who Jesus is. Remember, when you believe in Jesus as your Savior from sin, you are invited to worship with your talents.
    - We can steward our talents by using them to help other people.
        - For example, someone who is a really amazing guitar player can steward his music talent by using it to help other people. He could play for people who don't get to hear music very often, or he could play in a band at church to worship Jesus.
        - When someone sees who Jesus is—the amazing Forever Rescuer who loves us and saves us no matter what when we believe in him—they want to use *everything* to whisper, "Thank you, Jesus!" and to murmur, "I love you Jesus!" They even use their talents—the things they are very best at.

We get to steward our treasure.

- Your treasure means your money and other things you have that are really special to you.
- One way we can steward our money is by sharing it. In a book of the Bible called 2 Corinthians, God inspired Paul to tell us about giving money to help other people.
    - "Paul knew God wanted people to give for the right reasons. He wanted their hearts to be filled with love as they shared what they had with others. So the Holy Spirit inspired Paul to say in his letter that . . . 'God loves a cheerful giver.'"[151]
    - "Isn't it good to read about God's people sharing their money to help the poor? Paul tells us it was the gospel at work in their hearts that made them want to give. Before we know and love Jesus, we desire the treasures of the world. But when God helps us see how much Jesus has given us—forgiveness of sins and eternal life in heaven—the things of this world don't seem so important anymore. . . . And when we understand that everything we have comes from God—including our money—it is easier to share it with others. We know God will supply all we need."[152]
- What we spend our money on shows what we worship. It shows what we really, really love and live for.
    - If we share our money and things that are special to us with others, we are showing that we love other people and want to be generous with them like Jesus is generous with us.
    - If we keep all our money or spend it all on ourselves, we are showing that we really, really love ourselves more than God.
- The Bible says *a lot* about taking care of our money. Be sure to ask your parent or Community Group leader to tell you more about what the Bible teaches us about money.

Knowing Jesus, the best steward of all, makes us want to take care of things well.

- Taking care of our talent and treasure is only worship if we are really, really loving Jesus and living for him while we do it. If we are doing it to be good or to get a compliment from someone else, we are not worshiping Jesus.
    - Every day, we get it wrong. We do things for ourselves and disobey God because we sin.
    - But every day, seeing our sin also shows us that we need Jesus. When the Holy Spirit helps us see our sin, we get to tell Jesus that we are sorry and ask him to forgive us. First John 1:9 says, "If we confess our sins, he is faithful and just to forgive us our sins and to cleanse us from all unrighteousness."
    - Over and over, when we realize that he loves and forgives us every time, we get to remember that Jesus is the Forever Rescuer. We receive his grace and we *celebrate!* Because that's good news!

---

[151] Machowski, *The Gospel Story Bible*, 270.
[152] Ibid.

Gospel Link: How does what we know about stewardship connect to the gospel, the good news of God's Rescue Plan through Jesus?

- God's Rescue Plan shows us that God is the best steward of all. He promised to take care of his people by sending Jesus the Rescuer even though we disobeyed him by sinning.
- Because Jesus lived a perfect life as God and man, died to pay the penalty for our sin, and conquered death by rising to live forever with God, we can be part of the Forever Family of God—worshiping him forever—if we believe in Jesus as the Savior from sin.
  - In Acts, a book in the New Testament of the Bible, God tells us, "Believe in the Lord Jesus, and you will be saved."[153]
    - If you want to talk more about Jesus as your Rescuer, feel free to talk to your dad or mom, your teacher or Community Group leader, or to read the Bible and talk to Jesus.

APPLICATION

DISCUSSION:

- What are you really good at? How could you steward your talent well?
- How can you take care of your treasure? How does taking care of your treasure connect to Jesus?
- Describe a time when you did not take good care of your treasure. How does Jesus respond?
- How does God's Rescue Plan connect to you?

SCRIPTURE: *Review the Scriptures you began exploring last week.*

Read:

- Read 2 Corinthians 9:6–15 as a family and discuss the ways that your family stewards your treasure.

Explore:

- 2 Corinthians 9:9: "As it is written, 'He has distributed freely, he has given to the poor; his righteousness endures forever.'"

[153] Acts 16:31.

PRAYER:

- Thank Jesus for being the best steward of all so that we can be part of his family if we believe.
- Pray that Jesus will help you and your family to steward your talent and treasure in worship of who he is.

ADDITIONAL RESOURCES:

- Mark Driscoll and Gerry Breshears, *Doctrine: What Christians Should Believe* (Wheaton, IL: Crossway, 2010), 380.
- Marty Machowski, *The Gospel Story Bible: Discovering Jesus in the Old and New Testaments* (Greensboro, NC: New Growth Press, 2011), 270.

STEWARDSHIP: 4/5/6 Activity 1

Circle and color pictures that show kids stewarding things well.
Cross out pictures that show kids not stewarding well.

STEWARDSHIP: 4/5/6 Activity 2

Circle and color examples of treasure that you can share with others. Remember that you are worshiping if you are sharing in response to who Jesus is and what he has shared with you.

Cross out things that are not examples of treasure.

STEWARDSHIP: 7+ Activity 1

Re-read 2 Chronicles 2–4, then answer the questions based on the verses below to further unpack the example of stewardship in the Old Testament that you have already looked at.

Scripture	What is going on in this verse?	Do you think Solomon is stewarding God's gifts? Why do you think so?
2 Chronicles 4:7: "And he made ten golden lampstands as prescribed, and set them in the temple, five on the south side and five on the north."		
2 Chronicles 4:19–21: "So Solomon made all the vessels that were in the house of God: the golden altar, the tables for the bread of the Presence, the lampstands and their lamps of pure gold to burn before the inner sanctuary, as prescribed; the flowers, the lamps, and the tongs, of purest gold."		
2 Chronicles 5:1: "Thus all the work that Solomon did for the house of the LORD was finished. And Solomon brought in the things that David his father had dedicated, and stored the silver, the gold, and all the vessels in the treasuries of the house of God."		
Can you find another verse that describes Solomon as a good steward? Write it here.		

STEWARDSHIP: 7+ Activity 2

Scripture	In your own words, what is this verse saying?	What does this verse teach you about what it means to be a good steward?
1 Peter 4:10: "As each has received a gift, use it to serve one another, as good stewards of God's varied grace."		
James 1:16–17: "Do not be deceived, my beloved brothers. Every good gift and every perfect gift is from above, coming down from the Father of lights with whom there is no variation or shadow due to change."		
Matthew 6:24: "'No one can serve two masters, for either he will hate the one and love the other, or he will be devoted to the one and despise the other. You cannot serve God and money.'"		
Acts 20:35: "In all things I have shown you that by working hard in this way we must help the weak and remember the words of the Lord Jesus, how he himself said, 'It is more blessed to give than to receive.'"		
John 14:12: "'Truly, truly, I say to you, whoever believes in me will also do the works that I do; and greater works than these will he do, because I am going to the Father.'"		

KINGDOM: Lesson 1

PROCLAMATION

BIG IDEA:

Jesus is King of a Kingdom.

FOCUS VOCABULARY:

- **King:** The person in charge of a kingdom.
- **Kingdom:** The place that a king is in charge of and rules over.

OBJECTIVES:

- Kids can identify Jesus as King.
- Kids can describe Jesus' kingdom.

KEY POINTS:

Jesus is King.

- "Jesus is God. As God, Jesus is the king of all the earth and he is the one who makes its laws and who explains what they really mean."[154]
- There is no other king like Jesus. The book of Revelation in the Bible says that Jesus is the "Lord of lords and King of kings."[155]
- In the same book of the Bible, God tells us that Jesus is seated on a throne, ruling as King over all creation, "including all peoples, times, and places."[156]
- Not just that, Jesus is a warrior king! One day, Jesus will wear white and ride a white horse as he leads his army to go to war against people who do not believe in him. Jesus is Ruler over everything and everyone.[157]

Jesus rules a kingdom.

- "One day Jesus was telling people about God's kingdom. 'God's kingdom is wherever God is King,' Jesus told them. 'It's wherever God is in charge. It's where he fills your heart

---

[154] Meade, *Mighty Acts of God*, 183.
[155] Rev. 17:14.
[156] Driscoll and Breshears, *Doctrine*, 417.
[157] Ibid., 418.

up with his Forever Happiness and you stop running away from him and you love him."[158]

- In some ways, Jesus' kingdom is right here and right now. Right now, there are people who love Jesus and believe in him as the Savior from sin. In those people's hearts, God is in charge. God is King. He is already filling hearts up with Forever Happiness.
- In other ways, Jesus' kingdom is still coming. There is still sin in the world—there are sad things and broken things. Jesus is in charge of all things, but we are still waiting for his future kingdom to see all the sad things come untrue. He has promised to rescue the whole world and make it new. That part is still coming.

Gospel Link: How does what we know about Jesus' kingdom and the new earth connect to the gospel, the good news of God's Rescue Plan through Jesus?

- The new earth is a place for people who have believed in Jesus as the Savior from sin—people who know that no matter how hard they try to be good and keep the rules on their own, they have sinned.
  - In Acts, a book in the New Testament of the Bible, God tells us, "Believe in the Lord Jesus, and you will be saved."[159]
    - Jesus lived a perfect life as God and man, died to pay the penalty for our sin, and conquered death by rising to live forever with God. When Jesus changes your heart to believe this is true—to believe in him as the Savior from sin—you also become part of God's family. You get to live with him in Jesus' Forever Kingdom.
    - If you want to talk more about Jesus as your Rescuer, feel free to talk to your dad or mom, your teacher or Community Group leader, or to read the Bible and talk to Jesus.

APPLICATION

DISCUSSION:

- Who is King of everything? What does it mean to be king?
- What is God's kingdom?
- Do you need Jesus? Why do you think so?

SCRIPTURE:

Read:

- Read selections from Revelation together as a family. Identify the promises that you see Jesus make and the promises you see him keep in the text.

---

[158] Lloyd-Jones, *The Jesus Storybook Bible*, 250.
[159] Acts 16:31.

Explore:

- Matthew 6:10: "'Your kingdom come, your will be done, on earth as it is in heaven.'"

PRAYER:

- Thank God for inviting people who believe in Jesus to live with him forever in a better-than-before world.
- Pray that the kids in your family will worship Jesus as King.

ADDITIONAL RESOURCES:

- Sergio Cariello, illus., *The Action Bible: God's Redemptive Story,* ed. Doug Mauss (Colorado Springs, CO: David C. Cook, 2010). See especially "Praying Lessons" (597–599).
- Mark Driscoll and Gerry Breshears, *Doctrine: What Christians Should Believe* (Wheaton, IL: Crossway, 2010), 417–418.
- David R. Helm, *The Big Picture Story Bible* (Wheaton, IL: Crossway, 2004), 447–453.
- Sally Lloyd-Jones, *The Jesus Storybook Bible: Every Story Whispers His Name* (Grand Rapids, MI: Zondervan, 2007), 250, 342–348.
- Starr Meade, *Mighty Acts of God: A Family Bible Story Book* (Wheaton, IL: Crossway, 2010), 183, 288.

KINGDOM: Lesson 2

PROCLAMATION

BIG IDEA:

King Jesus is making all things new.

FOCUS VOCABULARY:

- **King:** The person in charge of a kingdom.
- **Kingdom:** The place that a king is in charge of and rules over.

OBJECTIVES:

- Kids can identify Jesus as King.
- Kids can explain what it means that Jesus is making all things new.

KEY POINTS:

Jesus is King.

- "Jesus is God. As God, Jesus is the king of all the earth and he is the one who makes its laws and who explains what they really mean."[160]
- There is no other king like Jesus. The book of Revelation in the Bible says that Jesus is the "Lord of lords and King of kings."[161]
- In the same book of the Bible, God tells us that Jesus is seated on a throne, ruling as King over all creation, "including all peoples, times, and places."[162]
- Not just that, Jesus is a warrior king! One day, Jesus will wear white and ride a white horse as he leads his army to go to war against people who do not believe in him. Jesus is Ruler over everything and everyone.[163]

King Jesus is making all things new.

- If you have believed in Jesus as your Savior from sin, you will have a better-than-before

---

[160] Meade, *Mighty Acts of God*, 183.
[161] Rev. 17:14.
[162] Driscoll and Breshears, *Doctrine*, 417.
[163] Ibid., 418.

body one day. God is going to make the whole world better than before. Right here on this earth, God is going to make a new creation! He is going to make all things new.

- God gave one of the disciples, named John, a vision of the new earth God promised to bring one day. He told John about the new earth that will be your Forever Home with Jesus if you believe in him.[164]
- God inspired John to write it down in the book of Revelation in the Bible so we could have a preview of what the world will be like some day. Listen to what it will be like:
    - "John saw the city where God's people would live. It was radiant with glory, having foundations built of jewels. The twelve city gates were twelve giant pearls, and the streets were paved with gold. (Now, before you expect that there really is a city just like this in heaven, keep in mind that the things John saw in his vision were symbols, pictures of what will be. Whatever these things will really be like, they will be at least as good as the things John saw in his visions.) The city John saw was a perfectly safe city, in which there could be no sin. It needed no sun or moon because Jesus himself was in the city, giving it all the light it needed. People from all the nations would live in this city. A river flowed down the middle of the city's main street. On the riverbank grew the tree of life, with twelve different kinds of fruit, and with leaves that brought healing to the nations."[165]
    - "The best thing about the city was this: 'the throne of God and of the Lamb will be in it, and his servants will worship him. They will see his face, and his name will be on their foreheads.'"[166]
    - "One day, John knew, Heaven would come down and mend God's broken world and make it our true, perfect home once again. And he knew, in some mysterious way that would be hard to explain, that everything was going to be more wonderful for once having been so sad. And he knew then that the ending of The Story was going to be so great, it would make all the sadness and tears and everything seem like just a shadow that is chased away by the morning sun. 'I'm on my way,' said Jesus. 'I'll be there soon!'"[167]
    - The King will say, "'Look! God and his children are together again. No more running away. Or hiding. No more crying or being lonely or afraid. No more being sick or dying. Because all those things are gone. Yes, they're gone forever. Everything sad has come untrue. And see—I have wiped away every tear from every eye! . . . Look, I am making everything new!'"[168]
    - "And then . . . John awoke from his vision. John smiled. John knew. All God's promises, all the things Jesus had told him years ago, were true! The old man could hardly write fast enough. He had seen the very good ending waiting for everyone who follows Jesus as God's king. God's forever people will one day live in God's forever place under God's forever rule. Can you believe it? Amen. Come, Lord Jesus!"[169]

---

[164] Driscoll and Breshears, *Doctrine*, 423.
[165] Meade, *Mighty Acts of God*, 288.
[166] Ibid.
[167] Lloyd-Jones, *The Jesus Storybook Bible*, 348.
[168] Ibid., 347.
[169] Helm, *The Big Picture Story Bible*, 447–453.

- We get to wait with "happy excitement" for the world that Jesus is bringing.[170]

Gospel Link: How does what we know about Jesus' kingdom and the new earth connect to the gospel, the good news of God's Rescue Plan through Jesus?

- The new earth is a place for people who have believed in Jesus as the Savior from sin—people who know that no matter how hard they try to be good and keep the rules on their own, they have sinned.
  - In Acts, a book in the New Testament of the Bible, God tells us, "Believe in the Lord Jesus, and you will be saved."[171]
    - Jesus lived a perfect life as God and man, died to pay the penalty for our sin, and conquered death by rising to live forever with God. When Jesus changes your heart to believe this is true—to believe in him as the Savior from sin—you also become part of God's family. You get to live with him in Jesus' Forever Kingdom.
    - If you want to talk more about Jesus as your Rescuer, feel free to talk to your dad or mom, your teacher or Community Group leader, or to read the Bible and talk to Jesus.

APPLICATION

DISCUSSION:

- Who is King of everything? What does it mean to be king?
- What will the new earth be like?
- Do you need Jesus? Why do you think so?

SCRIPTURE: *Review the Scriptures you began exploring last week.*

Read:

- Read selections from Revelation together as a family. Identify the promises that you see Jesus make and the promises you see him keep in the text.

Explore:

- Matthew 6:10: "'Your kingdom come, your will be done, on earth as it is in heaven.'"

PRAYER:

- Thank God for inviting people who believe in Jesus to live with him forever in a better-than-before world.
- Pray that the kids in your family will worship Jesus as King.

---

[170] Lloyd-Jones, *The Jesus Storybook Bible*, 342.
[171] Acts 16:31

ADDITIONAL RESOURCES:

- Sergio Cariello, illus., *The Action Bible: God's Redemptive Story,* ed. Doug Mauss (Colorado Springs, CO: David C. Cook, 2010). See especially "Praying Lessons" (597-599).
- Mark Driscoll and Gerry Breshears, *Doctrine: What Christians Should Believe* (Wheaton, IL: Crossway, 2010), 417–418.
- David R. Helm, *The Big Picture Story Bible* (Wheaton, IL: Crossway, 2004), 447–453.
- Sally Lloyd-Jones, *The Jesus Storybook Bible: Every Story Whispers His Name* (Grand Rapids, MI: Zondervan, 2007), 250, 342–348.
- Starr Meade, *Mighty Acts of God: A Family Bible Story Book* (Wheaton, IL: Crossway, 2010), 183, 288.

KINGDOM: Lesson 3

PROCLAMATION

BIG IDEA:

Jesus' kingdom has already begun.

FOCUS VOCABULARY:

- **Kingdom:** The place that a king is in charge of and rules over.
- **Already:** Something that has happened or started in the past.

OBJECTIVES:

- Kids can describe the pieces of Jesus' kingdom that have already arrived.
- Kids can connect Jesus' kingdom to themselves.

KEY POINTS:

Jesus is King.

- "Jesus is God. As God, Jesus is the king of all the earth and he is the one who makes its laws and who explains what they really mean."[172]
- There is no other king like Jesus. The book of Revelation in the Bible says that Jesus is the "Lord of lords and King of kings."[173]
- In the same book of the Bible, God tells us that Jesus is seated on a throne, ruling as King over all creation, "including all peoples, times, and places."[174]
- Not just that, Jesus is a warrior king! One day, Jesus will wear white and ride a white horse as he leads his army to go to war against people who do not believe in him. Jesus is Ruler over everything and everyone.[175]

Jesus' kingdom has *already* begun.

- Jesus' kingdom has already begun because Jesus has already lived, died, and risen from the dead.

---

[172] Meade, *Mighty Acts of God*, 183.
[173] Rev. 17:14.
[174] Driscoll and Breshears, *Doctrine*, 417.
[175] Ibid., 418.

- "Through the centuries of Old Testament history, God's people had waited for the perfect King he had promised to send them. When Jesus came to earth, the kingdom of heaven had arrived. When he began preaching, Jesus said, 'The time is fulfilled, and the kingdom of God is at hand; repent and believe in the gospel.'"[176]

  - Jesus' kingdom has already begun because Jesus has already started changing hearts to worship him.

    - "One day Jesus was telling people about God's kingdom. 'God's kingdom is wherever God is King,' Jesus told them. 'It's wherever God is in charge. It's where he fills your heart up with his Forever Happiness and you stop running away from him and you love him.'"[177]

      - Jesus has already begun his kingdom, because he is already changing hearts so that people love him and live for him. If you love Jesus and believe in him as the Savior from sin, his kingdom has already begun *right in your own heart!*

      - Jesus' kingdom isn't something that is far away or separate from us. God is in charge of our hearts. When he fills our hearts "with his Forever Happiness and [we] stop running away from him and [we] love him," God's kingdom is already here—smack dab in the middle of our hearts![178]

        - "Being where God is—being in his kingdom—that's more important than anything else in all the world."[179]

Gospel Link: How does what we know about Jesus' kingdom and the new earth connect to the gospel, the good news of God's Rescue Plan through Jesus?

  - The new earth is a place for people who have believed in Jesus as the Savior from sin—people who know that no matter how hard they try to be good and keep the rules on their own, they have sinned.

    - In Acts, a book in the New Testament of the Bible, God tells us, "Believe in the Lord Jesus, and you will be saved."[180]

      - Jesus lived a perfect life as God and man, died to pay the penalty for our sin, and conquered death by rising to live forever with God. When Jesus changes your heart to believe this is true—to believe in him as the Savior from sin—you also become part of God's family. You get to live with him in Jesus' Forever Kingdom.

      - If you want to talk more about Jesus as your Rescuer, feel free to talk to your dad or mom, your teacher or Community Group leader, or to read the Bible and talk to Jesus.

---

[176] Meade, *Mighty Acts of God*, 173–174.
[177] Lloyd-Jones, *The Jesus Storybook Bible*, 250.
[178] Ibid.
[179] Ibid., 255.
[180] Acts 16:31.

APPLICATION

DISCUSSION:

- Who is King of everything? What does it mean to be king?
- How has Jesus' kingdom already started?
- Do you need Jesus? Why do you think so?

SCRIPTURE:

Read:

- Read Revelation 22 as a family. Discuss what it teaches you about how Jesus' kingdom is already and not yet.

Explore:

- Revelation 21:4: "'He will wipe away every tear from their eyes, and death shall be no more, neither shall there be mourning, nor crying, nor pain anymore, for the former things have passed away.'"

PRAYER:

- Thank God for his Rescue Plan. Thank him for showing us that Jesus' kingdom has already begun.
- Thank God for being a promise keeper. Pray that he will help you to wait with happy excitement for Jesus' better-than-before creation, and that he will use you to help carry out his special mission between now and then.
- Pray that the kids in your family will be saved by God's grace and will get to enjoy a Forever Home with Jesus.

ADDITIONAL RESOURCES:

- David R. Helm, *The Big Picture Story Bible* (Wheaton, IL: Crossway, 2004), 366.
- Sally Lloyd-Jones, *The Jesus Storybook Bible: Every Story Whispers His Name* (Grand Rapids, MI: Zondervan, 2007), 250–255.
- Marty Machowski, *The Gospel Story Bible: Discovering Jesus in the Old and New Testaments* (Greensboro, NC: New Growth Press, 2011), 313.
- Starr Meade, *Mighty Acts of God: A Family Bible Story Book* (Wheaton, IL: Crossway, 2010), 173–174.

KINGDOM: Lesson 4

PROCLAMATION

BIG IDEA:

Jesus' kingdom has not yet fully arrived.

FOCUS VOCABULARY:

- **Kingdom:** The place that a king is in charge of and rules over.
- **Not yet:** Something that has not happened that you are expecting. It is still coming.

OBJECTIVES:

- Kids can describe the pieces of Jesus' kingdom that are still coming.
- Kids can connect Jesus' kingdom to themselves.

KEY POINTS:

Jesus is King.

- "Jesus is God. As God, Jesus is the king of all the earth and he is the one who makes its laws and who explains what they really mean."[181]
- There is no other king like Jesus. The book of Revelation in the Bible says that Jesus is the "Lord of lords and King of kings."[182]
- In the same book of the Bible, God tells us that Jesus is seated on a throne, ruling as King over all creation, "including all peoples, times, and places."[183]
- Not just that, Jesus is a warrior king! One day, Jesus will wear white and ride a white horse as he leads his army to go to war against people who do not believe in him. Jesus is Ruler over everything and everyone.[184]

Jesus' kingdom has *not yet* fully arrived.

- We get to wait in happy excitement for the parts of Jesus' kingdom that are not here yet.

---

[181] Meade, *Mighty Acts of God*, 183.
[182] Rev. 17:14.
[183] Driscoll and Breshears, *Doctrine*, 417.
[184] Ibid., 418.

- When a man named Pilate asked Jesus, "'Are you the King?' Jesus answered, 'My kingdom is not of this world.'"[185]
    - This shows us that there are pieces of Jesus' kingdom that aren't here in the world that we know.
    - Jesus tells us lots about the new earth in the book of Revelation. We learned lots of things about this better-than-before world last week.
    - If you have believed in Jesus as the Savior from sin, you know that the new earth, your Forever Home with Jesus, isn't here yet because there is still a lot of sin in the world. People get sick; there are wars; people get hurt. There is still a lot of sadness and wrong in the world. Jesus' all-things-new world where you get to live forever with God isn't here . . . Yet!

We get to worship Jesus as we wait for the "not yet" to arrive.

- We know that one day a world where everything is new is coming. While we wait with happy excitement, God lets us help bring that world about by carrying out his special mission if we have believed in Jesus: telling as many people as possible about Jesus the Rescuer.
- "The book of Revelation gives us a sneak peek at how everything in God's plan will finally happen. God's promise to step on the head of the serpent and bring people together from every nation will one day come true. Until Jesus comes back our faith can get stronger by reading the end of the story. If you put your trust in Jesus and what he did on the cross, one day you will be there with millions of others, worshiping at the throne of God. You will join all the believers who ever lived and take your place in the last chapter of God's gospel story. What a great day that will be!"[186]

Gospel Link: How does what we know about Jesus' kingdom and the new earth connect to the gospel, the good news of God's Rescue Plan through Jesus?

- The new earth is a place for people who have believed in Jesus as the Savior from sin—people who know that no matter how hard they try to be good and keep the rules on their own, they have sinned.
    - In Acts, a book in the New Testament of the Bible, God tells us, "Believe in the Lord Jesus, and you will be saved."[187]
        - Jesus lived a perfect life as God and man, died to pay the penalty for our sin, and conquered death by rising to live forever with God. When Jesus changes your heart to believe this is true—to believe in him as the Savior from sin—you also become part of God's family. You get to live with him in Jesus' Forever Kingdom.
        - If you want to talk more about Jesus as your Rescuer, feel free to talk to your dad or mom, your teacher or Community Group leader, or to read the Bible and talk to Jesus.

---

[185] Helm, *The Big Picture Story Bible*, 366.
[186] Machowski, *The Gospel Story Bible*, 313.
[187] Acts 16:31.

APPLICATION

DISCUSSION:

- Who is King of everything? What does it mean to be king?
- Is Jesus' kingdom here yet? How do you know?
- Have you put your trust in Jesus and what he did on the cross? What does that mean for your eternity?
- Do you need Jesus? Why do you think so?

SCRIPTURE: *Review the Scriptures you began exploring last week.*

Read:

- Read Revelation 22 as a family. Discuss what it teaches you about how Jesus' kingdom is already and not yet.

Explore:

- Revelation 21:4: "'He will wipe away every tear from their eyes, and death shall be no more, neither shall there be mourning, nor crying, nor pain anymore, for the former things have passed away.'"

PRAYER:

- Thank God for his Rescue Plan. Thank him for showing us that Jesus' kingdom has already begun.
- Thank God for being a promise keeper. Pray that he will help you to wait with happy excitement for Jesus' better-than-before creation, and that he will use you to help carry out his special mission between now and then.
- Pray that the kids in your family will be saved by God's grace and will get to enjoy a Forever Home with Jesus.

ADDITIONAL RESOURCES:

- David R. Helm, *The Big Picture Story Bible* (Wheaton, IL: Crossway, 2004), 366.
- Sally Lloyd-Jones, *The Jesus Storybook Bible: Every Story Whispers His Name* (Grand Rapids, MI: Zondervan, 2007), 250–255.
- Marty Machowski, *The Gospel Story Bible: Discovering Jesus in the Old and New Testaments* (Greensboro, NC: New Growth Press, 2011), 313.
- Starr Meade, *Mighty Acts of God: A Family Bible Story Book* (Wheaton, IL: Crossway, 2010), 173–174.

KINGDOM: 4/5/6 Activity 1

What will the new earth be like? Will it be a good Forever Home? Sketch a picture of what you think the new earth will look like in the box below.

KINGDOM: 4/5/6 Activity 2

We know that Jesus' kingdom is already and not yet. Look at each picture and ask yourself, "Has this part of Jesus' kingdom arrived already, or not yet?" Next to each picture, write "A" for already or "N" for not yet.

KINGDOM: 7+ Activity 1

Scripture	In your own words, what is this verse saying?	What does this verse teach you about Jesus' kingdom?
Revelation 1:12–16: "Then I turned to see the voice that was speaking to me, and on turning I saw seven golden lampstands, and in the midst of the lampstands one like a son of man, clothed with a long robe and with a golden sash around his chest. The hairs of his head were white, like white wool, like snow. His eyes were like a flame of fire, his feet were like burnished bronze, refined in a furnace, and his voice was like the roar of many waters. In his right hand he held seven stars, from his mouth came a sharp two-edged sword, and his face was like the sun shining in full strength."		
Revelation 1:17–18: "When I saw him, I fell at his feet as though dead. But he laid his right hand on me, saying, 'Fear not, I am the first and the last, and the living one. I died, and behold I am alive forevermore, and I have the keys of Death and Hades.'"		
Choose another verse from Revelation that teaches you about Jesus' kingdom. Write the verse here.		

KINGDOM: 7+ Activity 2

Read Revelation 22. Then re-read the verses below and answer the questions.

Scripture	Does this verse describe something that is already or not yet?	What does this verse teach you about Jesus' kingdom?
Revelation 22:6: "And he said to me, 'These words are trustworthy and true. And the Lord, the God of the spirits of the prophets, has sent his angel to show his servants what must soon take place.'"		
Revelation 22:7: "'And behold, I am coming soon. Blessed is the one who keeps the words of the prophecy of this book.'"		
Revelation 22:12–13: "'Behold, I am coming soon, bringing my recompense with me, to repay each one for what he has done. I am the Alpha and the Omega, the first and the last, the beginning and the end.'"		
Choose another verse from the New Testament that tells about how Jesus' kingdom is already and not yet. Write the verse here.		